UNITED STATES
WEST OF THE
MISSISSIPPI RIVER

palacios

By John Edward Weems

Death Song
To Conquer a Peace
Dream of Empire
Men Without Countries
Peary
Race for the Pole
The Fate of the *Maine*
A Weekend in September

Growing Up in Texas
(CONTRIBUTOR)
The Schiwetz Legacy
(CONTRIBUTOR)
A Vanishing America
(CONTRIBUTOR)
U.S.S. *Ashtabula:* Her History
(CONTRIBUTOR AND EDITOR)

Death Song

Death Song

THE LAST OF THE INDIAN WARS

by John Edward Weems

Doubleday & Company, Inc., Garden City, New York
1976

Library of Congress Cataloging in Publication Data
Weems, John Edward.
Death song: the last of the Indian wars.
Includes bibliographical references and index.
1. Indians of North America—Wars—1865-1895.
2. Parker, Quanah, 1854-1911. 3. Geronimo, Apache
chief, 1829-1909. I. Title.
E83.866.W32   973.8
ISBN 0-385-00728-0
Library of Congress Catalog Card Number 74-33668

To the memory of William Edward Weems, 1863–1945,
and to the future of Carol and Ernest

A PERSONAL PREFACE

Since the age of seven or eight I have felt an intimate association with "the last of the Indian wars." My birth date in 1924 precluded any firsthand experience during the dramatic and tragic years 1867–90 on the Great Plains, but at least one chain of events that occurred in that period meant much to me personally. Had there been different links in that chain I suppose I never would have made an appearance here on earth—or at least not when and where I did. My grandfather, who *did* live during those momentous years, told me about it when I was young.

He was seven or eight years old himself when he and his family left the frontier town of Mansfield, Texas (where he was born in 1863), for California greenery, traveling—of course—in a covered wagon. The family had arranged to rendezvous at Jacksboro, Texas, 125 miles northwest, with some other emigrants who included kinfolk, and together they would travel across the southwestern wilderness, generally following the route of the old Butterfield Overland Mail that had carried letters and passengers by semiweekly stagecoach in 1858–61 from eastern points to California destinations.

Because of a delay my grandfather and his family missed the wagon train. When their own canvas-covered bone shaker rumbled up to the meeting site they discovered that the others had left already. One lonely wagon with little more than a canvas top for protection surely would have been no match for the perils of a fifteen-hundred-mile journey that lay between the Jacksboro frontier and Pacific Ocean majesty, so the family began talking disconsolately of turning back. Before they gave up completely, however, they traveled on a short distance and came upon signs of Indians presumably on one of their frequent raids southward from the Indian Territory —presently Oklahoma. That served to confirm the decision. Back to Mansfield went their covered wagon, although that town itself was subject to occasional raids by the same reservation Indians.

My grandfather's turnaround was fortunate for me, and no doubt for him, too. Soon after he and his family had returned to Mansfield —on May 18, 1871—a band of one hundred or more Kiowa and Comanche Indians led by a medicine man named Sky Walker (Mamanti), White Bear (Set-tainte, or Satanta), Sitting Bear (Set-ankeah, or Satank), and Big Tree (Addo-eta), reaping what they considered justice in revenge for stolen lands and broken promises, swarmed down from their Indian Territory reservation and attacked a ten-wagon train only seventeen miles southwest of Jacksboro. The raiders killed seven men; several bodies later were found to have been badly mutilated. One man had been chained to a wagon wheel and burned.

The essence of this story I heard more than once from my grandfather during Christmas and summer visits to his blackland farm eight miles east of Temple, Texas. By that time he was around seventy (and a long-time resident of Bell County), with straggly gray hair and a drooping George Armstrong Custer mustache (also whitened by twentieth-century vicissitudes), but he was still lean, lithe, and young in spirit (like one of the army scouts he sometimes described, I thought), and he would recollect events of the past as long as anyone would listen. I can still hear him talking in his loud, deliberate, raspy voice, using out-of-date phrases like "on yonder hill" and "back in early day"—singular, not plural—as he recounted youthful observations of Indians or of his father's killing a bear on Big Elm Creek nearby (by now long devoid of those critters) or of his own breaking of virgin soil near Temple with a plow drawn by oxen, while he threw pebbles at prairie chickens swarming around him. On other occasions he might talk about something he had heard in regard to the shooting of Sam Bass, an event that occurred in olden days fifty miles south of his farm, or about the time (later) when Temple hurriedly passed a city ordinance requiring all trains carrying United States Presidents to stop in the city limits—thus halting Teddy Roosevelt's entourage that had planned to chug straight through the youthful village to greater things elsewhere.

On summer nights we would all sit on the darkened front porch—or "gallery," as my grandfather always called it. Nearby, ready for sleeping on clear nights, would be cots and mattresses placed in the yard or on the porch, to catch any fleeting breeze. The entire household would quietly retire, one by one, while my grandfather talked on, telling no one in particular now about the last great chief of the Comanche Indians, the half-breed Quanah (who later added his white-family surname Parker) and how Quanah seemed to have turned from "red" to "white" during the waning years of the Indian wars, or about the professionalism of Colonel Ranald Mackenzie, a U. S. Cavalry leader who helped to assure safety for small white boys then living in Mansfield, Texas, or about something noticed long ago in a newspaper or a journal—the only publications he read regularly.

I would soon be asleep. Those stories became tiresome to me. After all, I was a member of the new generation and was much more interested in today: the latest outrages committed by Clyde Barrow and Bonnie Parker, John Dillinger, "Pretty Boy" Floyd, or any number of other white savages; the passing records then being set by Texas Christian University football star Sammy Baugh; the activities in Germany of a new power-mad leader named Adolf Hitler; and the explorations in Antarctica of Richard E. Byrd. Those were the important events; I was living *today*. Stories of Indian raids and swarming prairie chickens (especially Indian raids) were interesting to a degree, but they were not worth staying up half the night to hear. I suppose my grandfather would talk on until he realized every last member of his audience was in bed asleep, then he probably would finish whatever story he happened to have been on at the time, would crawl into his own bed, and would be up before any of us the next morning.

Those stories stopped thirty years ago now, but as I said, I can still hear him rambling on about some old event. The happenings he recounted were often minor, sometimes even trivial, but taken together they gave a good picture of life in those days of a waning frontier.

My grandfather was a talking book of history. Occasionally he had some facts wrong (as I discovered much later), but he probably did not make many more mistakes than the ordinary historian-scholar. And I feel certain he had his people right.

Most of his stories concerned people. Mere recital of the facts and figures of history bored him, and this (in addition to an early halt in schooling) must have been one reason for his lack of interest in the old-style textbook history that told a reader what happened and when, but did not go much further into people than listing names. (But my grandfather was not a book reader anyway. A major reason for this, I am sure, was that he could not stop talking long enough to get involved in a book.)

Much of this narrative (especially when it treats of people) is told in a manner similar to the one my grandfather would have used orally, with the exception that I have more sympathy for Indians than he ever did. As a youth he had been told nothing of some now well-known wrongs perpetrated against native inhabitants of this country, beginning on the Atlantic Coast, then expanding westward. Instead, he knew only the raids, scalpings, murders, and mutilations inflicted by Indians on his very neighbors.

The idea for the book and the people therein came largely from a recollection of his own stories. I have, however, made an effort to verify accuracy, and I have listed sources in a "Notes on the Chapters" section toward the end of the book.

I have invented no dialogue or other direct quotations. Where they appear I have taken them directly from reliable sources as having been said at the time and the place indicated. In some quotations I have corrected misspellings and have sometimes changed punctuation, paragraphing, and capitalization, for easier reading today, but I have not tampered with the words themselves.

I have sought consistency in style, but also simplification. For example, in the use of Indian names I have tried for both consistency and simplicity, using English translations of those names whenever possible: White Bear, Sitting Bear, and so on. The last renowned Comanche chief was, however, universally known only by his Indian name, Quanah, which meant something like "Fragrant." Only

Quanah can suffice for him, although the translation possibly described him well after he had torn into a freshly killed buffalo with his hands, or after a hard ride or fight.

Similarly, it would be senseless to refer to Goyathlay, Go khlä yeh, Goyakla, or Goyahkla, or to an English translation of those Apache versions, or to any name other than Geronimo, by which that Indian leader was most widely known.

The text of this book, then, should not be considered a reference catalogue of names, dates, and statistics of the last of the Indian wars, or even a truly comprehensive recounting of them, but, instead, an attempt to tell the story of that long and sorrowful series of conflicts and to depict life style, color, drama, tragedy, and meaning mainly through the use of seven principal characters who participated in the wars and who left behind written accounts.

Some of the participants are well known. For their stories I have sought less widely known details and have avoided lengthy repetition (as in Custer's Little Big Horn campaign) of what has been thoroughly covered earlier. Other participants are not so well known generally.

The seven characters are these individuals, in alphabetical order here:

John G. Bourke, a well-educated freethinker who, as an officer with the 3rd Cavalry, fought the native Americans, but found himself frequently sympathizing with them.

Robert Goldthwaite Carter, a young officer with the 4th Cavalry whose nationalistic loyalties impelled him to endure many hardships while contributing to an "opening of the West."

Elizabeth ("Libbie") Custer, wife of the renowned general, whose devotion to her husband led her into frequent danger and depression.

George Armstrong Custer—ambitious, independent, and sometimes erratic—who became a cavalry general while still in his early twenties.

Geronimo, who led small bands of Apaches into several last stands against Mexican and American dominance and who also led troops of two nations into many futile chases.

Quanah, half-breed Comanche chief in whose veins flowed the

blood of conqueror and conquered, and who eventually gained the respect of both peoples responsible for his existence.

White Bear (Satanta), Kiowan "orator of the Plains" who infuriated white generals and alienated even some Indians by saying one thing and doing another during his ultimately ineffectual defense of the homeland.

The Indians' homeland it certainly was—a fact now freely admitted by all enlightened Americans, who have seen also how treaties were disregarded in the winning of the West. But this narrative is not intended to arouse sympathy for the natives (other authors have done that), nor is it meant to be an apology. Instead it is simply a story of people involved in the last of the Indian wars, together with some overview of the subject. Persons other than the seven individuals named enter the story, of necessity, but the focus is on the principal characters.

John Edward Weems

CONTENTS

CONTENTS

ILLUSTRATIONS

ILLUSTRATIONS

Oh, sun, you remain forever, but we Kaitsenko must die;
Oh, earth, you remain forever, but we Kaitsenko must die.

from the death song of Sitting Bear

PROLOGUE
DEATH SONG

The withered old Indian was singing a shrill, sad chant that amused several of the soldier guards who were taking him back to Texas. His wail was an echo from that dark, nebulous cave where lie unrecorded, and presently beyond reach of human knowledge, thousands of years of history. Possibly it was an echo from prehistoric Asia, where (many authorities say) the old man's ancestors lived before they used steppingstones around the Bering Strait for their passage into North America.

To some curious soldiers the Indian's voice might have seemed to quiver as he worked his lips. The shakiness would have been caused by high pitch or old age, however, and not by fear; for the man was a chief of the Kiowas, Sitting Bear. He was being returned to Texas from the Indian Territory with two other tribal leaders to face verdicts in a white man's court for alleged crimes.

Sitting Bear, accompanied by a guard on each side, was riding in the first of two rumbling, creaking army wagons that rolled along between two dusty columns of mounted men wearing the blue blouses of cavalry. The old chief, handcuffed and leg-chained as were the other two Indians who rode in the wagon behind, sat enveloped in a blanket despite the heat of this June 8, 1871.

As Sitting Bear continued his song some of the soldiers tried to mimic him, but this was not true of the Indians (on U. S. Army payroll) who also comprised part of the escort. They remained silent while the chief shrilled his personal lament.

1

Kaitsenko ana obahema haa ipai degi o ba ika;
Kaitsenko ana oba hemo hadamagagi o ba ika.

The white soldiers probably neither understood nor cared that "Kaitsenko" referred to an elite Kiowa society composed of the ten or so bravest warriors. This select group included Sitting Bear, who had proved himself one of the bravest of them all. Nor would the soldiers have understood the old man's announcement, spoken in Comanche for every Indian present to hear and to comprehend. "Take this message to my people," he said. "Tell them I died beside the road. My bones will be found there."

Minutes later he added, "See that tree? When I reach that tree I will be dead."

Then Sitting Bear lapsed into silence, while the army wagons lumbered on through the day's heat and dust toward the tree. No longer did he sing his death song, which had said (translated into English):

Oh, sun, you remain forever, but we Kaitsenko must die;
Oh, earth, you remain forever, but we Kaitsenko must die.

(FROM CHAPTER 13)

1

THE GREAT WESTERN PIONEER

Henry David Thoreau, no man to take Indian land for his own gain, nevertheless once expressed the lure of new regions to westward in poetic language beyond the capability of those countless nineteenth-century Americans who were on the move there in reality, and not in imagination.

> Every sunset which I witness inspires me with the desire to go to a West as distant and as fair as that into which the sun goes down. He appears to migrate westward daily, and tempt us to follow him. He is the Great Western Pioneer whom the nations follow. We dream all night of those mountain-ridges in the horizon, though they may be of vapor only, which were last gilded by his rays. The island of Atlantis, and the islands and gardens of the Hesperides, a sort of terrestrial paradise, appear to have been the Great West of the ancients, enveloped in mystery and poetry. Who has not seen in imagination, when looking into the sunset sky, the gardens of the Hesperides, and the foundation of all those fables?

By 1867 post-Civil War peace had forced many Americans toward the distant West: those who had lost kin or property during the war and who wanted or needed to get away; former soldiers who had developed an affinity for military service and whose only chance now to continue in that career required enlisting for Indian fighting; individuals who for some reason found the eastern establishment closed to their hopes for opportunity; and farmers whose lands had lost fertility through hard use. Many of these Americans would indeed find new opportunity in the West, but in time they would also find there a native population ready to die in homeland defense.

Postwar peace also allowed time in 1867 for thinking and planning—for the final phase of filling out the North American continent all the way to the Pacific Ocean. Already a transcontinental railroad link had become a major project; the work would be completed and the last spike, significantly a "golden" one, would be driven into place on May 10, 1869. Congress voted loans and lands for railroad companies. Boosters and speculators rode the boom westward, selling lots in many a metropolis that never would leave a paper-planning stage. New equipment helped to open farms on the fringes of the Great Plains, once presumed useless for agriculture. Between 1860 and 1900 more than 400 million western acres would be added to the nation's farming area, making the United States the world's greatest producer of cheap food. The combined effect of railroad, harvester, telegraph, and cable (the steamship *Great Eastern* had laid the last of the submarine link with the British Isles in 1866) would be to cut men's hours and miles with an efficiency that was considered almost miraculous then.

It was the nineteenth century, but the entire country was on the move toward the twentieth. Southerners began rebuilding ruined cities like Atlanta, Richmond, and Charleston, and they commenced replanting crops with a vigor that later amazed even the perceptive Georgia journalist Henry Grady, then in his teens. Fields that had run red with human blood in April, Grady remarked, came out green with the June harvest, although resurgence of the southern economy was to come much more slowly.

Northerners, bustling as usual, added prosperity to war victory. Enterprising men became wealthy. Rich men grew richer through profits of industries that drew mindlessly from vast natural resources. Millionaires multiplied; railroad mileage doubled during the first five years of peace. Living became easier, especially for those holding the greatest number of shares in the system. Natural gas became available for lighting and cooking (Fredonia, New York, 1865). In 1865 the federal government authorized free, city-

4

wide delivery of mail in towns with fifty thousand or more residents, eliminating the need for regular trips to a central location to call for any letters that might have arrived. Typewriters, patented in 1868, came into use, eventually swelling the volume of mail. The first paid firemen were employed by the city of New York (1865), and a firm there built the first elevated railroad (1867), running from Battery Place through Greenwich Street and Ninth Avenue to Thirtieth Street. For overnight rail passengers elsewhere George Pullman provided "luxurious" accommodations with his Palace Car Company, founded in 1867.

Contending with Northerners and Southerners for shares in a rebuilt Union were Westerners, newly influential economically and politically—not only through national expansion but also through gains made during the recent war. Western farms in Ohio, Illinois, and elsewhere had helped to feed Union armies and civilians; and in 1865 Chicago opened a stockyard that would utilize western and eastern rail connections to make the city the world's largest meat-trade center, replacing Cincinnati.

The white surge westward, all the way to the Pacific Coast, gave further indication of attaining great proportions now. On March 1, 1867, Nebraska became the thirty-seventh star on the red, white, and blue banner, after having experienced a railroad-inspired population increase of 90,000 (to a total count of 120,000) in seven years. Twenty-nine days later Secretary of State William H. Seward completed negotiations for buying Alaska from Russia, but "Seward's Folly" did not really represent a stride in the westward march then in progress. Not until many years later would the strategic and economic importance of that acquisition be realized.

The Civil War, two years ended now, and Abraham Lincoln's assassination still cast a pall and would continue to do so. Fighting had resulted in a million casualties on both sides: 617,000 dead (359,000 among Union armies) and 375,000 wounded (275,000 of them Union). In a day when the number "billion" was almost unheard of, both sides had spent $8 billion ($5 billion Union), and the United States Government had come out of the conflict burdened by debt amounting to $75 for every man, woman, and child in the country—highest ever to that time. But many of the 38 million Americans then living foresaw nothing but peace and prosperity ahead.

In the city of Washington any appearance of genuine peace proved to be superficial. The great mass of soldiers garrisoned there to protect the federal government from rebels had indeed disappeared. During the war as many as 150,000 troops had been quartered in Washington, in established posts, in tent-crowded parks, and even—in the case of one regiment—in the Capitol Building rotunda, under the unfinished dome. But though uniforms were rarer now, war ghosts remained. Temporary hospitals still cluttered parks. Cobblestone streets showed a need for restoration from the effects of constant wartime grinding under iron-reinforced wheels of horse-drawn guns and caissons. Many trees had disappeared, having been chopped down by soldiers for winter firewood or for cooking fuel in other seasons. Civic improvement had halted. Washington's stinking Tiber River still meandered through the city carrying raw sewage. An area around Dupont Circle lay barren of buildings, all development there having been delayed by the war. Neglect showed itself everywhere, and municipal officials could do little with the limited funds available. The federal government owned more than half the city land and paid no taxes on it.

So war ghosts continued to haunt Washington. The conflict had indeed brought a form of prosperity, but, as usual for war, it was inflated; and people who had accumulated some money craved more yet—not caring sometimes how they got it. Military authority remained pervasive. The most popular man in the city was Ulysses Grant, U. S. Army chief of staff and later Secretary of War.

One of the least popular men was the Chief Executive, Andrew Johnson, the former Vice-President who had succeeded Lincoln. Unfortunately for Johnson, a Tennessean, though a prewar supporter of the Union, many people considered him a Southerner or worse: plain "white trash." Mary Todd Lincoln dubbed him "the tailor," a spiteful reference to the President's early career. As a boy in North Carolina, Johnson, whose parents were illiterate, had not attended even one day of school. At the age of thirteen he had been apprenticed to a tailor. Eventually, in Greeneville, Tennessee, he had become established as an expert tailor himself and at the age of nineteen had married an attractive, intelligent, patient woman,

6

Eliza McCardle, who had tutored him in reading, writing, and arithmetic.

Johnson had mastered public speaking on his own, and in Greeneville he had broken into politics (first as city alderman, then as mayor), devoting particular attention to the plight of the poor and oppressed people from whose ranks he had come.

As a politician he never lacked physical attractiveness. He seemed sturdy and sound—175 pounds well arranged on a body just below six feet in height, all giving him a look of power: strong limbs, large shoulders and neck, broad head and beardless face ennobled by a dark complexion and by black, liquid eyes. But as his political career lengthened he began to antagonize people with an outspokenness that often blossomed into tactlessness.

On the eve of war Johnson had represented Tennessee in the United States Senate. Improving fortune had made him a slaveholder, and he voted consistently with Southern Democrats. But he also spoke against secession, and when the nation split he refused to leave Congress, becoming the only Southerner to stay. This led in 1864 to his nomination as Vice-President on Lincoln's coalition ticket, the "National Union Party," largely supported by Republicans, then to his accession as the seventeenth President.

"It is now peace," Johnson had said early in his tenure. "Let us have peace." But Andrew Johnson as President would have no peace.

Great trouble had begun for him as the incoming Vice-President at the 1865 inauguration. Ill, and possibly not very confident in the first place, he had taken a drink of brandy (or whiskey—accounts differ), then another, seeking to steady himself. His ensuing speech came out distorted and even incoherent, to the great embarrassment of Republicans. Later, as President, he encountered much more difficulty—specifically, a Congress sprinkled with Radical Republicans who demanded severe chastisement of the South, as opposed to the forgiving course desired by Lincoln and continued by Johnson. To the northern radicals the President's sympathies seemed more and more southern. Johnson's foes steamed and declared that the South must suffer longer for its transgressions—but there was another reason for their emotion. A readmitted

South could be expected to send Democrats back to Congress, thus eliminating the Republican majority there.

Johnson vetoed bills. Congress overrode, blazing with open anger. One fight developed over the admission of Nebraska. The President vetoed this bill, too, fearing the election of two more Radical Republican senators from that state to torment him. But Congress admitted Nebraska over his veto.

Nor did a presidential veto kill a Civil Rights Act, voted into law with the necessary two-thirds majority on April 9, 1866, although Johnson had called it a violation of states' rights. This legislation bestowed citizenship on all persons born in the United States, with the specific exception of Indians, guaranteed the same rights and privileges for all those fortunate persons included, and provided punishments for individuals guilty of restricting rights.*

"Let us have peace," Johnson had insisted. Instead, Congress (whether morally right or wrong) forced harsh years of Reconstruction on the South, from 1867 on, and reopened old wounds.

In the West, where all those pioneers were chasing the sunset, much more opened than old wounds: fresh opportunity, "vacant" lands, new wounds—open warfare. As it had inevitably developed, Indians could not be allowed sole possession of all that area, just as eastern tribes earlier had been pressed and squeezed and finally forced westward across the Mississippi River.

No one seemed truly concerned about the native Americans, with the exception that everyone felt they must be safely removed from the inexorable march of progress. The militant sympathy for Negroes that had helped to bring on the Civil War seemed to have monopolized emotions even of northern zealots. Indians enjoyed little white support at this time (and that mostly in the distant Northeast), little Caucasian understanding, no political representation, and no privileges awarded others under that Civil Rights Act. Congress had bestowed the rights of citizenship upon all natural-born residents of the United States, with the specific exception of native Americans.

By 1867 government officials had agreed on a plan for these pesky noncitizens. Fighting them had become too expensive in

---

* Questions regarding the constitutionality of this act arose and eventually led to passage of the Fourteenth Amendment.

money and men. Sioux Indians under Red Cloud, Crazy Horse, and other leaders had inflicted some notable defeats on the U. S. Army and had closed the white man's Bozeman Trail, which ran through their territory. In Kansas a poorly planned 1867 campaign by General W. S. Hancock had failed to do much more than provoke various tribes into new depredations. Therefore, all Indians were to be pacified by talk and by gifts, rounded up, and taken to live on specified areas of land—reservations—to be given them in return for their cooperation.

This policy would provide two-way protection. Not only could white men follow the Great Western Pioneer without interference, but the Indians, safely ensconced in their own abbreviated bailiwicks, presumably would be free from depredations of Americans engaged in their pursuit of land and wealth. A rationalizing official might even have considered this plan to be of greatest benefit to the endangered species.

2

LET US HAVE PEACE

So President Johnson found an opportunity to include the West in his hoped-for peace program. In 1867 a senator, John B. Henderson, from a western state with great interest in a placid frontier, Missouri, proposed in Congress the creation of a commission to travel into Indian lands to make peace with tribes west of the Mississippi River. His suggestion, passed in bill form by Congress, became law when signed by the usually veto-prone President, who this time agreed with the purpose and the legality of the legislation: to remove the causes of war, to protect frontier settlements and railroad construction, and to establish a system for civilizing the tribes by placing them on those reservations, where they would receive food, clothes, and shelter in return for their promise to live there quietly, except for occasional forays after buffalo.

One member of the commission was the man who had proposed it—Missouri Senator Henderson, a wealthy, learned bachelor with a law background who, more than most other legislators, wanted peace with the Indians, but not at any price. He also advocated punishing tribes who fought the federal government. Other members, consisting of prominent civilians and military men, represented a variety of attitudes ranging from sympathy with Indians to outright militancy against them. They planned to meet, at different locations, Indians of the northern and southern Great Plains. Southerly Indians (Comanches, Kiowas, Plains Apaches—or Kiowa-Apaches, Cheyennes, and Arapahos) would be assembled during the first full moon in October at a location in present Barber

County, Kansas, on Medicine Lodge Creek (sometimes called river)—or so the commissioners hoped when they dispatched gift-promising agents to summon the "nomads." The government intent was to place these five tribes on a reservation in present Oklahoma, to give them cattle, and to teach them agriculture and other civilized vocations.

Original selection of the southern council site had been a problem in itself. Few Indians—even those most desirous of discussing peace—would dare to congregate again in the vicinity of a white settlement or fort, with an inexcusable massacre of Cheyenne Indians buried in history by only three years.

In November of 1864 Chief Black Kettle had brought his people into a camp on Sand Creek, near Fort Lyon, Colorado, to await a meeting with United States officials, as requested by the chief. While Black Kettle and six hundred Cheyennes waited beneath a United States flag they had attached to a tepee pole that towered above their camp, an Indian-hating leader of the 3rd Colorado Cavalry, Colonel J. M. Chivington, in search of any or all red savages to eradicate, unleashed his larger force upon the unsuspecting Cheyennes and slaughtered them by the scores, mostly women and children, even though Black Kettle (who finally fled) had quickly hoisted a white flag on the same pole where the national ensign flew. Black Kettle escaped, but another chief, White Antelope, seventy-five years old, stood with folded arms under the flag and sang his death song, "Nothing lives long; only the earth and the mountains," until gunfire silenced him.

The site on Medicine Lodge Creek had been selected because it was far removed from the nearest white settlement of importance, and it lay in the heartland of the Kiowas, although some white men had poked around the countryside already and had begun to covet this oasis: a green valley, grassy and timbered with cottonwood and elm trees that lined the banks of the swiftly running creek and those of another stream, Elm Creek, that sent its clear water gushing into the Medicine here—two silvery, sunlit ribbons that contrasted sharply with the emerald landscape.

The Kiowas loved this locality for many reasons: the streams that watered the land; the verdant pastures of sweet, native grasses; the natural shelters provided by trees, bluffs, and canyons; and the abundance of game—buffalo, deer, antelope, and fowl—that flocked

11

into the valleys of the Medicine and of other streams nearby. But still another reason caused the Indians to cherish this section of earth: the main creek's healing capabilities, indicated by its name and fulfilled by its mineral content, which acted as a mild laxative.

Near the confluence of the Elm and the Medicine Lodge, Indians many years ago had built a structure they used as a primitive spa. From trees nearby they cut a number of long, slender logs, placed them on end to form a giant circle, and roofed the enclosure with branches, rushes, reeds, and earth. Inside the completed building they heated rocks, placed on them aromatic, healing herbs and plants, and splashed water on all of this, turning their lodge into a steam bath where various ailments could be sweated out of the body. For countless years Indians had come annually to this site and had set up tepees or tents for an interval of bathing and for drinking the medicinal waters.

By 1867, and probably well before that, other furnishings had gone into the lodge: objects with sacred meaning to the Kiowas, and war trophies. A U. S. Army officer commanding a force that once camped near the lodge visited the place (in the absence of its owners) and described it: "an immense structure . . . used by [the Indians] as a council house, where once . . . each year the various tribes of the Southern Plains were wont to assemble in mysterious conclave to consult the Great Spirit as to the future and to . . . engage in imposing ceremonies." The officer saw hanging from the rude ceiling those various herbs and plants used for healing (and for other purposes), and some grimmer articles: "trophies of the warpath and the chase, the latter being represented by the horns and dressed skins of animals killed in the hunt, some of the skins . . . beautifully ornamented in the most fantastic styles peculiar to . . . Indian art. Of the trophies relating to war, the most prominent were human scalps representing all ages and sexes of the white race." Many scalps, after having been lifted from the original owners and properly cured, had been brightly painted, and sometimes the hair had been dyed, "either to a beautiful yellow or golden, or to crimson."*

* The officer referred to this as the medicine lodge near the site of the council meeting. It is possible, however, that the structure he visited was a

A camp ground near that remote lodge was the destination of the government party that departed southward from Fort Harker, Kansas, early on October 9: Senator Henderson and five other peace commissioners (a sixth, General William Tecumseh Sherman, had been summoned to Washington, leaving towering, white-haired General William S. Harney, another commissioner, the ranking military officer present). Accompanying the commissioners were various other federal government officials; nine newspaper reporters, including the *Missouri Democrat's* Henry M. Stanley, who would later find personal fame and the long-absent missionary-explorer Dr. David Livingstone in Africa; a large group of aides, male secretaries, interpreters, cooks, and teamsters; and an escort of two hundred troopers of the 7th Cavalry.

The expedition formed a column nearly two miles long. In the lead, riding in mule-drawn ambulances, were commissioners, their aides, and reporters, followed by some two hundred wagons, each pulled by three span of mules and crammed with supplies and gifts for the Indians. Three days later more gift-laden wagons accompanied by two infantry companies riding in ambulances joined the entourage, but not even this addition made the expedition a match for the awesomeness of nature. From a distance men and vehicles would have appeared as mere insects moving imperceptibly across empty prairies that seemed to stretch into infinity under a blue-gray sky.

Nightfall usually brought realization of immediate danger: sweeping prairie fires, their presence indicated by distant, dim illuminations on the horizon. Had Indians—maybe vengeful Cheyennes —set these fires as their greeting, instead of extending the hoped-for other warm welcome, of peace? No one could say for sure, and at night mounted sentinels kept an especially close watch over the area, which was known as a favorite hunting ground. The presence of soldier escorts had been opposed from the beginning by Superintendent of Indian Affairs Thomas Murphy, who was accompanying the expedition, but his argument (that the sight of military units would upset the Indians) had not won out, and on dark nights many of the men would have slept better because of the soldiers.

Kiowa sun-dance lodge, built twelve miles down the creek. The two lodges were similar in appearance.

Near the Arkansas River, sixty miles from the meeting site, a group of colorfully dressed, brightly painted chiefs who had been invited to the council joined the white men for the rest of the journey. A teen-age U. S. Army employee from West Virginia, new to the Plains, gaped at the Indians and described them. They carried themselves regally, he said (with open-mouthed awe that seemed to stem half from adulation and half from fear); their splendid costumes and the fine horses they were riding contributed to this effect. Their every feature and action, he thought, revealed a racial pride and a haughty contempt of the white men they saw.

The West Virginia boy carefully studied one of the most imposing of the chieftains, a Kiowan of powerful physique who towered over the other Indians present and, in fact, over almost everyone else around, with the exception of that tall, cool, white-haired General Harney, a retired Indian fighter already well acquainted with this same Kiowa leader, whose name was Satanta, or White Bear. The towering chief was riding a black horse of such magnificence as to equal his own kingly appearance, the West Virginian thought.

Closer observation of White Bear showed a giant, grim-mouthed Indian with a large head and an oval face painted green, yellow, and red. Dominating his facial features were a prominent nose and two dark, fierce eyes that seemed to shoot arrows through narrow slits at the pale-faced men around him—that is, when his arms were not encircling them in dubious bear-hug greetings.

White Bear's long hair had been brushed back behind his ears. He stood more than six feet tall—and showed other impressive physical characteristics: broad shoulders and chest, thick arms, powerful legs. Although he was well into middle age, his body obviously had not been rusted by the encroachment. Another observer remarked that every one of the chief's strong features seemed to indicate bravery, forcefulness, and untamability. Altogether, White Bear fit the general description of Kiowas given by George Catlin in an 1844 book, *Letters and Notes on the . . . North American Indians:* "They are a much finer looking race than either the Comanches or the Pawnees—tall, erect, with an easy graceful gait— with long hair cultivated often to reach near the ground. They have generally the fine Roman outline of head."

White Bear had won the respect of his tribe while a young man, when he had proved himself to be a fearless, energetic, and cunning warrior—and, in time, an exceedingly talkative and boastful one, a characteristic that did not endear him to rivals. Years before 1867, upon the death of Kiowa chief Dohasan, White Bear had sought to grab tribal reins—and he had succeeded, although his rivals had continued to contend with him for leadership. Few could equal his early daring, however, and none could match his later ability as a speaker—certainly not in quantity of word flow. White Bear, who had become known by 1867 as "the orator of the Plains," appeared to have the ability to talk a buffalo out of his hide, and he could do this either in his native tongue or in Comanche or Spanish (which might have indicated his ancestry). He could speak also some Pueblo and a little English, a language he understood much better than he ever indicated. His main failings as an Indian leader were an inability sometimes to clamp his teeth together for the sake of his listeners and even for himself, and a marked weakness for whiskey.

Other failings had, in time, alienated certain white men and even some of White Bear's tribal followers. Unlike many other chiefs, White Bear fell far short of being a man of his word—and if he had learned this trick from some of his Caucasian adversaries it still did not heighten his stature. Earlier in 1867, for instance, White Bear had spoken of his desire for peace at a council attended by General W. S. Hancock and other officers of the U. S. Army, and journalist Henry M. Stanley, present also at that meeting, had recorded the words: "I want friends, and I say by the sun and the earth I live on, I want to talk straight and to tell the truth. . . . I want friends, and am doing all I can for peace. . . . I do not want war at all, but want to make friends, and I am doing the best I can for that purpose. . . . This prairie is large and good, and so are the heavens above, and I do not want it stained by the blood of war."

White Bear had spoken on and on (recording his speech had required several pages), but the gist of it had been that yearning for friendship and peace so emphatically stated. The Kiowa chief had impressed Hancock so favorably with his oration that the General presented him with an army officer's uniform. One month later, after having had a picture made in the outfit, White Bear had worn the uniform while leading an unsuccessful attack on the same army

15

post that had been the site of the council. This represented his own peculiar follow-up to still another message, one with a somewhat different tone, that he had sent Hancock before the peace discussion just mentioned had soothed the General's ruffled feelings: that he, White Bear, hoped army animals were well fed, since he would be over soon to capture the stock.

So, after a mighty first impression, White Bear had not worn very well among either whites or some Indians. His pomposity, selfishness, and ruthlessness repelled, but still he persisted. During raids he carried an army bugle (apparently acquired sometime around 1830, at Fort Leavenworth) and directed his men in their attacks by calls blown with great ostentation. His love affairs were legion and legendary, as were his alleged rapes of captured white women, who were thereafter usually slain into silence. But White Bear was an important Indian leader with whom the federal government had to deal—and not everyone saw the flaws in his façade. A government physician who had visited the Kiowa camp three years earlier had written (as reported in the *Annual Report* of the Commissioner of Indian Affairs for 1868):

> I was four days in . . . White Bear's village. . . . He is a fine-looking Indian, very energetic, and as sharp as a briar. He and all his people treated me with much friendship. I ate my meals regularly three times a day with him in his lodge. He puts on a great deal of style, spreads a carpet for his guests to sit on, and has painted fireboards twenty inches wide and three feet long, ornamented with bright brass tacks driven all around the edges, which they use for tables. He has a brass French horn which he blew vigorously when the meals were ready.

During the marches to Medicine Lodge, White Bear made himself obvious with his loud talk and raucous laughter and his occasional horseback gallops from some place far back in the column to the van, where he would from time to time engage his old friend General Harney, who was riding in the lead ambulance, in lengthy conversation. When (in late afternoon of October 12) a hunting party, quickly organized from among the white men present, galloped across a grassy prairie into a newly sighted buffalo herd, shooting and slaughtering, White Bear looked on with those dark

16

eyes flashing their warning signals and demanded that Harney stop the wanton killing of animals so necessary to Indian life. "Has the white man become a child that he should slay and not eat?" White Bear asked.

The General, fearing disruption of the entire council, ordered a halt to the sport. But that night men of the expedition feasted on tidbits collected from their kill—buffalo tongues and hump steaks, cooked over camp fires and served sizzling hot—while on the hunting ground the rest of the meat began to spoil and smell and, to the south, a glow on the horizon indicated the presence of another faraway prairie fire. Might it really have been set by those wrathful victims of Sand Creek as notice of what these white peace commissioners could expect?

Later that night a startling clatter of hooves signaled the approach of a body of horsemen, but the group proved to be friendly: General Christopher Auger, Platte Department commander recently appointed by President Johnson to serve as commissioner in place of the recalled General Sherman, and an escort that had accompanied the General from Fort Harker. Wary men awakened by the noise dropped off to sleep again.

The following dawn heralded the final marching day. Sometime before evening the expedition would arrive at the council site. Thomas Murphy, the Indian Affairs superintendent, began worrying again about a response to the sight of United States soldiers approaching, holding weapons as if ready to fire. Murphy had helped with preliminary arrangements for the council—had conferred beforehand with several chiefs, including a few Cheyennes he hoped might appear with their people despite grievances—and he could foresee the reaction of Indians who would observe those hundreds of armed men escorting peace commissioners to the camp site. The natives might either flee or open fire, he argued. In any event, they would not consider this gathering any sort of peace conference. They had seen or heard what white soldiers could do to Indians showing friendship toward the United States Government. Murphy complained again, and this time he was persuasive. General Harney agreed to move the military units to the rear and to call in his outriders. The long column lumbered on toward the valley of the Medicine—now with the peace commissioners far ahead and unguarded, and mostly at the mercy of the Indians.

That last day men of the expedition saw more buffalo, but this time no one shot at the animals, not caring to put those fiery flashes back into White Bear's eyes or to disturb in any way the Indians presumably gathered on the banks of Medicine Lodge Creek ahead. Instead, the men traveled on south quietly, as if subdued by the vastness of nature or by the prospect of meeting as many as five thousand Indians (as some preliminary guesses had gone) without any armed escort in front.

Did Thomas Murphy really know what he was doing? What were White Bear and the other accompanying chiefs thinking? Their presence should assure safety, but Indian chiefs, especially a leader like White Bear, could be unpredictable.

Horses' hooves drummed the earth. Wagons groaned under burdensome cargoes. Saddles made leathery creaking sounds. But when men talked, they usually talked in low voices, and they rode on southeastward across a rise that soon proved to be the last one. They saw lying ahead of them a green valley threaded by the two tree-lined creeks, Medicine Lodge and Elm, that joined there. Infinitely more impressive than the landscape, however, was the awesome sight of the occupiers. The government men gaped and perhaps worried again about that subordination of their military escort. As far as their vision extended they saw signs of encamped Indians: tepees, horses, dogs, and their owners, who were sitting, walking, loitering, gathered in groups, all awaiting the arrival of those white men who had declared, once more, their interest in peace. Later estimates of the native population ranged as high as the five thousand predicted in advance.

Off to the left the peace commissioners saw a tree-shaded slope and, awaiting them there, numbers of brightly dressed and painted Indians—chiefs, ready to extend greetings. The commissioners and their interpreters rode toward them, dismounted, and shook hands all around. Most of the chiefs added a bear hug to the welcome, something that might have proved discomfiting to wary recipients, but white men would not have been the only cautious people present. Enmity existed also between some of the Indian tribes present—like Comanches and Cheyennes.

Among the welcomers was Black Kettle, the Cheyenne whose

camp had been attacked by Chivington's force three years earlier and whose own life had been in jeopardy while he stood amidst gunfire under the United States flag. Old Black Kettle knew the days of Indian independence were gone.

Not many other Cheyennes admitted this, however, as the commissioners soon were to learn. One vigorous and influential Cheyenne chief, Roman Nose, whose following included hundreds of the bravest Cheyenne warriors—members of the much-respected society of Dog Soldiers—had refused to come to Medicine Lodge, although he had agreed to a compromise. Roman Nose and his people would wait in camp sixty miles away, on the Cimarron River, and follow developments through reports of couriers stationed in Black Kettle's camp. If proceedings proved agreeable to Roman Nose he and his people would join the council.

But Roman Nose also had other motivation for his planning. The couriers staying with Black Kettle could watch that old chief, too. Roman Nose did not intend to allow Black Kettle to sign away all Cheyenne rights in any treaty.

Roman Nose's reluctance disappointed the peace commissioners, who had hoped especially to conciliate the Southern Cheyennes and all those Dog Soldiers. Still, Indians aplenty already had gathered on the council grounds. Along the foot of the same tree-shaded slope where the chiefs had waited, the commissioners found encamped the Arapahos—near the banks of Medicine Lodge Creek and not far from a previously established ration camp that held enough staples to feed the Indians during the entire conference. Beyond the Arapahos, and farther downstream, were encamped the Plains Apaches, Comanches, and Kiowas. Black Kettle and his small band of Cheyennes had chosen a site that would be across the creek from the government people. Although the old chief desired peace—just as he had before the Sand Creek massacre—apparently he still harbored some doubt about the true intentions of these visitors.

The white men, in turn, reflected on the great numbers of Indians virtually surrounding them, and many had doubts of their own. The presence of two or three hundred soldiers and one or two Gatling guns hidden away somewhere in military equipment did little to calm the jitters aroused by the proximity of all those "untamed" people, and the first night passed slowly for some sleepers. But on the following morning all scalps remained intact, and the journalists ventured forth to observe the scene. Henry M. Stanley visited the Arapaho camp and discovered that picturesqueness vanished in relation to the distance covered:

> All was corruption and filth. Dressed in dingy buffalo robes which swarmed with vermin were the warriors, squaws, and papooses. . . . The camp was strewn with . . . tanned buffalo robes, axes, pots, kettles and pans, beadwork, old moccasins, chunks of lately killed buffalo, stews cooking in kettles, dog skins, antelope and elk hides, pipes, tomtoms, war clubs, bone grubbing hoes, stone hammers, headless arrows and broken bows, dolls, bone saddles in heaps, wicker cradles by the score, and howling and barking dogs.

The actual site of the council meeting, however, was scenic enough. A short distance downstream from the government camp, in a handsome grove of elms and cottonwoods, men cleared away shrubs and bushes and built a brush arbor. Underneath that they placed tables and stools for the use of commissioners and journalists, and logs for the Indians, who could sit there facing the white visitors.

Cheyennes under Roman Nose were still refusing to come in. Leaders of other tribes wanted to wait for them, but Black Kettle said those other Cheyennes were "making medicine" and could not appear for several days. The Comanches, Kiowas, and Plains Apaches agreed to begin the talks. The Arapahos would continue to wait for the recalcitrant Cheyennes, as would old and beleaguered Black Kettle, who knew as well as the peace commissioners that any treaty made without the approval of Roman Nose and other tribal chiefs would be worthless insofar as it concerned Cheyennes.

The Indians who began peace discussions were represented by chiefs bearing some striking names. Among those speaking for Comanches were Dog Fat, Gap in the Woods, Horseback, Iron Mountain, Little Horn, Painted Lips, Silver Brooch, Standing Feather, Ten Bears, and Wolf's Name; for the Kiowas, Crow, Kicking Bird, One Bear, Sitting Bear, Stumbling Bear, White Bear, and Woman's Heart; and for the Plains Apaches, Bad Back, Iron Shirt, Little Bear, Poor Bear, White Horn, and Wolf Sleeve.*

An early speaker was Ten Bears, a Comanche chief who had visited the city of Washington and who had observed there that the most important men, including Presidents like Lincoln (whom Ten Bears had met), often wore spectacles. The chief had brought a pair of specs back with him, and now he wore the glasses as he greeted peace commissioners. He added that he wanted no part of their proposed reservation system.

My heart is filled with joy when I see you here, as the brooks fill with water when the snows melt in the spring; and I feel glad, as the ponies do when the fresh grass starts in the beginning of the year. . . . My people have never first drawn a bow or fired a gun against the whites. . . . It was you who sent the first soldier, and it was we who sent out the second. Two years ago I came upon this road, following the buffalo, that my wives and children might have their cheeks plump and their bodies warm. But the soldiers fired on us, and since that time there has been a noise like that of a thunderstorm, and we have not known which way to go.

So it was upon the Canadian [River]. . . . The blue-dressed soldiers . . . came from out of the night, when it was dark and still, and for camp fires they lit our lodges. So it was in Texas. They made sorrow come in our camps. . . . You said that you wanted to put us upon a reservation, to build us houses and to make us medicine lodges. I do not want them.

I was born upon the prairie where the wind blew free and there was nothing to break the light of the sun. I was born where there were no enclosures and where everything drew a free breath. I want to die there, and not within walls. . . .

When I was at Washington, the Great Father told me that all the Comanche land was ours, and that no one should hinder us in living upon it. So why do you ask us to leave the rivers, and the sun, and the wind, and live in houses? Do not ask us to give up the buffalo for the sheep. The young men

* In some other accounts these names have been translated differently.

21

have heard talk of this, and it has made them sad and angry. Do not speak of it more. . . .

The Texans have taken away the places where the grass grew the thickest and the timber was the best. . . . The white man has the country which we loved and we only wish to wander on the prairie until we die.

Even White Bear, the great Kiowa orator of the Plains, must have realized the difficulty of equaling Ten Bears' poetry and persuasiveness, especially since some men had pointed out to him that his own speeches often showed more quantity than quality. But White Bear could not remain silent. Some time after the Comanche chief had spoken, White Bear rose from a campstool, which he had brought for himself (not caring to sit on a log like any common Indian) and had placed just in front of Sitting Bear and beside Kicking Bird. Grim-faced, White Bear began to address the peace commissioners, probably in the Spanish language. Accounts described him as having dressed for the occasion in the U. S. Army officer's uniform presented to him by General Hancock and as holding his famous bugle.

White Bear rarely spoke briefly, but this time the gist of his remarks could be given in only three of his sentences. "When a Kiowa is put in a pen he dies. My people want to remain on the prairies as long as there are buffalo. When they are gone we will be ready to live in houses."

White Bear and other Indians had agreed to gather here at Medicine Lodge, but they were hardly agreeable to yielding to the United States Government the comparatively small slices of land and liberty left to them now. Still, the peace commissioners pressed their argument—their demand—and the outcome, whether or not the Indians realized it, never had been in doubt. Senator Henderson replied to White Bear.

You say that you . . . like the buffalo. You say that you wish to do as your fathers did. You say that the buffalo will not last forever. They are now becoming few, and you must know it. When the day comes, the Indian must change the road his father trod, or he must suffer and die. We now offer you the way. Before all the good lands are taken up by the whites we wish to set a part of them for your exclusive use. On that land we will build you a house to hold the goods we will send you when you become hungry and naked. You can go there and be fed and clothed.

White Bear still had an answer ready, one with Indian logic entirely unacceptable to men preparing to flesh out a continent. After Senator Henderson had finished his talk, which also had included a summary of the treaty terms, White Bear again rose from his campstool throne and declared, "I ask the commissioners to tell the Great Father what I have to say. When the buffalo leave the country, we will let him know. By that time we will be ready to live in houses."

Eventually, however, the Comanche and Kiowa chiefs agreed to sign the treaty—on October 21—motivated by cajoling, the promise of immediate gifts, pressure, and a probable misunderstanding of specifics. They gave away much of their Great Plains homeland, including their beloved valley of the Medicine and the healing properties to be found there, and agreed to refrain from raiding white settlers and travelers, railroad builders, and army posts—all this in exchange for a small area to become known as the Wichita Reserve in present southwestern Oklahoma and for a government promise to provide storage facilities, farms, tools, carpenters, agents, teachers, and doctors. Additionally (and the signing actually hinged on this), Indians elicited from the commissioners a promise of hunting privileges south of the Arkansas River for "so long as the buffalo may range," unaware that at that very time some influential Americans were urging extermination of those animals as the only way to rid the West of Indians.

More immediate rewards came after the signing. Government men distributed gifts of blankets, beads, baskets, clothing, knives, ammunition, firearms, and hundreds of bugles like the one White Bear owned.

Plains Apaches signed a similar agreement a few days later, but that still left two tribes out of the fold. Many of the Cheyennes were still making their medicine on the Cimarron, and the Arapahos refused to sign any treaty without them. During the delay everyone passed the hours drinking, smoking, gambling, whittling, or showing off horsemanship—at which the Comanches excelled. Several teamsters engaged in a drunken brawl apparently ignited by the presence of an Indian woman. Many Comanches and Kiowas left the site—but not White Bear, who stayed around for the whiskey that he felt his treaty signing had earned. His drunken braggadocio fell far short of most of his council oratory and repelled journalists who had been favorably impressed earlier.

Some loiterers, both white and red, wondered about the real intentions of those distant Cheyennes. It would not be out of character, they reflected, for the Cheyennes to fall upon both white and Indian enemies at the council grounds and wipe them all out. Everyone knew the Cimarron Cheyennes had been keeping themselves informed of activity through those runners operating out of Black Kettle's camp.

As the commissioners became more frustrated and impatient Black Kettle and another friendly Cheyenne chief, Little Robe, agreed to visit the Cimarron encampment and to try persuasion on their kinsmen.

Little Robe returned to Medicine Lodge late in the afternoon of October 26 with word that the reluctant Cheyennes—five hundred armed warriors and their chiefs—would be riding in the next day. They would be firing weapons into the air, he warned, but this would be nothing more than ceremony. The Cheyennes wanted ammunition for hunting, he said, and if it were forthcoming as a gift most of them would agree to the treaty.

About noon of the following day the Cheyennes arrived— mounted and at a gallop. The same West Virginia boy who had observed White Bear saw them coming, and he never forgot the sight.

They first appeared cresting a ridge two or three miles south of the council site. Warm autumn sunshine and cloudless skies provided a striking backdrop: a giant blue curtain that dropped down and touched the browning plains at some far-distant point.

To the awed West Virginian the Cheyennes seemed to be rising from out of the earth itself as they raced over the ridge and toward the spot where he stood staring "dumbfounded." He saw that the Indians were armed, adorned, and resplendent in the noonday sun, a "glittery, gaily colored mass of barbarism." They were chanting

24

and singing and firing rifles and pistols into the air as they charged with the speed of "a whirlwind."

Near the youth stood tall, gray-haired General Harney pacing back and forth and urging other white onlookers to keep calm and not to show fear. Some of them already had fled for cover, however, and others had seized weapons for a last-ditch defense.

Then they all waited and wondered. As suddenly as the Cheyennes had appeared they stopped, not far from the now motionless Harney. Loud laughter, handshaking, and bear-hugging followed. Some commissioners who had vanished earlier reappeared and, after a few embarrassed moments, extended their own meek welcomes to these dashing, painted warriors.

More chiefs with colorful names spoke—for the Cheyennes, Black Kettle, Buffalo Chief, Bull Bear, Curly Hair, Gray Head, Heap of Birds, Lean Bear, Little Bear, Little Man, Little Robe, Slim Face, Spotted Elk, Tall Bull, Whirlwind, White Horse, and others; for the Arapahos, Little Big Mouth, Little Raven, Spotted Wolf, Storm, White Rabbit, Yellow Bear, Young Colt, and others.

None of them spoke enthusiastically about the reservation idea. Buffalo Chief called for joint ownership of the land north of the Arkansas where his Cheyennes had hunted for many years. Even after treaty signing commenced two Cheyennes, Bull Bear and White Horse, refused at first to add their marks to the document, but more prompting and pressure persuaded them to change their minds. Roman Nose never did sign (and later died fighting). But eventually it was decided: the Cheyennes and Arapahos would move to the Darlington Agency, north of the Wichita Reserve, and agree to other terms similar to those accepted by the first three tribes.

Next came more distribution of gifts, including ammunition for the Cheyennes and Arapahos, and adjournment—shortly before the arrival of a spell of severe autumn weather. Most Indians already had hurried away to gather supplies of meat for the approaching winter, but before the peace commissioners and their people could pack and leave a storm struck the council site.

Lightning flashed and thunder boomed. Wind velocity rose to a low moan, a howl, then a shriek, blowing tents and heralding a prairie rainstorm that soaked the ground. Southward, ahead of the rain, another huge grass fire glowed for a time on the horizon—set by lightning for certain, not by Cheyennes. A rainstorm moved in and put out the glow. On the following morning men sloshed through mud to load the last wagon, then commenced a dreary journey into a chilly north wind, comforted perhaps by the thought of their contribution to peace on the prairies.

They had reason to be pleased. Even White Bear, the mighty Kiowa warrior and orator, eventually had spoken in favor of taking the peace road. During a late council session he had left his camp-stool throne again to declare, at a length appropriate to him:

> It has made me glad to meet you, the commissioners of the Great Father. You, no doubt, are tired of the much talk of our people. Many of them have put themselves forward, and filled you with their sayings. I have kept back, and said nothing; not that I did not consider myself the principal chief of the Kiowa nation, but others younger desired to talk and I left it to them. Before leaving, however, as I now intend to go, I come to say that the Kiowas and Comanches have made with you a peace, and they intend to stick to it. If it brings prosperity to us, of course we will like it the better. If it brings poverty and adversity, we will not abandon it; it is our contract, and it will stand.
>
> Our people once carried on war with Texas. We thought the Great Father would not be offended, for the Texans had gone out from among his people, and become his enemies [during the Civil War]. You now tell us that they have made peace, and returned to the great family. The Kiowas and Comanches will make no bloody trail on their land. They have pledged their word, and the word shall last, unless the whites shall break their contract and invite the horrors of war. We do not break treaties. We make but few contracts and these we remember well. The whites make so many they are liable to forget them. The white chief seems not to be able to control his braves. . . . He sometimes becomes angry when he sees the wrongs his people commit on the red men, and his voice is as loud as the roaring wind; but like the wind, it soon dies away and leaves the sullen calm of unheeded oppression.

We hope now that a better time has come. . . . Before the day of apprehension came, no white man came to our village and went away hungry. . . . In the far distant past there was no suspicion among us. The world seemed large enough for both the red and white man. But its broad plains seem now to contract, and the white man grows jealous of his red brother. He once came to trade; he now comes to fight. He once came as a citizen; he now comes as a soldier. . . . He now covers his face with a cloud of jealousy and anger, and tells us to be gone, as the offended master speaks to his dog. We thank the Great Spirit that all these wrongs are now to cease, and the old days of peace and friendship to come again.

You come as friends. You have patiently heard our many complaints. To you they may have seemed trifling; to us they are everything. You have not tried, as many do, to get our lands for nothing. You have not tried to make a new bargain merely to get the advantage. You have not asked to make our annuities smaller, but unasked, you have made them larger. You have not withdrawn a single gift, but you have voluntarily provided new guarantees for our advantage and comfort. . . . You know what is best for us; do what is best. Teach us the road to travel, and we shall not depart from it forever. For your sakes the green grass shall not be stained with the blood of the whites; your people shall again be our people and peace shall be our mutual heritage. If wrong comes, we shall look to you for right; we know you will not forsake us. And tell your people to be as you have been.

I am old and will soon join my fathers, but those who come after me will remember this day. It is to be treasured . . . by the old, and will be carried by them to the grave and then be handed down, to be kept as a sacred tradition by their children. And now the time has come when I must go. Good-bye. You may not see me again; but remember [White Bear], the white man's friend.

Some truth and logic peculiar to the thinking of many wise old Indian chiefs appeared in this oration. But White Bear, like many other outstanding speakers, simply loved to see people swayed by his unusual power with words; and frequently he sought to influence them by telling them what he knew they wanted to hear.

White Bear, like many white men and a few other chiefs, could speak out of either side of his mouth. He had impressed General Hancock with all that peaceful talk, sufficiently to have received an army officer's uniform as a gift—then had worn it later during the raid on Hancock's post. White Bear could say, like Great Father Andrew Johnson himself, "Let us have peace," then raid, rape, and kill.

Sincerity in him proved to be hard to discern, but he certainly had meant one sentence: "When a Kiowa is put in a pen he dies."

3

RED RAIDERS

One young Comanche subchief who had listened to some of that talk at the Medicine Lodge Peace Council determined not to be penned in by any blue-bloused soldiers. Quanah, whose fine, erect body gave an impression of speed and power, was an Indian in his early twenties. He had come to the council site, but not all of his people seemed to have followed him in from their favorite hunting grounds far out on the flat Staked Plain (Llano Estacado), a vast region covering most of the Texas Panhandle, much of eastern New Mexico, and some adjacent areas.

Quanah was indeed as quick as his physical appearance indicated, and when he rode a horse he became pure Comanche, seeming to blend with the animal. Mounted Comanche braves like Quanah had earned an awesome nickname among some settlers: "Red Raiders of the Plains." That epithet struck terror into the hearts of Mexicans and Anglo-Americans alike—particularly those victims of previous Comanche raids who had somehow escaped with their lives. Frontiersmen and soldiers knew Comanches as being adept at using nature for their surprise attacks—like striking from the direction of a rising, bursting sun soon after break of day, then capturing or destroying property and people, and fading into the landscape. Comanches hated particularly the Texans (for taking their best hunting grounds), and they fought them savagely.

Quanah already had proved his own quickness in some raids although he had not yet become widely known as a leader, but even by sight he could be conspicuous. Taller than most other members of his Quohada ("Antelope Eater") band of Comanches (who had adopted him around the age of sixteen, after his father's death), he stood out among them much as did White Bear among his Kiowas.

Quanah even resembled White Bear in many ways. He had the same tall, muscular physique; the same dark, oval face—pronounced cheekbones, aquiline nose, thin lips, black hair parted in the center and brushed back around his ears; and the same furrows between his eyes that always made an Indian's frown look more menacing to white viewers.

But his appearance differed from White Bear's, too. Quanah's facial features seemed softer and smoother, and his eyes did not appear to take on a look of cruelty, as did White Bear's, when he peered at a displeasing sight.

Another difference required more than sight to perceive. Quanah's mother had been white—a woman who had been captured at the age of nine, who had then been raised by Indians, and who had been taken as wife by a Comanche chief when she was about eighteen. Quanah's coppery face gave no indication that any white blood flowed through his veins; nor did his raiding betray any affection for his mother's people. But Quanah obviously loved his mother, whom he had not seen in years now—not since she had been recaptured in 1860 by white men. He had retained the name given him as an infant, instead of taking a more resounding name (like Iron Jacket or Ten Bears), the way most young warriors did; and the fact that "Quanah" meant "Fragrant" or, according to other interpretations, "Fragrance," "Odor," or "Stink," might have attested further to the degree of his love for his mother and for the memories of his youth.

While still in boyhood the young Comanche chief had heard from his father and from other persons the details of his mother's original capture. The story of Cynthia Ann Parker certainly would not have frightened Quanah as it did many settlers on the Texas frontier at that time and for years afterward. Told from the whites' viewpoint, the only one documentable to any extent, the account evoked terror among frontier children and parents who were vulnerable to similar depredations.

Thirty-one years before that 1867 gathering at the Medicine Lodge Peace Council, the southeastern limit of the frontier had been in present East Texas, generally along the damp, low-lying Gulf Coast and farther inland to a distance of one hundred miles or so. At the beginning of the year 1836 Texas still belonged to Mexico, although most inhabitants of the region (with the exception of residents of San Antonio and a few other westernmost towns) were of Anglo-American ancestry.

Beyond the frontier, in what is now referred to as East Central Texas, a small colony of immigrants had erected a large, quadrangular stockade for protection and had settled in and around it. The structure, known as Parker's Fort, was located near the headwaters of the heavily wooded Navasota River.

The site had been chosen by a Baptist Church elder named John Parker, a seventy-nine-year-old native of Virginia who had moved with kinfolk and other church members from Illinois to Texas before the outbreak of the conclusive rebellion against Mexico. Some of the Parker immigrants had settled earlier, during a layover period, around Fort Houston, near present Elkhart, Texas, but the rest had traveled on westward and had built their private fort on a slight rise overlooking a gentle valley and the tree-lined river bottom nearby. The area lay far removed from the safety of any neighboring settlements, but it offered advantages for the eight or nine families—the Parkers, Plummers, Frosts, Nixons, Kelloggs, and others—who inhabited it. Fields were fertile, winters were comparatively mild, and Mexican authority was distant, affording religious freedom.

But the isolation had not precluded involvement in political affairs. When the men of Parker's Fort heard reports from the settlements about Santa Anna's "invasion" of Texas with a large Mexican army brought along to smother dissent among the increasingly restive Anglo-American colonists (who had settled, with Mexican permission, as a potential economic boon to the country), some of them joined the Texan army. Other occupants of the fort fled eastward to safety.

In May, after the victory of Sam Houston and his Texans at San Jacinto, Parker's immigrants had returned to their fort to recommence what certainly appeared to be an idyllic life, especially now

31

that Texas had won its freedom. By day the men went out into the fields to work their crops. At night they herded their horses and cattle into the fort, which had been walled with strong timbers and further protected by two watchtowers that provided a complete view of the countryside. After the last chore had been completed and supper eaten, the people who resided inside the fort bedded down in comfortable log houses for the night. Embers from evening fires burned low, then faded away, but darkness brought no worry. Outside, those strong walls silhouetted against the night sky would keep out nocturnal prowlers, and with the heavy gate closed and firmly secured only a dim light from the heavens could gain entrance.

But as time passed without trouble the people grew careless. They ignored a warning passed on to them by a friendly Indian who traded in their vicinity (if a bit of family history is correct). "The wild Indians of the northwest are going to destroy that fort," the friend had declared. Other records indicate a reason for this wrath: dishonest dealing in the past by a Parker's Fort settler, or at least by a person whom the Indians believed to have been a member of the group. As a result of the warning, two men living outside the stockade but near it were said to have left for the greater safety of Fort Houston.

The others refused to flee, and apparently they took no greater precautions. Sometimes they even neglected to shut the gate, and it lay open at nine o'clock in the bright and balmy morning of May 19, 1836, after some men had left for work in the fields. Inside, a child glanced out the entrance and saw a throng of Indians, all mounted and waiting a hundred yards or so away, staring back at the fort. Later estimates placed their numbers at five to seven hundred—many of them the feared Comanches, those red raiders from farther west. Comprising the remainder were Kiowas and Caddoes—none of them to be toyed with.

The child's screams brought the occupants running. Benjamin Parker, a son of Elder John Parker, strode out to talk with the Indians, who were displaying a white flag. He returned to the fort to say the unwanted visitors were professing friendship and were asking for beef and directions to a camp site with a water hole.

The last request, however, indicated other intentions. Not far away flowed the Navasota River, and these Indians surely knew it.

But Parker said he would return and talk to them, with the hope of warding off an attack. Despite pleas from kinfolk he walked back toward the waiting warriors.

The Indians wanted no more of his talk. They swarmed over Parker and killed him with lances, while horrified relatives watched. Then, yelling and chanting, the raiders rushed through the gate and attacked the fort, running down a number of screaming, crying occupants—spearing, stripping, and mutilating them: men, women, children. One baby they later roped and threw into a cluster of cactus, pulling the body back and forth until it had become an unrecognizable red lump.

Some persons inside the fort had managed to escape through the only other opening in the walls as soon as they heard the first sounds of rampage around the gate. At the far end of the stockade, away from the main entrance, builders had emplaced a small door just large enough to allow space for an exit to a spring of water located some fifty yards away. Through that door fled a number of occupants of the fort, including Mrs. Lucy Parker (whose husband, Silas, another son of Elder John Parker, would soon be killed outside the gate while trying to rescue a niece) and Lucy Parker's four children: Cynthia Ann, aged nine; John, six; Silas, Jr., about four; and Orlena, an infant. Some other women fled through the door, too, with the aim of alerting their menfolk working in fields nearby.

Cynthia Ann had been entrusted with carrying a bag stuffed with one hundred dollars in coins—probably Silas Parker's total wealth. The treasure had been grabbed up just before the quick departure and given to her. But all that weight slowed Cynthia Ann. She complained, and her mother told her to drop the money.

The girl threw the bag in a clump of bushes and ran on toward her mother, who was carrying Orlena, and her two brothers. Behind them lay the besieged fort, distant about a half a mile now, but still a bedlam that could be heard.

By this time the entire countryside seemed to be aswarm with mounted Indians who had fanned out around the fort. One young warrior named Tahkonuapeah, according to Parker family history, swooped down on the fleeing girl, seized her, and planted her firmly astride his pony. Another Indian leaned from his horse and grabbed John. Sister and brother, both of them yelling and crying, vanished from Lucy Parker's sight. Mrs. Parker herself certainly would have fallen victim, along with her two youngest children, except for the bravery of a man hurriedly returning to the fort from the fields. He held up his rifle in plain view of several threatening warriors and succeeded eventually in getting Mrs. Parker and her children into adjacent woods, where they remained hidden for many horrible hours.

Other occupants of the fort had escaped, too, but none of them dared to leave their various hiding places to look for survivors, or even to make a noise, until long after the Indians had galloped their horses away westward, carrying loot and captives.

That afternoon passed hot, dry—and slowly. Finally, at twilight, two men who had been working in fields when the attack came and who had sprinted to a hiding place in the adjacent river bottom crept back toward the now placid fort, to look after any wounded in need of help. "We could not see a single individual alive or hear a human sound," one of the men said later. "But [some] dogs were barking . . . cattle lowing . . . horses neighing, and . . . hogs squealing, making a . . . strange medley of sounds."

Fearful still of the presence of lurking Indians, the two men sneaked back to their hiding place and stayed there for the rest of the night. On the following morning, as cautious as ever, they returned to the fort, found a few saddles and some meal, bacon, and honey, packed the supplies on five or six horses still standing unharmed in a pen inside the fort, and returned again to their refuge, without taking time to bury the dead.

Not until night had covered the countryside did they dare to commence the journey to Fort Houston, some fifty miles to the east. They arrived safely, as did other survivors (including Mrs. Parker and her two youngest children) who had struggled across the prickly wilderness despite hunger, thirst, and some painful wounds. The count of survivors of the wild attack eventually reached twenty-three—surprisingly.

Twelve men from Fort Houston later traveled to Parker's Fort to bury the dead and to verify the fact that five persons were indeed missing and presumed captives: Cynthia Ann and John Parker, two women (one of them pregnant), and an eighteen-month-old son of the again expectant mother, Mrs. Rachel Plummer, the niece whom Silas Parker had sought to rescue.

Following her release after nearly two years of captivity Mrs. Plummer wrote a brief description of the raid and of some ensuing events. Her account represented the last Caucasian glance at the vanishing nine-year-old Parker girl, Cynthia Ann, who was Mrs. Plummer's cousin and who would one day become the mother of the Comanche subchief Quanah.

When the Indians' intention of attacking the fort had become clear, Mrs. Plummer recalled, she ran to get her young son, James, and sought to flee through the main gate to a field nearby, where her husband had gone earlier for another day's work. But even as she ran from the fort she could see the Indians lancing Benjamin Parker, who had hoped to ward off attack through his talk. Wild yells seemed to reach "the very skies" and to grow even louder as attackers spread out around the fort, seeking other victims.

A warrior in a group of raiders who had galloped ahead of the running woman knocked her down with a hoe. Other Indians grabbed her infant son. She fainted.

> [After that] the first I recollect, they were dragging me along by the hair. I made several unsuccessful attempts to [rise] to my feet before I could do it. As they took me past the fort, I heard an awful screaming near the place where they had first seized me. I heard some shots . . . [and] heard Uncle Silas shout a triumphant huzza! I did, for one moment, hope the men had gathered from the neighboring farms, and might release me.

But she hoped in vain. The Indians swept on with scant interference, and her Uncle Silas fell dead.

Mrs. Plummer's captors dragged her to the area where another uncle, Benjamin Parker, lay dead—his face mutilated and his body porcupine-like from many arrows shot into it. As other Indians passed by they thrust their lances into the red corpse. Mrs. Plummer, almost as bloody now as her uncle's remains, looked around for her son, did not see him, felt certain that he had been killed, and expected to join him in death. Then she saw the boy in the grasp of a mounted warrior and heard him sobbing the only word he knew: "Mother—mother!" She cried out. A Comanche woman rode over and struck her several times with a whip, apparently to encourage silence.

> I now expected [that] my father and husband, and all the rest of the men, were killed. I soon saw a party of Indians bringing my aunt, Elizabeth Kellogg, and Uncle Silas' two oldest children, Cynthia Ann and John; also some bloody scalps; among them I could distinguish that of my grandfather by the gray hairs. . . .
>
> I had a few minutes to reflect [before being taken away]. . . . As I was leaving, I looked back at the place where I was one hour before, happy and free. . . .
>
> They soon convinced me that I had no time to reflect upon the past, for they commenced whipping and beating me with clubs . . . so that my flesh was never well from bruises and wounds during my captivity. To undertake to narrate their barbarous treatment would only add to my present distress.

The details Mrs. Plummer left out would have pertained to rape, which in those euphemistic days was usually referred to by writers as "a fate worse than death," if mentioned at all. She certainly would have been badly used by the Indian warriors after they had put sufficient distance between themselves and Parker's Fort. Some contemporary but unpublicized reports have described how women were held or staked down for as many as twenty rapes. After that the victims were often murdered, mutilated, and scalped.

But Mrs. Plummer escaped this ultimate horror. Instead, she and her son and the other three captives traveled with the Indians in a northwesterly direction, away from the white settlements, during the afternoon and evening following the raid.

> About midnight they stopped. They now tied a plaited thong around my arms, and drew my hands behind me. They tied them so tight that the scars can be easily seen to this day. They then tied a similar thong around my ankles, and drew my feet and hands together. They now turned me on my face and I was unable to turn over, when they commenced beating me over the head with their bows, and it was with great difficulty I

36

could keep from smothering in my blood; for the wound they gave me with the hoe, and many others, were bleeding freely.

I suppose it was to add to my misery that they brought my little James Pratt so near me that I could hear him cry. He would call for mother; and often his voice was weakened by the blows they would give him. I could hear the blows. . . . The rest of the prisoners were brought near me, but we were not allowed to speak one word together. My aunt called me once, and I answered her; but . . . they jumped with their feet upon us, which nearly took our lives. Often did the children [Cynthia Ann and John Parker] cry, but were soon hushed by such blows that I had no idea they could survive. [The Indians] commenced screaming and dancing around the scalps; kicking and stamping the prisoners.

In a few days a band of Comanches rode off westward with Cynthia Ann and John Parker, and Mrs. Plummer never saw the two youngsters again. Her own captors traveled on north, generally mistreating her until one day, months later, she attracted admiration among men of the tribe by clubbing an Indian woman who had been trying to beat her. After that they called her "Fighting Squaw," and her tribal standing improved noticeably.

Subsequent treatment given Cynthia Ann and John Parker went unrecorded, but considering some narratives left by other young white captives it could only have consisted of a brutal initiation into Indian life.

A fourteen-year-old boy captured by Comanches seventy-five miles west of Parker's Fort (and thirty-one years after the attack there) described his own ordeal:

I was suffering severely from my wound [in the right leg, which had been pierced by an arrow], but to this they paid no heed nor applied anything to alleviate the pain, but after a day or two when it had gotten thoroughly sore, they would carry it through a process of twisting and wrenching every now and then, I suppose to increase my already excruciating pain. They would kick and knock me about just for pastime it seemed, whip my bare back until it was perfectly bloody . . . fire their pistols held so close to my head that the caps and powder

37

would fly in my face, producing powder burns and bruises, until I was very much disfigured.

In time the Comanches gave this lad an opportunity to join their tribe, as they did most white captives who survived various initiations, by offering him an Indian girl as a wife. But he rejected marriage, tried unsuccessfully to escape, and eventually was ransomed by a white trader for 250 dollars.

Another boy, captured at the age of ten years and eleven months by Apaches raiding near his Mason County, Texas, home in 1870, received similar treatment for many weeks. Each night when the Indians made camp during their journey home

> they caught me, tied a rope around my neck, and fastened the other end to a bush. They strapped my arms behind me and tied my feet together. This done, they secured a pole, each end of which was placed in a forked stick driven into the ground. These sticks were about six feet apart, so that I was suspended from the horizontal pole, face down, so near the ground that my breast barely touched the sand and the least pressure would draw the cords deep into my flesh.
>
> Not content with placing me in this extremely painful position, they then placed a heavy stone on my back, pressing my face and nose into the sand, and there I was compelled to stay all night long, with no covering except that large rock on my back.
>
> It was damp and cool, and I suffered all the agonies of death, but when I would groan an Indian would jump up and pull my hair and ears and beat me.

As this youth survived his excruciating initiations without many whimpers (somewhat the same as Indian boys themselves were forced to do) he became accepted by the tribe and grew to be an Apache warrior. Since his own family presumably had been killed by the same Indians who had captured him, the transition to another life perhaps came more easily. In time he learned to love the freedom enjoyed by Indians: the unfenced landscape topped by an inviting horizon; a day's routine regulated only by desire (but sometimes restricted by necessity) and not dictated by any man-made, mundane employment; willing females ready to fulfill his manhood free of many barriers constructed by other societies—a liberty that seems to have been mentioned most often by white men who gave reasons for joining Indian tribes.

He learned to swim, as did Indian boys themselves, by being tossed in a river with a rope tied around his waist. He became adept at forecasting weather by observing spider webs: a long, thin web meant dry weather; short and thick indicated rain. He acquired an Indian's appetite and satisfied it in typical fashion after killing an ox:

> We . . . sucked the paunch and lower intestines, stripped the colon with our hands, tied up one end and filled it with water to carry with us. We ate the hearts, livers, lights, melts, and kidneys raw, while warm, and sucked up all the blood we could get. We made a fire, roasted the ribs and neck, and had a feast.

He came to hate white settlers and the danger they posed to his free life, and he tortured captives along with the Indians with whom he roamed. Like his fellow tribesmen, he feared the frontier minutemen known as Texas Rangers, whose weapons always seemed to be loaded and unerringly aimed, and who slept in the saddle and ate while they rode—or traveled hungry. His respect for United States regulars stood on a lower level. Those soldiers were much slower getting ready for a march.

Even after fleeing from the Apaches (following his slaying of a medicine man) and joining a band of Comanches, this white youth remained completely Indian. Eventually, after government officials had reunited him, mostly against his will, with his dimly remembered family (who had not been killed during the attack, as he had supposed), his first desire was "immediately to go back to the tribe," but he lived out the rest of his life as a white man, one always yearning for the vigorous days of his Indian youth.

In the soul of captive Cynthia Ann Parker a similar transformation would have taken place. Soon separated from her brother John (who would eventually forsake Indian life, marry a Mexican girl, and establish a ranch in Mexico), Cynthia Ann thus broke the last link with her past.

Time proved to be an anesthetic. An Indian family adopted her, and her treatment would have improved after that. Desire to escape would have given way to a primary interest in self-preservation wherever she was living. Further, countless wild animals and hundreds of roadless, thirsty, hungry miles lay between her and any white settlement, even assuming she knew the specific location of one. In addition to that (she probably thought), all members of her immediate family, with the exception of John, had been killed. Cynthia Ann had been left with a life to live while still young enough to bend to meet the environment, and the longer she stayed with the tribe the more Indian she became—the same as had the Mason County, Texas, boy captured by Apaches. In time Cynthia Ann Parker would forget her native language, would almost forget her white name, and except for a pair of blue eyes would have the look of any sun-gilded Indian who roamed the land proud and free.

Even while she began riding with those unfenced lords of the Plains she became a legend back home. Her family constantly sought her return, and both the United States and Texas governments instructed their agents to look for her and to ransom her when found. But no one saw Cynthia Ann Parker for nearly five years after her capture.

In 1840 two white traders and a Delaware Indian guide came upon her band of Comanches. One of the white men, Len Williams (later known as a Texas Indian agent), sought to ransom her from the Comanche brave into whose family she had been adopted. But the Indian glared so menacingly, Williams said, that his fierceness "warned . . . of the danger of further mention of the subject."

Williams did get to see the girl, now about fourteen. The same Indian grudgingly allowed Cynthia Ann to come out and to sit down by the root of a tree while Williams tried to engage her in conversation.

The trader was familiar with her story, as were most people on the frontier. He gave Cynthia Ann information about her relatives and some of her former playmates, and he offered to carry back any message she wanted to send. But the girl spoke not a word and appeared to show no emotion, except reputedly for one brief quiver of her lips, perhaps indicating that at this time, at least, she had not become totally Indian. But Cynthia Ann Parker's story has been

40

fictionalized by sentimental authors, and the lip quiver might never have occurred. She might not have understood Williams' talk, or she might not have cared to answer. Whatever the reason for her silence, Texans could scarcely believe that an Anglo-American captive would actually prefer Indian life.

For another eleven years white people heard nothing new about the girl. As would be learned later, however, at the age of seventeen or eighteen she became the wife of a Comanche chief, Peta Nocona. Probably in May of 1845 she gave birth to Quanah (the flowers of springtime might have been responsible for calling him "Fragrant") at a location said by many students of Parker history to have been near the shore of a large, desolate body of water, now alkaline, named Cedar Lake, lying isolated amid a flat expanse of Plains dreariness near present Seminole, Texas. The birth represented a quiet fusion of blood that flowed elsewhere from countless wounds.

Whatever the date and wherever the location, the event would have been conducted in the style of the Comanches, to whom the mystery of life and the need for additional strength through greater numbers made birth an occasion of greatest moment. The girl once known as Cynthia Ann would have isolated herself beforehand in a tepee or lodge provided with some special, if primitive, equipment: long stakes embedded in the earth for an expectant mother to clench during the pangs of childbirth; and two holes, one for holding afterbirth and the other for making a steam bath. A few women might have assisted, but no man would have been around (with the exception of a shaman—medicine man—if the birth proved especially long and difficult).

The arrival of a boy always brought particular rejoicing, although Comanches welcomed infants of either sex. A woman attendant would have cut the umbilical cord, and other women would have bathed the baby, wrapped him in velvety skins, and placed him in a primitive cradle. Later the boy could be expected to come under his father's instruction.

Within two years a baby brother, Pecos, joined Quanah in the Nocona household.

Cynthia Ann Parker's relatives in East Texas, knowing nothing of these events, continued to hope for her release from what they presumed to be a terrible captivity, but years passed without any

41

further sighting of the girl. About 1851, fifteen years after the raid at Parker's Fort, "a party of white hunters, including some friends of her family, visited the Comanche encampment on the upper Canadian [River], and recognizing Cynthia Ann—probably through the medium of her name alone, sounded her in a secret manner as to . . . a return to her people and the haunts of civilization"—if a piece of dubious writing by a Texan named Victor M. Rose can be believed.

> She shook her heard in a sorrowful negative [Rose continued] and pointed to her little, naked barbarians sporting at her feet, and to the great greasy, lazy buck sleeping in the shade near at hand, the locks of a score of scalps dangling at his belt, and whose first utterance upon arousing would be a stern command to his meek, pale-faced wife. . . .
>
> She retained but the vaguest remembrance of her people—as dim and flitting as the phantoms of a dream; she was accustomed now to the wild life she led, and found in its repulsive features charms. . . . "I am happily wedded," she said to these visitors. "I love my husband, who is good and kind, and my little ones, who, too, are his, and I cannot forsake them!"

The likelihood was that Cynthia Ann now spoke no English (and certainly no such fancy words as were quoted), but whatever was said, and whether or not "a party of white hunters" actually ever saw her, part of Rose's account in time proved accurate. In December of 1860, more than twenty-four years after her capture, a Texas Ranger captain named L. S. (Sul) Ross (later state governor) led a mounted force of 120 men against some of Peta Nocona's Comanches, whom he found in the act of breaking camp around sand hills bordering the Pease River—near the present Oklahoma-Texas line. A wailing north wind and billows of stinging sand enabled Ross to surprise the Indians, who proved to be mostly women and children, and to hurry their already commenced departure with a generous and lengthy fusillade that knocked some Comanches off their ponies and left them lying sprawled and bleeding on the thirsty ground. The attackers galloped after the rest.

Ross and another officer identified as a Lieutenant Tom Kelliheir pursued several Indians fleeing on horseback. After a mile-long chase they neared the hindmost rider. Ross aimed his pistol and was ready to fire when he saw his target: a woman, holding up a child for both men to see. Kelliheir halted to look after these two prisoners, but Ross sped on, shot two other Indians (one a girl and the other a man he erroneously thought to be Peta Nocona), and rode back to where Kelliheir was waiting.

> [I] found him bitterly cursing himself for having run his pet horse so hard after an "old squaw" [Ross said]. She was very dirty, both in her scanty garments and person. But as soon as I looked on her face, I said: "Why, Tom, this is a white woman. Indians don't have blue eyes."

Another member of Ross's force—a man named James H. Baker, later a teacher, whose previously unpublished diary of that expedition came to light in 1937—studied the "old squaw" and wrote this notation: "The woman is of white parentage and was undoubtedly taken by the Indians when a child, has married an Indian and has a family, looks just like an Indian, except that she has blue eyes."

Ross immediately suspected the woman to be the long-lost Cynthia Ann Parker, but he found that this woman, whoever she was, spoke no English and apparently remembered nothing of her early life. From the moment of her capture she showed little emotion other than anguish—first crying, then assuming a look of silent sullenness at having been deprived of her freedom. A brief interlude, however, came that evening. James Baker also recorded it in his diary.

> As we sat about the camp fire I picked up a tiny moccasin and after looking at it decided to keep it as it was a beautiful one. On glancing around I noticed the woman looking at me intently and I looked at her and the little child and noticed it had only one moccasin on, so I held up the one I had picked up. She nodded her head and I held it out and the child came over and got it and the mother put it on for her.

Ross sent the woman and her daughter back to the settlements. He immediately informed an uncle of Cynthia Ann's, Isaac Parker, of his discovery and suggested that Parker might ascertain her identity.

Isaac Parker visited her, found her as silently sullen as Ross had left her, saw that she indeed apparently possessed no knowledge of the English language or of the attack on Parker's Fort so long ago, and prepared to leave. But before he departed he said to her, "The name of my niece was Cynthia Ann."

Later, in a letter to an early Texas historian, Isaac Parker described how the sound of a name not heard for nearly a quarter of a century stirred dormant memories in the woman and caused her to break her silence. "The moment I mentioned the name," he said, "she straightened herself in her seat, and, patting herself on the breast, said 'Cynthia Ann, Cynthia Ann.'"

Cynthia Ann's daughter proved to be named Prairie Flower (Topasannah), another child by Chief Peta Nocona. Neither mother nor daughter flourished in white civilization. Cynthia Ann sought to escape, to return to her family and to her wild, free life, and she had to be watched almost constantly.

She and her daughter lived for a while with the uncle who had identified her and, later, with her younger brother who had escaped capture during the attack on Parker's Fort.* In time she reacquired the use of her native tongue, but only gradually, and she rarely relaxed—not even in the company of relatives. Once, a short time after her recapture, and before her knowledge of English had returned to any extent, friends of the Parker family took her on a visit to the State Capitol at Austin, where (on the eve of Civil War) a convention planning secession happened to be in session. They sat in the gallery listening to arguments for some time before Cynthia Ann's companions realized their guest had become alarmed by a belief that the delegates must be members of some council discussing punishment for her, and they had difficulty in reassuring her of safety.

For more than three agonizing years Cynthia Ann Parker survived white captivity—sometimes like an animal in a cage, when curious Texans visited her place of residence to stare at her. Always she yearned to return to her husband and her two sons, somewhere on the Staked Plain.

Then her daughter died. Her own death followed quickly—in

* Lucy Parker, Cynthia Ann's mother, had been dead for years.

1864, while residing with her brother. Away in the vast but constantly shrinking land of the Comanches, her husband and her youngest son, Pecos, also died, leaving Quanah an only survivor.

At the 1867 Medicine Lodge Peace Council the young subchief learned from white men the story of his mother's and sister's death three years earlier. To commemorate the memory of his mother he took on the surname Parker, previously unknown to him.

The death of father, mother, brother, and sister in the wild struggle to survive made Quanah Parker more Indian than ever (as Quanah's own son would remark to a historian many years afterward). Quanah rode away from the site of the council meeting with an over-the-shoulder taunt that meant something like, "Tell the white chiefs that the Quohadas are warriors and will surrender when the blue coats come and whip us." He rejoined the rest of his people far out on the Staked Plain, where they continued to organize and to carry out forays that earned them and other much-feared bands the name "Red Raiders."

Some of Quanah's attacks were to be aimed at a frontier area in present North Central Texas particularly open to ravages of marauding Indians: Parker County, whose seat of administration was at Weatherford. But this was mere coincidence. Quanah probably did not know at the time that the county took its name from his mother's uncle, Isaac Parker, the man who had helped to reclaim blue eyed Cynthia Ann for white civilization and who had, at the same time, brought on her death and the ensuing rage of her Indian son.

4

DISHONEST WORDS
AND BROKEN PROMISES

Peace and tranquillity continued to elude people of the West, even after the signing of Laramie and Medicine Lodge treaties. Some Indian chiefs, like Quanah and other leaders more widely known than he, never had agreed to the terms, of course, and they continued their attacks on invaders of their hunting lands. Some others obviously never intended to abide by the treaties, although they signed —with the primary intention of getting presents. But even those Indians who had honestly pledged to be peaceful soon became restive, and with good reason.

The fault lay mostly in Washington, with the United States Congress, where treaty approval and the promised tribal assistance went unacted upon for months. Of greater importance to most congressmen was the looming impeachment of President Johnson, which occurred formally in the House of Representatives on February 25, 1868, after much preliminary maneuvering. The Senate trial occupied most of the time, then, until late May of the same year.

In waning 1867 and early 1868 few officials of government outside the West had opportunity or desire to devote attention to the Indians and to those promises. In the South, northern fortune hunters ("carpetbaggers") supported by occasional southern opportunists ("scalawags") were marshaling newly enfranchised Negroes for their own greedy purposes and preparing to leave in their Reconstruction wake a desolate path of scandal, extravagance, fraud, and some enormous debts and taxes.

In the West, many Indians who had sincerely agreed to either of the treaties waited a while for the expected assistance to arrive. But autumn of 1867 browned into a barren and icy winter, and still no supplies came. Most Indians, being provident in regard to the coldest season, survived well on their own stores, but they could not ignore what they considered to be dishonest words and broken promises. Conscientious agents distributed the small amounts of food obtainable and sought to explain the cumbersome workings of the government, but without much success. Spring of 1868 brought lengthening days, vanishing stores of food, and more menacing grumbles. Give us arms and ammunition, Indians said, and we can obtain our own food. That request went largely ignored, too, although an agent friendly to Indians, Edward Wynkoop, did distribute (courtesy the Indian Bureau) a number of antiquated rifles and pistols to "peaceful" Cheyennes and Arapahos at Fort Larned.

Wynkoop's action angered senior army officers, who not only feared the eventual aim of those weapons, but who also resented civilian authority over people the Indian Bureau "fed in the winter" and the Army "fought in the summer." These officers thought the simplest solution would have been to place Indians under military control and supervision. When some of the Cheyennes and Arapahos used their old firearms to carry out raids the anger grew.

Fiery General Philip Sheridan, a small, bullet-headed commander of the Department of the Missouri whose ready fund of profanity bespoke his giant temper, ordered the 7th Cavalry out to punish the Indians. In approval, Sheridan's superior, tall, red-headed, fierce-faced General William Tecumseh Sherman, announced that a state of war existed with the Cheyennes and Arapahos. Agent Wynkoop resigned in protest. Away rode General Alfred Sully, commanding, and eleven troops of the 7th. But Sully, who tended toward a belief that the best way to get rid of a wild savage was to civilize him, rode in an army ambulance, not on horseback, and the Indians outmaneuvered and outfought him. Sully and his cavalrymen groped their way back to Fort Dodge late in the same summer of 1868 that the United States Senate was finally getting around to ratifying the Medicine Lodge treaty (on August 19).

Sheridan seethed at Sully's failure. Fighting continued, and it

47

blazed especially in Kansas. This brought no Washington disavowal of the recently designed reservation policy, but it did require primary reliance again on force to herd the Indians onto their assigned plots of land. Sherman, who tended toward a belief that the best way to get rid of a wild savage was to exterminate him, said that agents should conduct all peaceably inclined Indians to their reservations in the Indian Territory, south of Kansas, but he added a significant observation that all Indians, peaceable or hostile, looked alike.

The officer who should have commanded the 7th Cavalry during its recent campaign was not Sully, as the exasperated Sheridan would have agreed, but ambitious George Armstrong Custer, a horseback hero of the Civil War who had been brevetted major general at the age of twenty-five and who (with his cavalrymen) had won great acclaim for harassing General Robert E. Lee during the retreat from Richmond and for hastening surrender at Appomattox.

Custer would have been leading the 7th except for a vagary of fate. As a result of a court-martial stemming from some of his actions while commanding the regiment during General Hancock's poorly thought out 1867 campaign, he had been suspended from rank and command for one year, with loss of pay. While Sully toured Indian-infested prairies in his ambulance Custer was enjoying greater creature comforts with his wife, Libbie, in Monroe, Michigan, a town located on the western shore of Lake Erie—close to good hunting, boating, and fishing.

The chastened officer might have had a hankering to end his enforced holiday and to get back to his regiment, but along with ambition he had an obvious affinity for life away from military duty and the discipline it imposed. He could endure hardship, as he had shown, but he also enjoyed comfort whenever it was obtainable. Probably he was not extremely fretful, especially since he already had won national renown and would have been basking in it during his sojourn in Monroe. Custer was a man whose being seemed to demand fame as well as food to flourish, but for the moment he could have subsisted on glory already stockpiled.

In the fall of 1868, when Sully and the 7th Cavalry struggled back to their post, Custer was twenty-eight. History already had recorded him as a hard-riding, hard-fighting cavalry leader who deliberately cultivated an image by allowing his thick, curly, golden hair to grow to such length that it would fall around his shoulders. Certainly he would have gazed approvingly at his top-to-bottom appearance in uniform before a full-length mirror. Those blond curls cascaded from beneath a broad-brimmed cavalry officer's hat and contrasted colorfully with its army blue. A pair of bright blue eyes were deep-laid in a hawkish face that featured a sharp nose, harsh, high cheekbones, and a thick, drooping yellow mustache overtopping a clipped tuft that grew below his lips and de-emphasized the shallowness of his chin. Ample shoulders and slim hips set off a slender, sinewy body—just under six feet from head to toe—clad in a close-fitting, flat-collared blue jacket splotched with gold buttons, shoulder straps, and insignia of rank; and blue trousers with two thin yellow stripes running along the outside seams. A pair of black top boots, well polished and affixed with cavalryman's spurs, completed the uniform. A favorite pose of Custer's showed him standing, arms folded across his chest, with left leg placed slightly forward of the other and bent as if in a half step. A pair of gloves as bright as the trousers' stripes hid his large-knuckled hands.

He looked the cavalry officer that he obviously thought himself to be, but the quiet pose did not betray a nervous abruptness of body movement when dismounted. Any unknowing observer would have had to be told another physical flaw. During campaigns Custer sunburned badly, and he never tanned. Nor were some mental weaknesses evident at a glance.

Custer seemed in many ways to have been a boy who never matured—just as he never outgrew the family nickname "Autie," a result of his early mispronunciation of "Armstrong," the name his father had preferred to call him. He and his brother Tom, who served with him in the Army, never overcame an enjoyment, acquired paternally, of the rudest kind of practical joking. Nor did he ever outgrow a childlike selfishness and a tendency to use men badly in his quest for self-gain—even easygoing superior officers, unless they scolded him and thus usually won his respect and sometimes sycophancy. Further, he never put behind him a romanticism reminiscent of youthful daydreaming, and he could be emotionally carried away by plays, books, and certain music, without showing much sensitivity sometimes to real-life sadness like human suffering. He would describe with relish the death throes of the first man he ever killed, during the Civil War, and he liked to show off the victim's sword, which he frequently wore.

But in some actual situations of excitement he might betray other emotions, through a voice that grew high and piercing and through a fast flow of words and phrases repeated over and over with agitation—like "all right—all right—all right!" The night before certain combat, observers have said, Custer would scarcely sleep, and the next morning he might be flushed and jittery, but in battle he showed remarkable calm, and he rarely used even the palest profanity—then or any other time.

As a cadet at the United States Military Academy (1857–61) Custer did not show promise of potential generalship or give any indication of excessive vanity. When his long blond curls earned him the nickname "Fanny," he cut his hair short, to be less conspicuous. Friendly and easygoing to a degree that slipped into slovenliness, he called forth neither enmity nor admiration. An accumulation of demerits nearly forced his expulsion once, but through an early instance of the good luck that some historians said followed Custer throughout most of his military career, that particular rule seemed to have been changed in time, and Custer stayed on to graduate thirty-fourth in a class of thirty-four.

His very last duty at the Academy resulted in a court-martial, when as officer of the guard he refused to intervene in a fist fight between two other cadets, declaring instead that they should be allowed to have a fair fight. Later he admitted error (something rare for him) in a written statement:

> My duty as officer of the guard was plain and simple. I should have arrested the two combatants and sent them to the guard tents for violating the . . . regulations of the Academy. But the instincts of the boy prevailed over the obligation of the officer of the guard.

The court-martial delayed his reporting for army duty until July 1861, but he made up for lost time in a hurry. Events that quickly followed showed his ecstasy at being largely on his own and out of the uncongenial atmosphere of learning and discipline. His craving for fame would have been a major motivation, too.

Custer began to attract favorable attention among superiors— first as a courier of daring and dependability, then, after senior officers had recognized his splendid horsemanship along with other qualities, as commander of the Michigan Cavalry Brigade, at the age of twenty-three, with the brevet rank of brigadier general.

Early in 1864 he married the twenty-one-year-old daughter of a prominent Monroe, Michigan, widower, using his newly won renown to overcome the future father-in-law's—and, in fact, all Monroe's—snobbish distaste for Custer's plain-folk parents, father and stepmother, and especially for his father, a raucous advocate of the Democratic Party in an area not fond of Democrats.

Elizabeth Bacon, a romantic herself, would have been awed by young General Custer's dash and reputation. They were married in the First Presbyterian Church at Monroe. For the ceremony Custer cut his curls and dressed in the personally designed full uniform of a brigadier general.

Libbie dazzled him and probably everyone else with her own appearance: dark eyes that reflected every smile, brown hair parted, brushed back behind her ears, and knotted at the back of a delicate neck, and girlish figure with a petiteness that could not be hidden by the hoop skirt or by the long bulging sleeves of her green wedding dress, which she had trimmed with a braid of cavalry yellow.

After a honeymoon trip to Cleveland, West Point, New York, and Washington, Custer returned to the business of fighting, and Libbie insisted on going with him for a time into the war theater, despite Custer's desire that she remain in Washington. This manifested a characteristic that would, in time, become obvious. Libbie's love overflowed into worship. Despite her complete femininity she repressed her great fear of various risks and her dislike of firearms and other aspects of rough military life to accompany her husband wherever possible—and sometimes only an order from a superior officer concerned about her safety kept her away. In marrying the "boy general," Libbie, a gently spoiled only-surviving daughter of an indulgent father, gave up her entire upbringing: the comfort of a neatly kept home, the mood and leisure for reading George Eliot, Tennyson, and Shakespeare and for engaging in her favorite hobby—watercolor painting—and the strict maintenance of religious practices that called for no work on Sunday, no dancing anytime, and no close association with persons who used liquor. Her wedding denoted no sudden or extreme departure from past beliefs, but thereafter "the General"—as Libbie always referred to her husband publicly—received first priority.

After the Civil War the Custer comet seemed to have vanished, although it was still remembered. Custer had been brevetted a major general, but his permanent rank was only captain. Now, however, the nation had little use for commissions of any rank. Some officers gave up their Civil War promotions to enlist in the Army, but Custer in time enjoyed better fortune. After the end of the war he was sent to Texas—to be near Mexico, where conflict seemed to be impending because of the importation there of a foreign ruler, Maximilian, and some French troops, despite well-known United States doctrines prohibiting such practice.

Headquartered in a vacated two-story stone "Blind Asylum" in Austin, Custer continued an indulgence in his rank by taking Libbie, guests, and the local army band to nearby Mount Bonnell, where the chosen ones picnicked while military entertainers serenaded them with music like the "Anvil Chorus," a Custer favorite. When France withdrew its troops and a Mexican faction executed Maximilian, Custer left Texas.

The West, however, still offered him military opportunity. As part of the postbellum drive against Indians the War Department created the 7th Cavalry and chose Custer as its commander, to hold Regular Army rank of lieutenant colonel. Libbie accompanied him to his new job. At Fort Riley during the fall of 1866 and the winter of 1866–67 Custer and a few other West Point graduates molded into something of a military regiment an odd mixture of humanity: Civil War veterans, several of them having resigned commissioned rank to enlist and stay in the Army; drunkards and other escapees from various self-disciplines imposed by polite civilian society; indolent men who anticipated giving scant work in return for their upkeep; and energetic recruits who hoped to hack out a career. They all came together at Riley, a fort composed of buildings constructed around a parade ground and located amid prairies a hundred miles west of Fort Leavenworth on a rise of level, treeless land overlooking the junction of the Smoky Hill and Republican rivers. Cold, late-autumn wind whipped across the plains and flung sand, then snow, into the faces of people caught outdoors. Moldy, weevily foodstuffs sold to the Army by crooked suppliers added to the general misery, and fresh foods proved exorbitant, with butter a dollar a pound and eggs a dollar a dozen. Drunkenness and even desertion became common. A soldier's bleary glance on westward into destiny brought into view an awesome scene of dead-brown desolation extending to the horizon.

The battle music "Garry Owen," selected by Custer himself for the 7th Cavalry, seemed entirely appropriate to his rough, frustrated unit. "Garry Owen," an old drinking song with a galloping cadence, glorified the gaiety of knocking out street lights in Limerick, Ireland, and of mauling bailiffs there.

Custer's first campaign with the 7th during that year of 1867 had only detracted from his earlier military accomplishments, and it had emphasized some odd paradoxes in the man. Reflective observers joined earlier critics in pronouncing him to be a man who could give his dogs and horses treatment worthy of human beings, then treat his own men like dogs; a campaigner who could endure the worst of hardships, yet aggressively seek comfort when available nearby and loll in it selfishly; an officer whose Military Academy record shouted of his own slovenliness, but who now demanded of subordinates a spick-and-span discipline; a commander, impulsive and swashbuckling, who wasted little patience on those who would not throw themselves completely into his planned campaigns, yet who exhibited temperance back on the post, preferring the quiet and private company of Libbie to drinking, gambling, and other carousing with army companions.

A few of his officers and men idolized him. Most eventually hated him. Part of the Army called him crazy.

The record of Custer's 1867 campaign brought out this random information:

The 7th Cavalry, encumbered by wagons and other heavy equipment, had proved to be incapable of carrying out its assignment against Indians mounted on fleet ponies that could feed on plentiful spring and summer grass and drink from numerous water holes.

53

Frustrated by being outridden, Custer pushed his command hard, far, and fast—eventually at entirely too great a pace.

Once Custer sent word for his wife, waiting in safety at a frontier post, to ride out to him at an isolated location on the plains in the company of a wagon train carrying supplies. For reasons of safety the post commander refused to let her go. This infuriated both Libbie and her husband, and not even an ensuing Indian attack on that very wagon train entirely pacified them. (Had Libbie been there and had the raid verged on success she probably would have been killed by one of the officers, who would have had the unwanted job of shooting her himself rather than allowing her to fall into Indian captivity. Libbie referred to this as her "double danger" while traveling in Indian country.)

On another occasion Custer ordered his men on a one-day march of sixty-five miles across an area known to be waterless. By noon alkali dust, searing sunshine, and empty canteens had begun to enfeeble already weakened men and animals. Pet dogs died; their carcasses were left behind on baked ground to putrefy. Afternoon waned, but promised refreshment at the Platte River still lay far distant. Custer left the command and with three companions rode ahead, later claiming he went in search of a camp site. But after reaching the Platte he and the others drank heartily, then slept while waiting for the regiment to come up.

On yet another occasion Indians attacked stragglers from the regiment and killed them. Custer made no effort to pursue the Indians or to recover the victims' bodies.

The mutinous spirit inspired by Custer's insensitive leadership provoked a wholesale overnight desertion of twenty or thirty men. Custer ordered officers out to bring in the fleeing soldiers, and he yelled at one lieutenant to "bring in none alive." A massacre did not ensue, but one enlisted man died from bullet wounds.

Near the end of the campaign Custer again left the main body of the regiment and with seventy-five of the best men and animals for an escort and with three officers for company rode 150 miles in fifty-five hours, with only a six-hour period for rest and sleep, to a post, there to have supplies rushed out to the rest of the regiment (as he claimed). The dash resulted in permanent disablement of some of the horses, and it brought more desertions from the ranks.

Eventually Custer ended his forced march at Fort Riley, where Libbie happened to be staying, and thus he raised some questions among senior officers that helped to bring on his court-martial and his twelve-month suspension.

Years later General D. S. Stanley, in command of another expedition Custer once accompanied, would describe the young officer (in his *Personal Memoirs,* 1917) as a cold, dishonest, unscrupulous man "universally despised by all the officers of his regiment, excepting his relatives and one or two sycophants."

But that description would come later. For the present Custer had some important friends, and one of them was General Sheridan, in 1868 the Missouri Department commander.

Custer had been under Sheridan's command when, as a "boy general," Custer had won most of that Civil War glory. Sheridan admired the youthful vigor and the dashing looks of his remarkable subordinate; and Sheridan's fiery temper would have precluded any attempt by Custer to test this particular senior and thus ruin the relationship. After the surrender at Appomattox, Sheridan had purchased for twenty dollars in gold coin the table General Lee used, and he had given it to Custer as a gift for Libbie (who also would have attracted Sheridan) with this note:

> My dear Madam: Permit me to present to you the table upon which were signed the terms of surrender of the Army of Northern Virginia, under General Robert E. Lee; and in conclusion let me add that I know of no person more instrumental in bringing about this most desirable event than your most gallant husband.
>
> I am, madam, most truly your friend
> PHILIP M. SHERIDAN, Mj. Gen. USA

Now Custer, relaxing with Libbie in Monroe, Michigan, received another message from Sheridan, who wanted him back at once to command the 7th Cavalry in its forthcoming campaign against marauding Indians made even more irate by the dishonest words and apparently broken promises of Medicine Lodge and Laramie.

This time the campaign would be handled differently. Army units organized for fast marching would hunt their enemy during winter months, too, instead of waiting for spring, and thus they would not allow the "hostiles" those periods of welcomed easy breathing.

Custer would be the officer to command the campaign. In Monroe he read a telegram:

HEADQUARTERS DEPARTMENT
OF THE MISSOURI,
IN THE FIELD, FORT HAYS, KANSAS,
September 24, 1868.

General G. A. Custer, Monroe, Michigan:

Generals Sherman, Sully, and myself, and nearly all the officers of your regiment have asked for you, and I hope the application will be successful. Can you come at once? Eleven companies of your regiment will move about the 1st of October against the hostile Indians, from Medicine Lodge Creek toward the Wichita Mountains.

P. H. SHERIDAN,
Major General Commanding.

56

5

RED MOON

Early in October 1868, Custer rejoined his regiment, which he found encamped at a bleak site thirty miles southeast of Fort Dodge on a tributary of the Arkansas River called Bluff Creek. Custer had taken a westward-bound train out of Monroe the very next day after receiving the telegram and had traveled to Fort Hays, from where he and a small cavalry escort had set out southward, on horseback, across more empty plains for Fort Dodge and, eventually, the Bluff Creek encampment. Custer arrived one afternoon, formally resumed command, and sat down to dinner with an appetite intensified by his recent ride. Before he could sample a bite of food a small band of mounted Indians raced toward the camp and opened fire. Officers and men scrambled for their weapons.

Custer recognized the Indians' strategy at once. The attackers hoped to attract pursuit by a large force, which they would then ambush somewhere in the vicinity. No pursuers rode forth to chase the raiders.

Other attackers rode up and pressed even more closely, dashing into view singly or in groups of two or three from behind a rise not far away that served as a sort of staging area. Mounted on fast ponies, they displayed for the still-surprised white men some fine horsemanship. In single file they raced past the camp, risking death for a distance of at least two hundred yards.

To Custer pony and warrior seemed to become one. The mount appeared "possessed of the . . . wishes" of the rider and raced by

57

apparently "unguided by bridle, rein, or spur," while the rider fired his weapon, loaded, and fired again, then repeated the action—all from his precarious, jolting position. When return fire whined by too closely the warrior threw himself over the opposite side of his animal so that Custer could see only a foot (hooked around the pony's back) and a face (peering from under the animal's neck). When the rider vanished this way Custer sometimes heard a gleeful shout from a recruit who presumed his latest shot had been well aimed. "The old soldiers . . . were not so easily deceived," he said, "and often afterwards would remind their less experienced companion of the terrible fatality of his shots."

Eventually the Indians withdrew and joined others who had been waiting, hidden, to ambush those unsuspecting pursuers who never followed. Custer watched them ride off on the open plain. Some turned occasionally to shout a distant insult or to make a last defiant gesture.

When Custer had time to discuss the attack with other officers he learned that raids like this one had become a daily occurrence. He determined to teach those "hostiles" respect in a manner that Sheridan and Sherman would thoroughly approve.

Late in November, after a brief period of campaigning and a halt for reorganization and refitting, Custer was ready to take his regiment into the field for the recently planned winter operations, which would be fought on army terms and not on those favoring Indians (who, in most of spring, summer, and fall, could roam at will around the countryside and find food and water). During winter the tribes encamped, usually at southern sites far removed from military posts.

Custer meant to find them. His 7th Cavalry would march in accordance with these orders, from Sheridan:

> To proceed south in the direction of the Antelope Hills, thence toward the Washita River, the supposed winter seat of the hostile tribes; to destroy their villages and ponies; to kill or hang all warriors and bring back all women and children.

Although the orders failed to mention it, not every Indian in that specified area could have been classified as hostile. The Medicine

58

Lodge treaty left "any lands" south of the Arkansas River open as hunting grounds "so long as the buffalo may range thereon."

Four o'clock reveille in morning blackness of November 23 brought troopers out of their tents at what had become their new base—Camp Supply, in present Oklahoma near the Kansas line— and into a dismal winter scene, especially for any man who had to ride through it. A blustery snowfall that had commenced the night before had continued all night, and now the ground lay blanketed to a depth of a foot or more.

"How will this do for a winter campaign?" one officer asked sarcastically.

"Just what we want," came a cool reply.

But no one seemed truly elated by the subfreezing weather, and troopers finished grooming their horses more quickly than usual.

After a hurried breakfast around fitful camp fires that flickered in the cold gusts men took down tents, packed wagons, and exhaled dark puffs of fog into the air as their exertions increased. Then, as each group finished, its leader trudged off through new snow to report readiness to move. Sometime around a sunrise that could only have been imagined and not seen a bugler sounded the quick notes of "Boots and Saddles."

From out of the morning darkness came leathery sounds of troopers implanting saddles on the backs of horses, then arranging straps and buckles.

While they worked, Custer rode his already saddled horse over to the vicinity of the headquarters tents for a last word with General Sheridan, who was visiting the new base. Most tents lay ghostlike in the gusting snowstorm, but in front of Sheridan's canvas quarters a chilled sentinel paced back and forth. Custer dismounted, but he supposed the General to be sound asleep inside—until he heard a familiar voice announce that he was indeed awake and had been listening to the preparations for departure. Then Sheridan invited Custer inside and asked about the snow.

"I replied that nothing could be more to our purpose," Custer said. "We could move and the Indian villages could not. If the snow only remained on the ground one week, I promised to bring the

General satisfactory evidences that my command had met the Indians."

Custer mounted his horse to ride back. At the opening of a tent nearby one of Sheridan's staff officers, a friend of Custer's awakened by the conversation, called out from inside the folds of a large buffalo robe: "Good-bye, old fellow; take care of yourself!"

After Custer had rejoined his men he found them waiting for further orders to march. The call "To Horse" sent each trooper to a position at the head of his animal. Then the commands "Prepare to Mount" and "Mount" put him in the saddle, quickly and quietly and in unison with other troopers, who then awaited only the final signal, "Advance."

With that, the 7th Cavalry struggled out of Camp Supply into the full storm. Clogging snow deadened the thud of hooves and the rumble of wheels to some degree, but at the head of the column, just behind the scouts and friendly Indian guides in the lead, the regimental band—riding horseback, too—made plenty of noise, blaring forth "The Girl I Left Behind Me."

The music was nothing more than frozen formality. The 7th usually marched out to the rhythm of that tune. At masculine Camp Supply "the girl" would have been left far, far behind already.

Once on the open plains Custer sought to peer through the snowy curtain but could see only a white blanket covering the land everywhere. Still the thick flakes fell, breeze-whipped, "in almost blinding clouds." Weather continued so heavy that any straggler would have risked losing the regiment and his life in the whirling white desolation, but no one ventured away from the column.

Even the Indian guides Custer was using had trouble deciding on a course. Finally they admitted their helplessness. They could see no landmarks.

Custer, like most other cavalry officers, always carried a compass. He took it out, now, and using it with a map of the area set a course for the evening's proposed camp site—on Wolf Creek, which was supposed to have been an easy twelve- or fifteen-mile first-day march.

At two o'clock that afternoon the cavalry arrived at this destination, but the wagons had lagged far behind. Troopers and their officers began collecting firewood, and the exercise apparently warmed and cheered them all. Custer listened to men laughing and joking. "It was . . . gratifying to witness the contentment and general good humor everywhere prevailing throughout the command." This was a different regiment than the one that had marched out of Fort Riley for the first campaign. Many of those misfits had left the Army, one way or another.

By the time the mule-drawn wagons rolled onto the scene cavalrymen had managed to start enough fires in the various company areas to drive away most of the gloom and much of the cold. While troopers' cooks and officers' servants prepared dinner, men and officers pitched tents—an operation made more difficult by the weather this particular evening. Snow had to be removed from any spot to be covered by tent flooring; otherwise the area would melt into a sloshy puddle of mud when heated from above. But the snowfall continued to be so heavy and the atmosphere so windy that even "the most energetic efforts of two persons were insufficient to keep the ground properly clear." They did the best they could with their tents, then devoured a warm dinner, finished it off with a cup of hot coffee, and relaxed in robes or blankets while, outside, unfortunate sentinels squinted into the storm for the unlikely sight of strangers.

In a tent shared with his adjutant Custer lay in warm, quiet comfort on a bed of buffalo robes. In the center of the shelter a small fire crackled. The General watched a lazy column of smoke rise through a small opening at the top of the tent. There the warm vapor met and melted the flakes still blowing down from the heavens, but the interior remained snug.

"I consoled myself with the reflection that to us [the blizzard] was as an unpleasant remedy for the removal of a still more unpleasant disease," Custer said. "If the storm seemed terrible to us, I believed it would prove to be even more terrible to our enemies."

By four-o'clock reveille the next morning "the travelin' was good overhead," as one of Custer's scouts known as California Joe liked to say when referring to clear skies. The 7th moved on through deeper snowdrifts, following the valley of Wolf Creek. Custer intended to strike the Canadian River in the vicinity of Antelope Hills. During the next few marches he and his men saw, standing huddled against the cold in occasional leafless groves and other partially sheltered areas, herds of buffalo, which the Medicine Lodge treaty allowed friendly Indians to hunt in this region. But Custer was not anticipating seeing any friendly Indians; nor did many people besides those "Indian lovers" among the government agents expect such a discovery. Kansans had been suffering badly at the hands of warriors who would now be encamped for the winter somewhere in this southern area. Those victimized people counted these casualties (possibly incomplete) for a six-month period of 1868: 157 white settlers slain, 57 wounded (41 of whom had been scalped), 14 women raped and then killed, 29 men, women, and children taken captive, 1,627 ranch animals stolen, 24 ranches or settlements destroyed, 11 stagecoaches attacked, and 4 wagon trains demolished—all this against reported Indian losses (surely minimized by frustrated and furious settlers) of 11 warriors killed and 1 wounded. White Westerners eagerly awaited word of revenge.

At the Canadian River, now a swollen stream whose frigid red current carried along bobbing chunks of snow and ice, Custer detached three troops and ordered them to ride along the north bank and look for signs of Indians. Commander of this detachment would be Major Joel Elliot, a likable, zealous man of younger years than many officers junior to him. Custer ordered Elliot to march without wagons or other burdensome equipment for fifteen miles and to pursue any Indians whose trail might be found, meanwhile sending back word of the discovery to the main body.

If Elliot found no trail the two groups were to reunite at the headwaters of the Washita River and continue the sweep southward down its valley.

As soon as Elliot and his men had made an early-morning departure Custer began moving the rest of the regiment across the brimming Canadian, a slow, dangerous task. After each unit and each wagon had crossed the river at a ford selected by California Joe it proceeded southward for a short distance toward Antelope Hills, a series of five sandstone rises (to heights of three hundred feet above the surrounding plain) that now loomed in Custer's front "like towering battlements." Then men halted horses and wagons, and waited for the rear guard to cross.

From one of the hillocks Custer observed the landscape: to his left the reddish-brown ribbon of the icy Canadian, winding in from the southwest and curving northward before disappearing off to the east; and all around him a white horizon encircling a blanket of snow with wrinkles that indicated the presence of a frozen brook or a covered ravine.

Custer saw that the last cavalryman had crossed the river—well before noon. He was on the verge of turning to his bugler waiting nearby and ordering "To Horse" when he noticed, far off, a dark object on the surface of the snow: a horseman approaching from the direction of Elliot's probable location. As the man rode nearer Custer could make out through his field glass the familiar form of one of the Major's scouts, Jack Corbin, riding as hard as he was able.

Minutes lengthened, and an hour or more seemed to pass before Corbin galloped up to the impatient Custer and reported that Elliot, after traveling up the north bank for about twelve miles, had found the fresh trail of a war party some 150 strong headed southeast, no doubt after a raid into Kansas. The Major had ordered his three troops across the river in pursuit.

Custer gave the scout a fresh horse and sent him back to Elliot with word that the rest of the 7th would follow his trail and join him as soon as possible, and that if the regiment had not come up by 8 P.M. Elliot was to stop and wait. Then Custer ordered his bugler to call officers. He passed on all this information and told them his plan. The cavalry would ride on with minimal supplies of ammunition and food, leaving the wagon train to follow under the guard of eight men and an officer detailed for this inglorious work. After a twenty-minute period allowed men and officers for hurried repacking Custer finally ordered his ever-waiting bugler to sound "To Horse" and all the other calls that eventually sent the regiment into the advance across open plains covered by more than a foot of snow.

Midafternoon overtook the struggling 7th, whose horses were becoming fatigued, and still no sign of Elliot's trail had been discovered by the scouts and Indian guides traveling far ahead and on the flanks of the main body. "The snow seemed unbroken and undisturbed as far as the eye could reach." The sun leaned farther and farther westward, lengthening shadows. In waning daylight a scout finally found Elliot's trail, and the rest of the regiment followed it now "with lighter and less anxious hearts"—into a valley, toward a distant stand of timber, and on into darkness. At nine o'clock they finally came upon Elliot and his men encamped near a deep-banked stream whose rushing water below cut through the snow cover.

Where were the hostiles? No one knew, but Indian scouts said the trail Elliot had been following was less than twenty-four hours old. Thus the war party might be camped not far ahead. Hot coffee seemed essential for the bone-cold troopers, however, and Custer let them have it, with hard tack, ordering further that fires for boiling be kept small and well hidden under the steep banks of the stream. The date happened to be November 26, Thanksgiving Day, and this was their dinner. Horses, unsaddled for a rest, received a better "feed"—of oats.

After a one-hour rest the reunited 7th rode on—without bugle calls to start them now, in column of fours, through moonlight that put a ghostlike glimmer on the snowy landscape. The temperature drop that came with evening had crusted the surface. It popped and cracked underneath horses' hooves and made men uneasy.

Two Osage scouts, on foot several hundred yards ahead, preceded the cautious column. They followed the trail of the war party with moves that seemed pantherlike to Custer, who was riding a short distance behind them. The Osages apparently glided (rather than walked) across the frozen white surface. After those two came other Indian guides and some white scouts, in single file.

The 7th Cavalry had moved forward several miles in this manner when Custer realized that the two Osages in the lead had stopped. Quietly he ordered the regiment halted, rode forward, and asked, "What is the matter?" One scout who spoke a few words of English said, "Smell fire."

Custer sniffed the air. So did other officers who had joined the group by this time. No one else could smell anything resembling wood smoke. Custer ordered the two scouts to continue, and they went on with great reluctance.

Half a mile farther they stopped again. Once more Custer rode up. "Told you so," the same Osage whispered, and he pointed to faintly visible embers of a used camp fire smoldering some seventy-five yards off to the left.

Were hostile Indians asleep near the coals? Had they been awakened by noise? The fire surely would have been made by the war party whose trail the 7th was following, Custer reflected. He asked for willing scouts and guides to creep over and look around. The volunteers commenced their risky probe with fingers on rifle triggers, but after an inordinately long time they returned to report the area deserted. The Osage scouts added a bit of intelligence arrived at from their own native deductions. This camp fire had not been made by the war party, but by villagers living somewhere nearby while tending ponies herded out for the scant grazing available.

"Hope and excitement" stirred Custer's soul. Many more Indians than he had been expecting to find apparently awaited him—as did greater glory. The column advanced more slowly and cautiously than ever, with those same two Osage scouts in front and Custer riding close upon them.

He watched as the same scout who had discovered the fire edged ahead in the moonlight, peered over the crest of a hill, then crouched down and crept back.

Custer asked, "What is it?"

"Injuns down there," the Osage replied, pointing in the murky direction of his previous gaze.

Custer dismounted and walked to the crest, crouching so that his figure would not be silhouetted. He peered into midnight and saw in a valley below what seemed to be a herd of animals—a large black spot on the whitened fields. Inside the dark blotch there seemed to be movement. After a long, silent look he concluded that the animals, if any, might easily be buffalo roaming the prairies, and he asked the guide why he suspected Indians nearby.

"Dog bark," the Osage replied. Indian villages were famous for having great numbers of those watchful animals—but dogs never accompanied war parties because of the noise they might make.

Custer looked and listened for a while longer. From deep woods off to the right of the animal herd, or whatever it was, came the sound of another bark—providing Custer and his scout with specific information about the village location. Then Custer heard a distant metallic tinkling and realized the noise would have been made by a small bell hung around the neck of the leader of a pony herd.

He had turned to summon his officers when he heard yet another faint sound from the distance: "the . . . cry of an infant." Custer talked later of feeling a pang of regret that the ensuing fight might have to claim innocent lives, but he went on with the planning with no apparent loss of enthusiasm. He intended that the attack on this village and its hostile occupants would help equalize those Kansas statistics, would subtract some warriors from availability for future raids there, and (no doubt) would add to his own laurels. He did not know what tribe or band inhabited the village, but this probably would have made small difference to him.

Custer instructed all of his officers to remove their sabers (and the possibility of sending forth warning clinks of their own), to sneak up to the crest, and to look over the terrain. Then, having returned to the place where they had left their swords, Custer told them his plan. During the rest of the night he would surround the village and at daylight would attack, on signal by the band playing "Garry Owen." He divided the regiment into four nearly equal detachments of some two hundred men each, assigned commands, and sent them off, with probably needless orders to light no fires and to make no unnecessary noise. He would not have a reserve force in case his plan went awry, but he was usually lucky as well as impetuous.

The moonlit hours grew even colder. While awaiting the attack some men and officers wrapped themselves as snuggly as possible, lay in the snow, and slept. About two hours before dawn the moonlight forsook them. During the darkness time seemed to freeze along with the men.

When predawn that November 27, 1868, began to powder the eastern sky Custer assembled the officers of his detachment and whispered orders to prepare for the attack. Sergeants awoke still-sleeping troopers by touching them. Men rose, mounted, and cautiously advanced on horseback over crusted snow, which again snapped underfoot with sharp sounds, but any half-awake Indians in the village apparently presumed the noise came from their pony herd. Directly behind the commander rode the band, ready to strike up his beloved battle song.

A distant rifle shot apparently fired by some nervous member of another detachment brought Custer's order for "Garry Owen" sooner than he had intended. As the notes frolicked across the once-quiet valley for a few moments before the musical instruments froze with breath moisture and fell silent, men yelled and cheered from all sides and bugles joined in the summons to charge. Troopers urged their horses into a gallop, making the cold ground quake.

Men of Custer's own detachment saw surprised Indians run from lodge entrances for the shelter of trees and the Washita River bank nearby. They were carrying rifles and arrows and bows seized before their panicky departure. Defiant whoops soon mingled with the 7th Cavalry's battle din, and the sharp cracks of Indian rifles began answering the heavier reports of cavalry carbines.

Soldiers won possession of the village quickly, but they faced a dangerous fire aimed from woods and river. Typically, young Indian boys joined in the battle, firing pistols or arrows with practiced efficiency.

Elsewhere, villagers had sought to break through the squeeze. Some succeeded. Others surrendered. Many fell dead or wounded, their bodies oozing dark red blotches on the trampled snow. Sharpshooters picked off some of the fleeing Indians and helped to clear woods and riverbank of other villagers who were seeking to defend the place.

The day's fighting lasted only a short time altogether, despite Custer's literary attempt later (in *My Life on the Plains*) to describe a fierce battle and despite an ensuing counterattack by Indian reinforcements. When shooting stopped, the victorious troopers counted 103 dead Cheyennes and 53 prisoners—women and children, most of whom had never left their lodges, where they had huddled in terror during the fight. In his report Custer described all the slain as warriors, but some other participants (including Indians queried later) disputed this. One compiler said that only eleven of the dead Cheyennes had been true warriors and that many of the slain were indeed women and children.

Custer's own losses proved to be comparatively slight, at least on first count: four officers and eleven enlisted men wounded. Major Joel Elliot and nineteen men had vanished sometime after making the dawn attack. Nothing had been heard from the group, with the possible exception of some distant firing, but Custer devoted himself not to an extensive search of the area (although he claimed later that he did), but to having the village burned and every one of the many hundreds of captured ponies shot.

Two officers later gave incriminating accounts of Custer's conduct at this time. One of them, Frederick W. Benteen, an able officer whose prematurely gray hair set off a ruddy, rugged face, wrote in the *Missouri Democrat* (February 9, 1869):

> Our chief [Custer] exhibits his close marksmanship and terrifies the crowd of frightened, captured squaws and papooses by dropping the struggling ponies in death near them. Ah! He is a clever marksman. Not even do the poor dogs of the Indians escape his eye and aim as they drop dead or limp howling away. But are not those our men on guard on the other side of the creek? Will he not hit them?
>
> "My troop is on guard, General, just over there," says an officer.
>
> "Well, bullets will not go through or around hills, and you can see there is a hill between us," was the reply, and the exhibition goes on.

Another officer, E. S. Godfrey, recalled later:

> I told [Custer] that I had heard that Major Elliot had not returned and suggested that possibly the heavy firing I had heard on the opposite side of the valley [where Elliot was to have charged] might have been an attack upon Elliot's party. He pondered this a bit and said slowly, "I hardly think so as Captain Myers has been fighting down there all morning and probably would have reported it."

Then Custer ordered Godfrey to help with destruction of the village, but the commander saw to it that one Cheyenne lodge was spared to take home as a souvenir.

Speed became essential to Custer now. Through his field glass he had observed, gathering on surrounding hills, many Indian reinforcements, probably with only one concern delaying their attack: what would happen to the Indians the white men were holding? From a captured woman Custer learned that the place he had struck was only one of several winter villages established along the

Washita by Cheyennes, Kiowas, Arapahos, Comanches, and Plains Apaches, all of whom Custer considered hostile. Worried about the growing numbers of armed warriors now collecting—Arapahos, Kiowas, and no telling how many others—and worried about the safety of his supply train (as he said later), he decided to withdraw. But how could this be done, he reflected, without drawing an attack from all those vengeful Indians?

Custer's practical joking background might have helped him devise a clever ruse. He gathered his wounded, assembled the command, mounted prisoners on ponies, unfurled the regimental flags, ordered the band to strike up "Ain't I Glad to Get Out of the Wilderness," and marched forward, directly toward heights where large numbers of warriors waited. Not expecting Custer to launch another attack and puzzled by his apparent preparation to do so, they broke and fled. Later, in darkness, the 7th countermarched, found the supply wagons, and eventually returned to Camp Supply.

Custer, who never failed to sweeten Plains austerity with as much pleasure as possible, reputedly picked another victory plum—the nightly warmth of comely young Monahseetah, daughter of a chief, Little Rock, killed in the battle. Custer certainly never admitted this, but contemporary army gossips rejoiced in passing on the rumor. Frederick Benteen said it was true; and many Cheyennes, who would have known, asserted it was so—further, that the girl later bore Custer's child.

More information about the Battle of the Washita came with the passage of time. The victimized village had belonged to Cheyennes, as Custer had learned after examining dead and wounded villagers. The trail Elliot had discovered originally would have been made by a party of their young warriors traveling southward after a Kansas raid. When those warriors returned home shortly before the attack they related their triumphs and sparked a celebration. Drums throbbed for a scalp dance that lasted well into the night.

About the same time the warriors returned, their old chief, a man who constantly sought peace for his tribe, had come back from a visit with usually friendly Colonel William Hazen, commander of Fort Cobb, newly established as an agency headquarters. The chief had heard talk of more soldiers coming to fight—the Medicine

Lodge treaty having accomplished so little—and he had asked Hazen's permission to move his village near the fort for protection.

Colonel Hazen knew that Cheyennes from this group had participated in raids. He knew about Sheridan's order to Custer, and about Sheridan's plans regarding the destruction of Cheyennes and Arapahos. Hazen did not want these Indians in his vicinity, and he told the old chief to return to his Washita River village. If the young warriors stayed there instead of raiding, Hazen implied, the village would not be attacked. In any event, Hazen said, the old chief would have to make his peace with someone else. The matter was out of his own hands.

The chief himself knew that numbers of his young Cheyennes had been away from time to time pillaging Kansas, along with other raiding parties. Whenever they returned he would censure them gently, but he would always accept them back. No Indian leader had the power to dictate to his people. Further, the post-Medicine Lodge hiatus in regard to treaty implementation had not been to his own liking.

After the latest Cheyenne raiding party returned from Kansas the chief criticized their judgment, as usual, and he did not join in the scalp dance. Instead, he and another leader sat in a tepee, smoking and discussing prospects while those drums throbbed. The chiefs hoped to avoid another massacre like Sand Creek, by a cavalry regiment they had heard to be on the move in their vicinity—and probably even now following the trail of that returned war party.

The old chief had not been without reason for fearing another Sand Creek. He was a renowned survivor of that tragedy: Black Kettle, the Cheyenne leader who had hoisted a United States flag over the peaceful village and who had nearly died in Chivington's infamous slaughter. Later, Black Kettle nevertheless had met and welcomed those peace commissioners upon their arrival at Medicine Lodge.

On the night of November 26 Black Kettle had stayed up late, but he had awakened shortly before dawn, as usual, and had peered outside his lodge at the snowy landscape and the clear sky. He had heard a woman somewhere shout, "Soldiers!"

Black Kettle's first thought would have been: this must not be another Sand Creek. Apparently to warn his people (to flee, as some said, or to fight, as others claimed, or possibly to seek a conference with the soldiers' leader, as a few contended), he seized his rifle, aimed it skyward, and fired. This would have been the lone shot that Custer and his advancing troopers had heard shortly before the band opened up with "Garry Owen." Black Kettle then placed his wife on a pony and jumped astride the animal himself. Together husband and wife raced off in the direction of a Washita ford. At river's edge a volley knocked the old chief into the icy water. Another round brought his wife's dead body down near his own.

Soon after that, but in another area, Major Joel Elliot had observed a group of Indians escaping along the valley and had hurriedly collected nineteen men to accompany him in pursuit. Before he had ridden away Elliot turned to a lieutenant and yelled, in the spirit of Custer himself, "Here goes for a brevet or a coffin!" Then he and his troopers had begun taking potshots at figures of fleeing men, women, and children until they were suddenly stopped by the appalling sight of hordes of Cheyenne and Arapaho warriors riding in from nearby villages.

Elliot and his men turned to gallop back to the regiment, then realized that another swarm of warriors in their rear had them cut off. Although Elliot had been caught on a piece of low, grassy ground he ordered his men to dismount, to lie down in the long blades, and to open fire—thus virtually admitting defeat. From positions above them bullets and arrows hurtled into their poor shelter, and finally a furious charge by Indians ended all resistance. Knife- and hatchet-wielding Indian women completed the work.

A few days after that bloody November 27 had begun passing into history General Sheridan officially congratulated Custer for his efficient services and sent a report to the War Department boasting of the victory over "savage butchers" and of the death of old Chief Black Kettle, "worn out and worthless."

Indian survivors described the Battle of the Washita with more brevity and vividness than did either Sheridan or Custer. They saw the crimson trails left by their wounded ponies struggling through the snow, and they called that time the "Red Moon."

6

RED SUN

Participants in some other fighting might have called it a red sun that peered down on violence ablaze in a dehydrated land eight hundred miles southwest of the Washita battle site.

In a large, barren area of desert plains broken by sterile mountain ranges and dry arroyos raged a conflict that burned out most human juices. At the southern edge of present Arizona, around what has become known as the 1854 Gadsden Purchase, another group of natives waged a war for survival—more effectively than had Black Kettle's overpowered villagers on the banks of their icy river. Washington's moves toward peaceful accord with Indians did not seem able to stretch as far as Arizona; nor did the natives concerned really care.

An Athapascan-speaking people known as Apaches—never numbering more than five or six thousand and by now split into many bands, groups, and clans—had settled in that thirsty land centuries earlier, after migration down the eastern slopes of the Rocky Mountains from Canada, and now they were seeking to hold on to a wilderness nobody else would have wanted at this time except for two developments: the omnipotent Great Father was coveting a safe southern passage to the Pacific Coast across the continent he claimed as his own; and some of his people had discovered the presence of valuable minerals hidden far below the sun-scorched earth.

The Apaches were masters at holding on to their sector. Several hundred years earlier they had broken the northward thrust of a mighty empire—not many more than those few thousand Apaches against the power of Spain. With that development these Indians became the only North American tribe to succeed in resisting European invasion over a long period.

These tribesmen adapted for their own defensive use the harshness of the land to which they were so well attuned, and Spain never established itself north of the area where it encountered the several branches of fierce warriors generally labeled Apaches—a Zuñi word meaning "Enemies." In time the name became affixed solely to the particular group that would win renown in United States history as having been tenacious enemies not only of whites but also of most other Indian tribes. Occasionally bands of Apaches allied themselves temporarily with Spain, but mostly for protection against other enemies—like the Comanches. Spain eventually sought to implement a program of extermination of Apaches, but brought upon itself and upon citizens of its New World territory only more misery and barbarism. When Spanish rule in Mexico ended, the Apaches and other warlike Plains Indians "were more powerful, far richer, and in control of more territory than they were at the beginning of it," said Great Plains historian Walter Prescott Webb. "The problem of subduing them had to be solved by another race."

Unfortunately for that race, the Spaniards inadvertently had given Apaches some good ideas about how to handle unwanted visitors; so that when Anglo-Americans arrived in the region and began exerting their own various pressures those white men learned they were not contending against an entirely innocent native people lacking experience in dealing with clever newcomers.

At first, however, Apaches showed no great animosity toward the white intruders, who came only infrequently in those early days, and they even indicated a desire for friendship. In the view of Apaches, Mexicans had taken the place of Spaniards, and they hoped the pale-skinned strangers might become allies in their fight, yet still remain few enough in numbers to pose no great threat to the Apaches themselves.

Mexicans and Apaches reciprocated brutalities—rape, capture, murder—and the Mexican government offered bounties for scalps.

Mexicans (as had Spaniards) excelled in the taking of slaves, and they held in captivity hundreds of Apaches—especially women and children usually forced into prostitution and other degradations. Later, Anglo-Americans residing in what would become the states of New Mexico and Arizona also possessed Indian slaves—a total of two thousand, some historians have estimated, as late as 1866, three years after Abraham Lincoln's Emancipation Proclamation. The various debasements forced on slaves by Spaniards and Mexicans proved to be influential in giving remaining tribesmen that reputation for exacting revenge in a remarkably cruel way—such as having "prisoners hung head downward over small fires, their uncontrollable jackknifing affording amusement for hours while their brains slowly roasted until they died."

Anglo-Americans exhibited savagery of their own, and some of their early activities helped also to bring on that terrible retaliation. In the 1850's a group of them tied and whipped an Apache chief of the Mimbreños group, Mangas Coloradas (Red Sleeves), until his muscular back had been cut into bloody strips of flesh, and they created in the chief an implacable enemy. Later, in 1861, an army lieutenant and a detachment of soldiers working under a truce flag questioned another Apache leader (this time of the Chiricahuan group), Cochise, about the disappearance of a white youth the year before. When Cochise honestly denied responsibility the skeptical lieutenant retained as hostages the chief and five of his relatives who had accompanied him—this despite the truce flag. But Cochise escaped, and after rejoining his warriors captured three white men, whom he then sought to exchange for his relatives.

The lieutenant refused. Cochise, infuriated, ordered the three men tortured to death—by mutilation with lances, an old Spanish custom the Apaches might have acquired. The lieutenant in turn hanged three men from among those five relatives. Cochise, who had helped California-bound Anglo-Americans to cross Chiricahua country in the years immediately following 1856, then joined Mangas Coloradas in a war of revenge.

During the next several years, while most Anglo-American soldiers were away fighting each other, Apaches almost wiped out the white race in Arizona, leaving to them only one settlement of any importance—Tucson, with a permanent population of two hundred. The "stupidity" of the lieutenant who had violated that truce caused five thousand American deaths and an inestimable loss of property, said historian Thomas E. Farish (in the second volume of *History of Arizona*, 1915). But the casualties over a long period certainly were not one-sided. The "Apache wars" brought on by the lieutenant's blunder would not cease for a quarter of a century, and before they ended both sides would have recorded plentiful examples of the exquisite cruelties human beings are capable of inflicting upon each other.

The Anglo-American program of Apache extermination actually began in 1862, maintained separately by both Union and Confederate officials. That year a Confederate military governor of Arizona instructed his soldiers (who had pressed westward from Texas), "You will . . . use all means to persuade the Apaches or any tribe to come in for the purpose of making peace, and when you get them together kill all the grown Indians and take the children prisoners and sell them to defray the expense of killing the Indians. Buy whiskey . . . as may be necessary."

Higher Confederates overruled the governor and eventually removed him from office because of his harshness, but then the Federals took over the work. A three-thousand-man "California Column," marching eastward, entered the territory that same year, and its commander issued these instructions: "There is to be no council held with the Indians. . . . The men are to be slain whenever and wherever they can be found."

The program was slow in gaining speed, but occasional victories proved satisfying to the people who supported it. When Mangas Coloradas, weary and wounded from fighting, was tricked into appearing for a truce-guarded peace talk in 1863 he was taken prisoner. An eyewitness, Daniel Conner, said (in *Joseph Reddeford Walker and the Arizona Adventure*, 1956) that soldiers apparently following orders poked the tips of heated bayonets against Mangas Coloradas' feet and legs until the enraged chief began shouting (in Spanish) and gesticulating, then they shot him. A bystander cut off the chief's head and boiled away the flesh, and someone eventually sent the skull to the Smithsonian Institution. The official report said Mangas Coloradas had been killed while attempting to escape.

During the ensuing year, 1864, the program moved forward, with 216 Apaches reportedly slain, but actually not many warriors among that number. Some army officers (like Colonel Kit Carson)

refused to follow extermination orders, and they accepted surrenders—a development that surely would have reduced the toll—
but because of the harsh success of the program Anglo-American
existence in Arizona had become slightly less risky, and people
began moving back. Still, no white person could consider himself
safe living in or traveling through the land. No Apache band had
been conquered or obliterated.

In this habitat the Apache warrior was a hard man to catch—or
even to see. He refrained from painting himself in the garish
manner of other Indians, preferring instead to blend with the
withered desolation about him. Always watchful, he could glimpse
an intruder, but the intruder rarely saw him. Whenever that did
happen (usually too late) the dark, dusty warrior appeared as if rising from out of the badlands, almost like one of the cactus plants.
He might be showing a bit of color on his turban or on the war
band worn around his head, but that would be the limit. On his
desert-burned face a scowl implanted by centuries of hardship and
hate compounded the menace of his appearance. Around the waist
of his long-sleeve, hip-length blouse he fastened a belt for carrying
ammunition, a knife, and other weaponry. As protection while
walking or riding through a multitude of prickles he wore a pair of
sloppy leggings covering part of his otherwise bare legs that showed
plenty of strength—or sometimes he wore the leggings with baggy
trousers whose bottoms had been tucked inside the protective
pieces. Moccasins covered leathery feet with soles so calloused
(some observers said) that a smoker could strike his match on
them. But most noticeably the Apache would be carrying in his
hands a Winchester or an equally lethal bow ready for shooting, although he preferred to fire either one from a concealed position
somewhere in his arid fastness. He preferred also to strip almost
naked for a surprise attack, to wrap head and shoulders in a bundle
of yucca shoots or coarse sacaton grass and to smear the rest of his
body with clay or sand, then to wriggle like a rattlesnake into position for the strike, using a noiseless lance or bow to make his kill.

Apaches possessed horses, which they had begun stealing from
Spaniards centuries earlier, but because of the perennial food short-
age in their land they ate them almost as readily as they rode them.
More animals were always available, anyway, from the nearest
ranch. Unlike some people (early Californians, for example) who

depended entirely on horses for transportation, Apaches never surrendered completely to those animals. An Apache, man or woman,
could walk forty miles or more a day—and cover seventy-five miles
on horseback—living off a country that offered most white men
nothing but death. The Apache's only weakness, in fact, seemed to
evolve from his feisty self-reliance. He usually showed no appreciation of the necessity for Indian solidarity in his survival fight—even
less than did other tribesmen. He preferred instead to go with his
own small group, and he frequently rejected helpful alliances even
with other Apache bands. But because of the type of warfare this
forced him to wage it also contributed to his fearsome reputation.

Apaches liked to travel in small bands for their raids into Mexico
or for their plunderings of Arizona ranches and settlements. They
moved silently and speedily: attacked, looted, and killed—then
vanished. Their fighting methods were to be re-examined many
years later and adapted for use by twentieth-century guerrilla commanders.

In 1868, by the time of General Custer's attack on Black Kettle's
sleeping village, there had emerged another respected participant in
Apache raids—a man who would one day rank as a leader with the
likes of Mangas Coloradas and Cochise: Geronimo, then about
forty, whose broad shoulders indicated great strength packed into
his tall bulkiness and whose round face, beneath stringy hair parted
in the center, indicated an accompanying businesslike attitude
through a squint of his flashing eyes and a scowl on his broad, thin
lips. The "Human Tiger" of the southwestern frontier (later admired and emulated to a degree by twentieth-century guerrilla Che
Guevara) would not have been surprised as had been trusting Chief
Black Kettle; for Geronimo, whose warriors seldom numbered
more than seventy-five, relied on craft, cunning, distrust of others,
and deceit to survive and to flourish.

His training had begun early. As the fourth child in a family of
four sons and four daughters, he had plenty of playmates from his
own household; and two favored early games showed Apache
influence: hide-and-seek (or whatever term they had for it) and
something like "practice stealing"—always pretending their victim
to be an enemy.

Childhood did not last long for him. During Geronimo's youth
his father died. Later, at the age of seventeen, Geronimo became a

warrior and a tribally accepted man. He married and fathered three children while still taking care of his mother, who never remarried. During a peaceful tribal trading expedition into Mexico in the 1850's led by Mangas Coloradas Geronimo lost all five of his beloved, and the manner of their deaths helped to make him the war leader he would become.

The entire tribe had encamped outside a Mexican town. By day the men went into the place to trade,

> leaving our camp under the protection of a small guard so that our arms, supplies, and women and children would not be disturbed during our absence [Geronimo said].
>
> Late one afternoon when returning from town we were met by a few women and children who told us that Mexican troops from some other town had attacked our camp, killed all the warriors of the guard, captured all our ponies, secured our arms, destroyed our supplies, and killed many of our women and children. Quickly we separated, concealing ourselves as best we could until nightfall, when we assembled at our appointed place of rendezvous—a thicket by the river. Silently we stole in one by one: sentinels were placed, and, when all were counted, I found that my aged mother, my young wife, and my three small children were among the slain. There were no lights in camp, so without being noticed I silently turned away and stood by the river.

Prevailing Mexican government bounties for scalps would have brought someone $175 for Geronimo's family—$50 for a woman's scalp, $25 for a child's—but other unfortunate Mexicans would be called upon to make a terrible reimbursement. Geronimo's (and Mangas Coloradas') group, weakened by the attack, crept back northward into Arizona, reorganized, solicited reinforcements, and in time returned to the scene of the tragedy.

"I was never again contented in our quiet home," Geronimo would say years later. Maybe he would not have been happy there, anyway, since raiding was a way of life for the Apache. But Geronimo had another reason for his depredations now.

> There were the decorations that Alope [his wife] had made—and there were the playthings of our little ones. I burned them

78

all, even our tepee. I also burned my mother's tepee and destroyed all her property.

. . . I had vowed vengeance upon the Mexican troopers who had wronged me, and whenever I . . . saw anything to remind me of former happy days my heart would ache for revenge.

Geronimo and his people enjoyed their vengeance. During the return journey into Mexico they captured, killed, and scalped eight Mexican villagers who had ridden out to talk peace, and thus the Apaches deliberately elicited an attack by Mexican troopers—the same ones, it happened, who had demolished their camp and who had murdered their kin. After the bloodbath that followed, "the fierce Apache war whoop" rang out over a battlefield almost carpeted red with the bleeding bodies of Mexican soldiers—and Geronimo won recognition as a warrior worthy of leadership.

In all the battle I thought of my murdered mother, wife, and babies—of my . . . vow of vengeance, and I fought with fury. Many fell by my hand, and constantly I led the advance. . . .

Still covered with the blood of my enemies, still holding my conquering weapon, still hot with the joy of battle, victory, and vengeance, I was surrounded by the Apache braves and made war chief. . . . Then I gave orders for scalping the slain.

Geronimo vastly extended his period of vengeance, leading raid after raid into the land of those hated Mexicans, who retaliated with some raids of their own whenever possible and who eventually would appeal to the United States Government for help in halting the forays of those furious Indians whose homes lay to the north.

But in 1868, the year Custer fought his Battle of the Washita, American military forces operating in the southwestern desert were thoroughly engaged in trying to protect citizens of their own country and, whenever possible, to do some exterminating. They had little time for thinking about the sanguinary activities of Geronimo that continued mostly south of the border. Arizona's raw red sun illuminated enough trouble without looking elsewhere for more.

7

A BREEZE THAT WHISPERED

Like the Arizona military commanders, Sheridan and Custer planned more exterminating, but at this time they were forced also into some side activity resulting from Major Elliot's disappearance during the Battle of the Washita.

Sheridan's congratulatory message after that battle (dated November 29, 1868) obviously had included some dubious information supplied by Custer. Sheridan had said:

> The Major General commanding announces to this command the defeat, by the [7th] Regiment of cavalry, of a large force of Cheyenne Indians, under the celebrated chief Black Kettle, reinforced by the Arapahos under Little Raven, and the Kiowas under [White Bear], on the morning of the 27th instant, on the Washita River . . . resulting in a loss to the savages of one hundred and three warriors killed, including Black Kettle, the capture of fifty-three squaws and children . . . the complete destruction of their village, and almost total annihilation of this Indian band.
>
> The loss to the [7th] Cavalry was two officers killed, Major Joel H. Elliot and Captain Louis McL. Hamilton, and nineteen enlisted men . . . [and three officers and eleven enlisted men wounded].

Custer could not have been certain about the deaths of Elliot and the nineteen men, however, because he had never found their bodies and had not even looked carefully for them. Five days after his December 2 return to Camp Supply he was marching southward again toward the Washita River with wagons replenished and with his troopers reinforced. He was to attack any other Indians found and to search for the bodies of Elliot and his men.

Sheridan accompanied the expedition. The General wanted to look around the battleground.

Custer found the site much as he had left it. Frozen bodies littered the area: Indian victims, massacred ponies, dead dogs. Small groups of men fanned out in a search for Elliot's detachment, and someone soon discovered seventeen bodies (three never were found)—"stark, stiff, naked, and horribly mutilated," as the official report would say, ". . . lying within a circle not exceeding twenty yards in diameter." Some bodies, including Elliot's, lacked hands or feet. Two corpses were headless.

Night had fallen when the enlisted men's bodies were buried by torchlight in cold ground atop a knoll. Elliot's remains were to be removed to Fort Arbuckle (in present Oklahoma) for burial.

Later, while poking around an abandoned Kiowa camp nearby, searchers discovered two more bodies: those of a young white woman, whose skull had been crushed, and her child. Obviously they had been slain at the time of Custer's appearance before Black Kettle's village, shortly before the Kiowas had joined other Indians in flight. White Bear, known for some killings and suspected of many more, must have executed the two prisoners, Custer mused.

Sheridan's report, based on that information supplied by Custer, had stated that White Bear and his Kiowa warriors had fought as reinforcements with Black Kettle's Cheyennes, but this Kiowa camp showed evidence of a quick flight, as did other villages located along twelve miles of riverside. Custer himself said, "Nothing could exceed the disorder and haste with which these [Kiowa and other] tribes had fled from their camping grounds." But Sheridan and Custer now determined to follow those refugees—and not the escape trail of the remaining Cheyennes and Arapahos, which led southwestward toward the Red River. The panicky villagers had rushed down the Washita toward the agency at Fort Cobb, where they obviously hoped to find the protection to which they were entitled—with the exception of the Kiowa murderers of the woman and her child.

After seven days of torturous traveling across hard country that sometimes forced men to cut a way with picks, axes, and shovels, Custer's Osage scouts early one morning—December 17—rode back in a gallop from their position in the lead. Accompanying them was a mounted messenger from Fort Cobb. The scouts reported that many Indians were waiting ahead; one of them carried a truce flag. The Fort Cobb messenger, who had just left the company of those Indians, delivered a note dated "9 P.M. December 16, 1868" that read:

> To the Officer, commanding troops in the Field.
>
> Indians have just brought in word that our troops today reached the Washita some twenty miles above here. I send this to say that all the camps this side of the point reported to have been reached are friendly, and have not been on the warpath this season. If this reaches you it would be well to communicate at once with [White Bear] or Black Eagle, chiefs of the Kiowas, near where you now are, who will readily inform you of the position of the Cheyennes and Arapahos, also of my camp.
>
> Respectfully,
W. B. HAZEN, Brevet Major-General.

Hazen felt certain of his facts. He had "issued rations to 9/10th of all the Kiowas" under his charge on November 26, the day before the Battle of the Washita, and that night White Bear and all other "main Kiowa chiefs" had slept in his tent. They had not departed until ten or eleven o'clock the next morning, several hours after the 7th Cavalry attack had commenced.

Nevertheless, Custer's anger increased as he read through the note, and his face would have reddened, as it usually did, the more excited he became. Indian agents were softheaded fools, he reflected, even if this one was an army officer who had "superior opportunities for studying the Indian character . . . had participated in Indian wars, and at the very time he penned the . . . note . . . was partially disabled from the effects of an Indian wound." Custer wanted to attack the Indians ahead, but Sheridan, having read Hazen's note, too, advised a delay to ascertain the situation.

Among the waiting group of mounted Indians was White Bear, the Kiowa chief with a singularly black reputation, and the man Custer assumed to have been the killer who had executed the young white mother and her child. White Bear's career to date indeed had been crammed with violence and violations of the Great Father's laws, but good evidence showed that for a time after the Medicine Lodge treaty even White Bear had calmed down, if only to get the government gifts promised—those presents that had not come because of Senate delay in treaty ratification.

White Bear himself always insisted that the United States Army first broke the Medicine Lodge agreement, and he pointed to Custer for specific criticism, because of the attack on that peaceful Washita village. Since agreeing to the treaty no Kiowa had killed any soldiers, White Bear declared to anyone who would listen, although some warriors had continued to raid into Texas. But Kiowas still could not believe that Texans really mattered, because Kiowas never had made or talked peace with those people. Further, the days when Texas had been, first, a republic, then a Confederate state—and thus beyond the responsibility of the Great Father in Washington—were not long past.

The Kiowa chief knew, too, that not all of his people had been encamped on the Washita when Custer came, even though Sheridan's congratulatory message implied otherwise. Many Kiowas had moved down the valley of the Washita to a site near the mouth of a small creek called Rainy Mountain. There they had received word of the attack, and from there they had moved again. Some Arapaho and Cheyenne survivors of Washita soon joined them.

White Bear, no placid cooperator like Black Kettle, had mulled over all-out war in alliance with Cheyennes and Arapahos and anyone else who would fight the bluecoats, but the temporarily indecisive tribesmen refrained from attack. Instead, the Kiowas continued moving, largely in confusion, and most of them had encamped not far from Fort Cobb and presumed safety when Sheridan and Custer and all those troopers came along.

Kiowa scouts had reported to White Bear on December 16 the approach of a large cavalry force closing in from the northwest. He and some other tribal leaders, stifling their contempt for government agents, hurried to Hazen for help. Hazen in turn repressed his disgust with White Bear's previous intrigues and his distrust of Kiowas generally and wrote the note "To the Officer, commanding troops in the Field" that he felt compelled by honesty to send.

Now, White Bear, waiting under that truce flag, wondered about Custer's and Sheridan's reaction to the note. He rode forward with another Kiowa chief, Lone Wolf, toward the halted blue column and saw a group of mounted officers riding toward him. When White Bear reached them he extended his hand to the nearest officer—a lieutenant colonel.

The colonel ignored White Bear, who then offered to shake hands with the yellow-haired commander himself. Custer also refused. White Bear, peering around, saw nothing but a menacing array of faces.

Custer, peering around also, said he saw on surrounding heights hordes of Kiowa warriors, plumed and painted for battle and armed for attack. But Custer always showed a tendency to exaggerate numbers and designs, whether deliberately or not. Further, he did not explain why Indians had come directly to him flying a truce flag and carrying a peaceful note if they really had contemplated ambushing his force.

Custer's thinking at this time reflected his general outlook. The Army was bound to fight Indians, and vice versa. No peace was possible—which happened to be fortunate for a glory seeker like Custer; for only a few newspaper stories would be devoted to anyone as nondramatic as a peacemaker. The easiest way for Custer and other officers like him to deal with the Indian problem anyway was to annihilate the whole bunch, and not to consider pleas for peace and security on individual merit. That would have required too much intellectual exercise, because all Indians looked and acted almost alike.

The waiting group of Kiowas that Custer and Sheridan met certainly looked alike. All were chiefs, colorfully attired. After a conference "eighteen or twenty" of them agreed to accompany the regiment to Fort Cobb. The Kiowa chiefs promised Custer and Sheridan to bring their people into camp there, and thus to prove their peacefulness. The generals then could feel free to attack any other outlying villages as hostile.

The agreement was a generous one for officers like Custer and Sheridan to make, but Custer still doubted the chiefs' sincerity, and he wondered what might be their real intention. They all seemed exceedingly friendly, he thought, but he also felt they "bowed too low."

During the day two Indian messengers left, with Custer's (and certainly Sheridan's) approval, to tell tribesmen to come in.

Around a camp fire that night the chiefs told Custer of their desire "to abandon forever the dangers and risks of the warpath." Custer listened, but he did not believe. Instead he ordered the guard officer to have his men "keep a watchful eye upon those untutored sons of the forest [sic], as I felt confident their plans boded us no good." Through an interpreter he advised the chiefs not to wander away from the camp fire, else "sentries might mistake them for enemies and fire upon them."

Even if the chiefs had been sincere about their desire for peace they would have become as suspicious of Custer as he was of them after receiving that bit of advice—and after reflecting further on Custer's attack at the Washita River. On the following day more and more of them received permission to leave, ostensibly to tell their people of the peaceful assembly at Fort Cobb. "When their number had dwindled down to less than half the original party," Custer said, "I saw that instead of acting in good faith this party of chiefs was solely engaged in the effort to withdraw our attention from the villages." Still, Custer left unexplained the illogicality of such a large number of chiefs meeting him with the truce flag and the peace letter, then placing themselves in his power even for a short time.

When only White Bear and Lone Wolf remained—the two most prominent Kiowa chiefs—Custer ordered some officers nearby to draw revolvers and arrest them before they, too, wandered off. Through an interpreter Custer told the pair they were prisoners. Later White Bear's son, "a tall, trimly built warrior . . . of perhaps twenty," rode into the vicinity, possibly to see about his father and not, as Custer guessed, "as a decoy to cover the escape of [White Bear]." After more negotiation the young man joined the entourage, with his safe passage assured by Custer.

Predictably, Sheridan and Custer found no masses of Kiowas en-

85

camped around Fort Cobb now. Some villagers who had collected there earlier had fled upon hearing of the arrests of their chiefs. Nor were there to be found any Cheyennes or Arapahos—other "hostiles." Sheridan, through Custer, told White Bear and Lone Wolf that unless the entire Kiowa tribe came in at once he would dispatch soldiers to complete the work begun (on Cheyennes) at the Washita River.

White Bear's son carried this message to the people, but they refused to come in until their chiefs had been released.

After some delay Sheridan one day announced another ultimatum—a reflection of his thinking that "the only good Indian is a dead Indian." If the Kiowas had not come in by sunset tomorrow, he said, White Bear and Lone Wolf would hang and soldiers would be sent to attack the village, wherever it might be. On the following day the Kiowas arrived, preceded by the rest of their chiefs.

White Bear and Lone Wolf remained prisoners, but for some reason both Sheridan and Custer became temporarily more generous in their attitude toward Indians, as ensuing activity would show. Some influence for this might have been exerted by William Hazen, the army officer-agent at Fort Cobb. Or perhaps information about a remarkable Indian policy proposed by President-elect U. S. Grant (whom Custer despised, but Sheridan liked) had seeped in. Grant hoped to assure peace for the Plains not by exterminating Indians, but by placing them on reservations under the supervision of the least temperamental human beings imaginable—members of the Society of Friends (Quakers) and other religious denominations.

Whatever the reason, Custer, with Sheridan's approval, set out to entice peacefully onto a reservation the still-absent Arapahos. He took with him only a small force: forty sharpshooters, a few guides, scouts, and interpreters, and mule-drawn supply wagons—insufficient, actually, even for much defense, in the event those "hostiles" chose to fight. One of his interpreters was the comely daughter of dead Chief Little Rock, which might also have accounted for his geniality during this expedition.

Surprisingly, Custer the impetuous—fame-driven and immature—succeeded in bringing back both the Arapahos, then the recently frightened Cheyennes, without using a single bullet. He also talked

Cheyennes into freeing two white girls from captivity. For the most part he relied on courage, determination, psychology, and persuasion to accomplish his mission, as well as on some Indian reluctance to engage in any more fighting, and not on the firepower that had made him famous. This least known of his feats—an indictment of the mentality that requires smoking guns to make a hero—probably was his most difficult and daring, and it showed how history might have been written differently by men with a little more patience, understanding, selflessness, and willingness to look at another view besides their own.

With Kiowas, Cheyennes, and Arapahos on the reservation, at least for the moment, fighting waned on the Southern Plains. Sheridan finally released White Bear and Lone Wolf, but White Bear did not return to his people as an untarnished hero. Some Kiowas accused him of "acting the woman" while an army prisoner, presumably to influence his captors favorably.

Custer led his 7th Cavalry Regiment to Fort Hays and not into another debilitating campaign. Libbie Custer joined her husband at Hays for a serene summer, 1869—one of those happy interludes that made quite bearable for this very feminine woman the vicissitudes of life lived with a noted Indian fighter.

The 7th went into bivouac three miles from the fort, on the banks of Big Creek. Custer exercised his command option, as usual, and erected his own tents farther upstream than anyone else's. The shelters lay spread out in a breeze that whispered through the shade of a huge cottonwood tree. A giant hospital tent served as living room, three wall tents for dining room, guest room, and bedroom, a Sibley for a kitchen, and the souvenir Cheyenne lodge captured at the Washita for a Negro cook's quarters.

In March that year Ulysses Grant had become the eighteenth President of the United States, ending Andrew Johnson's executive ordeal, and had inaugurated the new Indian policy aimed to emphasize peace more than ever before, with those Quaker agents involved. Advisers—not Grant alone—were no doubt responsible for most aspects of the new program, as well as for pleas contained in Grant's inaugural address for "proper treatment of the original occupants of this land" and a promise to favor "any course toward them which tends to their civilization and ultimate citizenship." But

Grant himself (despite some criticism as being a man with a feeling for poor animals but not for war-suffering humanity) did indeed hope to civilize Indians instead of killing them off. His aim was to concentrate all tribes in either of two large areas: on public lands to the north of Nebraska (the Sioux reservation) or to the south of Kansas (the Indian Territory). Later, in a further effort to force his idea of help on reluctant tribesmen, he would sign (in 1871) an act nullifying all treaties and making Indians national wards.

Two months after Grant's inauguration the transcontinental railroad was completed. A May 1869 ceremony at Promontory Point, Utah, commemorated the event that linked East Coast and Far West and, incidentally, permanently divided the Plains and its Indian inhabitants into northern and southern segments.

With completion of the new railroad, inauguration of Grant's Indian program, and successful completion of its own military endeavors, Custer's 7th Regiment seemed to have worked itself out of a job. In early autumn came orders that moved everyone to Fort Leavenworth for the winter. With little else to occupy his hours, Custer began writing biographical articles for an eastern magazine, *Galaxy*. Subsequently in one of them he made a statement strange indeed for a man of his military mind, but still consistent with his notorious inconsistency. Perhaps he was thinking of the expedition with Monahseetah and of his own adventurous days on the Plains, or perhaps nostalgia for a way of life that seemed at this time to be ending for him as well as for those "hostiles" caused him to write this unconscious indictment of his own labor:

> If I were an Indian, I would greatly prefer to cast my lot among those of my people who adhered to the free open plains rather than submit to the confined limits of a reservation, there to be the recipient of the blessed benefits of civilization with its vices thrown in without stint or measure.

Oddly, the declaration more or less aligned Custer with that old Kiowa reprobate, Chief White Bear, who had pleaded at Medicine Lodge, "When a Kiowa is put in a pen he dies."

8

BEWILDERING KALEIDOSCOPE

Most Apaches in southern Arizona were as emotional as White Bear about being confined anywhere, and they had not slackened their guerrilla warfare against that threat. The still-lingering extermination policy, practiced locally but with severity (despite some few changes the Grant administration had effected in other areas), had forced most Apaches into mountain hiding places by now, but those Indians could strike almost any southwestern locality at any time, it seemed. They would sneak out of their remote refuges, cover many forbidding miles with that incredibly fast pace of theirs, raid any of the small ranches or villages scattered about the arid countryside, then hurry back to their havens with speed and efficiency that left victims wondering where the attackers had come from and where they had gone.

On a clear, cold, windy morning in March 1870 more troopers arrived at old Camp Grant (located toward the southeastern tip of present Arizona) to join the battle against those feared marauders. With the soldiers rode a lively officer of ranging and inquiring mind: Lieutenant John Gregory Bourke of the 3rd Cavalry, three months removed from his twenty-fourth birthday.

Bourke's background was not that of the usual frontier officer. His Irish-born parents had wanted him educated in the manner of young scholars who studied in their native Galway, although the Bourkes had moved to Philadelphia before the birth of their son; so young Bourke learned Latin, Greek, and Gaelic from a Jesuit priest in the Pennsylvania city. But when Bourke reached the age of six-teen his conduct suddenly became more conventional for a youth who would choose a military career. He ran away from home and in 1862 enlisted in the 15th Pennsylvania Cavalry, claiming to be eighteen. Following the Civil War his earlier study helped him to win an appointment to the United States Military Academy, where he graduated in 1869.

His attractive personality—one of vigor, intelligence, wit, humor, and kindness—was matched by his interesting appearance. Deep-set gray eyes gleamed under a pair of thick brows. A prominent nose underscored by a heavy mustache and a strong chin indicated his ancestry. His muscular frame—not tall, but not short—gave an impression of endurance.

His study of the classics obviously had helped to discipline his mind, and it must have helped him acquire linguistic ability in Spanish and French. Bourke wrote and left behind historical accounts that evinced knowledge and wit, and he contributed scientific articles (especially in ethnology) notable for close observation and careful scholarship and an avoidance of generalizations. When he came to Arizona, however, he tended at first to lump together all human beings of red ancestry and to accept General Sheridan's pronouncement that "the only good Indian is a dead Indian." Youthful ambition and opportunity for a military career, all warped further by a lack of frontier experience, had narrowed him temporarily. But his study certainly had not been restricted, and he could speak knowledgeably on many subjects—on the writing of Italian poet Dante Alighieri, for instance (and he could even spell the name correctly). Bourke referred to that poet's *Divina Commedia* (*The Divine Comedy*, as it would become known) in recording his first impressions of Arizona:

> Dante Alighieri . . . made the mistake of his life in dying when he did . . . five hundred and fifty years ago. Had he held on to this mortal coil until after Uncle Sam had perfected the "Gadsden Purchase," he would have found full scope for his genius in the description of a region in which not only purgatory and hell, but heaven likewise, had combined to produce a bewildering kaleidoscope of all that was wonderful,

weird, terrible, and awe-inspiring, with not a little that was beautiful and romantic. . . .

In no other section [of the United States than "the Territories of Arizona and New Mexico"] can there be found such extensive areas of desert crossed in every direction by the most asperous mountains, whose profound *cañons* are the wonder of the world, whose parched flanks are matted with the thorny and leafless vegetation of the tropics, and whose lofty summits are black with the foliage of pines whose graceful branches bend in the welcome breezes from the temperate zone. Here one stumbles at almost every step upon the traces of former populations, of whom so little is known, or sees repeated from peak to peak the signal smokes of the fierce Apaches, whose hostility to the white man dates back to the time of Cortés.

Bourke might have used the famous line from Dante Alighieri about the regions of the damned to comment on his arrival at Camp Grant that wind-chilled morning in March 1870: "All hope abandon ye who enter here." But Bourke, young and hopeful, perhaps did not think of it. Instead he said simply (and later), "Arizona was . . . separated from 'God's country' by a space of more than fifteen hundred miles, without a railroad, and the officer or soldier who once got out there rarely returned for years."

Nevertheless, disappointment at first flooded his soul, even though he had been warned what to expect. Army men who had been stationed there declared that the post named Grant was the most thoroughly forsaken station of all those included in the federal budget. Now their description seemed not at all exaggerated.

Bourke and the rest of F Troop came front into line upon arrival. Then the Lieutenant squinted into blowing sand around a gravelly parade ground and saw in the cold sunshine of that early morning a nondescript assortment of buildings slapped down on this dismal plot of desert with no apparent plan except for one general arrangement: they all followed the old army pattern of enclosing a bare quadrangle—the same parade ground from which Bourke was peering. He saw that some buildings had been constructed of adobe. Others had been fashioned from logs placed upright and chinked with mud that the climate had long since baked almost to brick. These "buildings" then had been roofed with tree branches and more mud. Some shelters were nothing more than tattered canvas tents that had done their best flapping in other wind gusts.

Bourke observed among these structures the usual variety of units, all facing him: a row of officers' quarters, an adjutant's office, a post bakery and guardhouse, storehouses, enlisted men's quarters, and sutler's store. A short distance behind the storehouses were located blacksmith's forge, butcher's corral, and cavalry stables. In the expanse beyond the outbuildings the desert rolled away to a dust-clouded horizon.

This original Camp Grant had been thrown up at the supposed confluence of two streams, but the source of water thus provided was little more than a dry joke among Grant soldiers. For much of the year whenever wind began to whine around the sun-baked beds of Aravaipa Creek and San Pedro River, those streams sent their own share of sand blowing into eyes and teeth of cursing garrison personnel. That certainly was the case this morning, as Bourke looked around.

After completion of the usual inflexible military formalities officers dismissed their men to lead horses to the stables, then to find their own quarters. Bourke and other commissioned personnel met and shook hands with opposite numbers of the 1st Cavalry, already quartered at Camp Grant. Then Bourke was shown to his quarters in a large adobe building (which had housed Camp Grant's first kitchens when constructed thirteen years earlier): a room nine feet wide and fourteen feet long, further cramped by having been given only eight feet of space beneath a low ceiling. Bourke eyed the furnishings with dismay, then, with typical resilience, reflected that at least they would not cause him any anxiety in case of fire: a cot, rocking chair, trunk, bookshelf, small washstand soon to be topped by a mirror he provided, and two chintz window curtains. One curtain covered the only window, which Bourke found to be clouded by dust and fly specks; the other hid a row of pegs provided for hanging saber, forage cap, and uniform. A small, little-used fireplace overlooking a rammed-earth floor completed the "appointments." Later, after the room had been painted thoroughly and brightened by the addition of a few items like two Navajo throw rugs and a color print by Louis Prang, Bourke felt better about it. Further, the thick walls shielded an occupant against sun and wind—security not enjoyed by inhabitants of the tents standing along officers' row—even if those same thick walls also protected a museum of Arizona entomology: tarantulas, centipedes, and scorpions. Bourke began catching and bottling the pests, along with rattlesnakes and other outdoor life, and he displayed his fauna in a neat row.

Desert flora fascinated him, too, and this was fortunate for him. Except for a study of Arizona nature and some textbook subjects Camp Grant offered little serious activity other than scouting after hostile Apaches, "who were very bold and kept the garrison . . . occupied." His unflagging interest and curiosity prevented surrender to the melancholy that captured other souls through boredom, sickness (though held down somewhat by the dry air), heat, bad water, flies and other insects, sandstorms, and utter isolation. Numbers of individuals turned to unfortunate diversions to pass away the time: drinking and gambling, and both usually led to tragic excesses.

The sutler, with his eye always on profit, made it easy and inviting to engage in both. For that purpose he maintained a "pleasant, cool room, with a mimimum of flies, the latest papers, perfect quiet, genial companionship, cool water in *ollas* swinging from the rafters, and covered by boards upon which, in a thin layer of soil, grew a picturesque mantle of green barley, and, on a table conveniently near, cans of lemon-sugar, tumblers and spoons, and one or two packs of cards." The huckster could provide no ice, and his most recent newspapers (delivered with the weekly mail) had been published ten or fifteen days earlier in San Francisco and five or six weeks earlier in New York, but with the noon temperature in a man's quarters idling at anywhere from 90 degrees Fahrenheit in fall and winter to 120 degrees in spring and summer,* the store offered unique comfort and set some individuals' habits for the rest of their lives.

Post routine occupied some time, but obviously not enough for

---

* Camp Grant comedians were fond of saying, over and over, that sometimes the heat required two thermometers fixed together to record all the degrees.

everyone's well-being. Reveille roused the garrison at an early hour that ranged from cold in the winter to cool in other seasons. After that, whatever the time of year, the day almost always began to heat up.

For cavalrymen, work began at the stables, caring for horses. Animals not needed for the day's military duties were sent out into the vicinity under a strong mounted guard in search of any blades of grass that might exist in the shade of some sheltering mesquite thicket. In camp, guard mounting preceded breakfast (or followed it, according to the season and the daylight), then came the rest of the daily routine: light drill or other employment—like courts-martial—then dinner, afternoon stables, supper, and dress or undress parade at sunset. Sprinkled throughout the day and enduring into evenings was "general ennui, unless the individual possessed enough force to make work for himself."

Bourke devoted his spare time to studying Spanish language and literature, mineralogy, botany, history, law, and belles lettres, although "it was no easy matter to study with ink drying into gum almost as soon as dipped out by the pen, and paper cracking about the edges when folded or bent."

He began also to study Apaches. Several tired Indians came into Camp Grant to give themselves up or to escape wrath of tribesmen: a woman whose nose had been cut off by a jealous husband; two other women surprisingly seeking something better than medicine-man help for a boy, accompanying them, who had been bitten by a rattlesnake; an old man who knew that fighting was for males younger than himself. The Camp Grant commander kept Apache refugees as prisoners, but mostly for the purpose of preventing their communication with tribesmen still at large. The Indians themselves seemed happy enough to remain in the safety of the camp and to receive their share of rations.

Bourke observed finer physical specimens, too: friendly, army-paid Apache couriers who came in occasionally from other isolated posts miles away. Their long black hair, kept out of eyes by bands of red flannel, and their massive chests and muscular legs showed him something about the renowned Apache quality that helped to overcome the absence of quantity.

Hostile Apaches appeared near the fort on a hot day in late

spring. Bourke and all other Camp Grant personnel were made aware of their presence by the arrival of a bloody, nearly naked Mexican man who stumbled into the post and trotted across the parade ground to the commanding officer's quarters. Two grizzled cavalry sergeants looking on knew what the man's arrival portended, and they sprinted for horses, mounted them, and galloped out to order guards to bring in the grazing herd.

Word spread around the post almost with the speed of sand blown by the desert wind, although on this particular day the flag hung listlessly at the top of the pole and the flies hummed everywhere in warm leisure. An Apache raiding party had surprised a wagon train loaded with supplies and carrying thirty Mexican laborers (including women and children) bound for a ranch located a few miles down the San Pedro River from Camp Grant. Teamsters and other men had fought off the Indians until the women and children could be hurried to terrain nearby that afforded some shelter, but a number of men had been killed or wounded. The Apaches had begun plundering wagons then, ignoring the Mexican refugees (who eventually reached Camp Grant safely).

Every cavalryman available was mounted and sent off, without regard to companies, less than twenty minutes after the Mexican had staggered into the post. Bourke rode with the motley detachment. A second group accompanied by a wagon loaded with water, rations, and medical supplies would follow.

The first detachment struggled through loose sand into a country broken by hills, ravines, and canyons. Excitement of the moment did not blind Bourke to the scenery. He maintained presence of mind and noticed that springtime glories still had not faded with the approach of summer. Myriads of golden crocuses and multicolored verbenas brightened the fields of grass that grew in more sheltered and fertile areas. Elsewhere, atop barren canyon walls, he saw stands of giant cactus looking down like sentinels. Bourke would have examined the bluffs for lurking Apaches, too, but none appeared.

The western sky began blazing its desert-sunset motif of scarlet and gold, and still the troopers rode on without finding the object of their search. That wagon train must have been farther away than reported. Then the soldiers slackened their pace, and they commenced deploying as skirmishers. Bourke heard a distant coyote greet dusk with a cry; at first he mistook it for a human wail. Gloom spread throughout the command like the night that was quickly covering it.

Another coyote called. Or was it really that? Men speculated as they edged ahead, even more cautiously.

"Hel-lup! Hel-lup!" No coyote could sound like that. The advance came upon one of the two Anglo-American owners of the ranch for which the wagon train had been bound—a man named Kennedy, "weak and faint and covered with his own blood," lying at the bottom of an arroyo, where he had fallen during his flight. The featherless shaft of an arrow protruded from his chest and the pain was intense: "Jes' like . . . I'd swallowed a coal o' fire, boys," he gasped to the troopers who found him. For hours Kennedy had refrained from calling out, he said, because he feared the Apaches would find him and torture him until he died. During the interminable wait he had tried to pull out the arrow, but he had only broken off the feather end.

A sergeant and some men stayed with Kennedy. Bourke and the rest went on and soon found the remains of the wagon train. Its wreckers had vanished. Bourke described the scene.

> There were the hot embers of the . . . wagons, the scattered fragments of broken boxes, barrels, and packages of all sorts; copper shells, arrows, bows, one or two broken rifles, torn and burned clothing. There lay all that was mortal of poor Israel [Kennedy's ranch partner], stripped of clothing, a small piece cut from the crown of the head, but thrown back upon the corpse—the Apaches do not care much for scalping—his heart cut out, but also thrown back near the corpse, which had been dragged to the fire of the burning wagons and had been partly consumed; a lance wound in the back, one or two arrow wounds . . . a severe contusion under the left eye, where he had been hit perhaps with the stock of a rifle or carbine, and the death wound from ear to ear, through which the brain had oozed.

The scene scarcely induced sleep, but the men remained there for the rest of the night, beneath a majestic star-filled sky. Sentinels watched anxiously from behind bushes, wondering whether those unpredictable Apaches would double back and strike again. The soldiers knew the advice of wise frontiersmen: "When you see Apache 'sign,' be *keerful;* . . . when you don' see nary sign, be *more* keerful."

Nothing exciting occurred. The sergeant and his troopers brought in Kennedy, and, later, the supply wagon and its escort rumbled up from out of the darkness to the watchful camp, bringing welcomed food and water—and orders from the Camp Grant commander to return the next morning. The commander intended to send a pursuing force after the raiders, whose fresh trail had been discovered and reported to him. Soldiers lifted Israel's body and that of the mortally wounded Kennedy into the supply wagon. Camp Grant would have two funerals of frontier brevity.

After the austere burials F Troop, commanded by an experienced lieutenant, cool and wiry Howard Cushing, rode out in search of the marauders. This time the soldiers were provisioned and armed for a fifteen-day scout. Two "tame" Apache guides accompanied the detachment. Bourke went, too. It would be his first real scout.

When the troop came upon the Indian trail the native guides latched on to it and were not fooled by endeavors of their fellow Apaches ahead to throw them off. Every dodge proved to have been in vain; the fleeing Indians had not suspected the Army's use of such knowledgeable human beings to track them during their escape.

To the mouth of the San Pedro the troopers rode, always following the patiently searching guides, then across the Gila and to the head of Disappointment Creek in the Mescal Mountains, on into the Pinal foothills—and almost to the very summit. From that vantage point the pursuers saw smoke rising to the northeast.

Bourke heard Cushing express a yearning for the sun to set behind the Superstition Mountains off to the west, so he could then ride into the valley for an immediate attack, but his Apache scouts advised caution. One of them motioned Cushing back, then crept on hands and knees to a crest and peered down. Below him were resting the people—his people—this army was seeking. Smoke from smoldering camp fires curled skyward. The scout crawled back out

97

of sight from below, then reported to Cushing. Bourke soon learned that F Troop would wait throughout the night and attack as soon as returning daylight permitted Cushing to see his hand in front of his face.

The night grew cold. Time lagged with the dismal halt. Then a cry startled them all. A chilled Indian from the camp below had walked out in search of wood to add to the fading embers and had somehow discovered their presence. The Apache ran toward his camp, yelling to everyone about the presence of soldiers.

The men of Troop F raised a great shout of their own and wreaked destruction on the Apaches. When fighting ended and sunrise illuminated the scene Bourke saw another "ghastly spectacle, a field of blood won with but slight loss to ourselves." For once the fast-paced Apache raiders had not escaped, but their lack of success had been due to the exertions of other Apaches, equally swift and clever.

Young Lieutenant Bourke, still an adherent of the General Sheridan principle, observed plenty of good Indians lying on the ground there. "The only use to make of [them] was . . . fertilizer," he had reflected a short time earlier, with disdain of gore made possible by distance from it. Now, however, he peered at the dead Apaches and concluded, "I do not care to [elaborate] upon the scene."

9

HAPPINESS AND HARSHNESS

Five months after John Bourke survived his first real encounter with hostile Apaches another cavalry lieutenant reported for duty on the frontier. Robert Goldthwaite Carter, twenty-five, arrived with his bride of two and a half months, Mary, at Fort Concho, near present San Angelo, Texas, there to join Troop E of the 4th Cavalry as previously ordered. The construction of Concho, one of a series of posts newly opened along the Texas frontier, had not been completed when the Carters arrived.

Lieutenant Bob Carter was eight months older than Bourke, but he had graduated from the United States Military Academy a year later—in June of 1870.

In some ways he resembled the lieutenant fighting those Apaches in distant Arizona. Like Bourke, Carter was an Easterner, born in Bridgton, Maine, and educated in the public schools of Portland. When his father moved to Massachusetts in 1857 to practice law Carter went, too, and (like Bourke) volunteered for service in 1862 at the age of sixteen by claiming to be eighteen. Carter thus exchanged association with Phillips Academy at Andover for life as a private with the 22nd Massachusetts Volunteer Infantry, an outfit that was thoroughly bloodstained by war's end.

But military life still attracted Carter. He liked the discipline and the camaraderie. Further, he had family ties (unlike Bourke) that would have encouraged such a career. Twenty of his kin had served in earlier wars, including the American Revolution.

Carter did not look much like a fighter and certainly not like a brawler, which Irishman Bourke, by appearance, might have been (but was not, either). Except for a sharp, prominent nose Carter's face was soft-featured. Liquid eyes, drooping slightly, seemed to look out upon the world in sympathy, not in military scorn. Even his light hair and his thick mustache (viewed in a photograph made later) appeared to be almost as soft as down. But Carter's mildness ended largely with facial features. He had a soul mostly military, particularly in regard to Indians. Still, he could fluctuate to some degree.

Perhaps his mental makeup could be described best by a statement regarding religion he once made; it showed him to be neither a hammer-and-tong atheist nor an emotional man swayable by various preachments. Carter was talking about army life in the open country when he said:

Here in this great solitude of nature we found our deepest study spread out before us, and gathered "sermons from the stones," "books from the running brooks," and "God in everything." . . . In these magnificent temples made with His hands we gathered inspiration and from this self-communion added to that breadth of knowledge and experience which come not in the life of every man, even when traveled, fully educated, and intellectually developed. . . . Hardships, dangers, privations, and sacrifices—quiet conceits—remove selfishness, filter the dross, purify and elevate, and make all mankind akin. It has been said in ecclesiastical circles . . . that soldiers and sailors lack the true essence of religion in their makeup. . . . This is not true. Most professional soldiers and sailors are neither atheists nor infidels . . . [but] always [hold] fast to the hope of . . . the immortality of the soul. . . . Yet, by such close contact with nature . . . and sleeping perhaps for years under the canopy of heaven . . . they accept pretty largely the theory of the *God of Nature* and leave the mere theology of religion with all the various beliefs, creeds, etc., etc., to be taken care of by religious quacks and scientists who are lacking in their own service experience.

To Carter the Army was everything, and he gave it all his loyalty and energy. He was a man who believed peace must be fought for before it could be secured, and he spoke with consistent scorn of pacificists: "spineless . . . jellyfish . . . pussyfooters." He approved of President Andrew Jackson's earlier removal of southeastern tribes to lands west of the Mississippi as "one of the best and most farsighted strokes of practical statesmanship that the country ever experienced. There were no more Indian troubles east of the Mississippi."

Yet Carter could occasionally admit another side to view, perhaps as a vague reflection of upbringing by a father who had served for years as a judge. Later, when a fellow officer fell dead during a skirmish in that western area to which Indians had been removed, Carter remarked, "One more splendid soul offered up in the sacrifice of 'Winning the West,' that civilization might advance, and the development of that wild country by seekers of gold, cotton, oil, etc., might satisfy the insatiable ambitions of the white man, then pressing on to and beyond the border already allotted to the Indian."

Carter's immediate grief over the death of the man and his ensuing resentment of civilians who might benefit by it must have motivated him to make that statement, because the Lieutenant rarely expressed such views. Writings he left behind characterized him as a military disciplinarian first of all, one who followed orders and gave them as appropriate without questioning morality. His country was expanding westward; something had to be done with the Indians there; and that was that. He cast from his mind other thoughts, if they ever intruded, and in this way differed most noticeably from his distant colleague in Arizona, John Bourke. Carter was not much of a thinker. He was a follower and a plodder, but one who learned well his job and those hard lessons taught by the frontier.

All that would come slowly, of course. When he and Mary arrived at forsaken Fort Concho after a hard trip through Indian country from San Antonio (and an earlier journey from points all the way back to Boston) neither the Lieutenant nor his wife possessed the background to take up frontier life without a pang of concern. The junction nearby of the North Concho and the Main Concho rivers, a bit of geography that has changed since then, offered more water than did those two streams that flung sand at

Bourke and his Arizona colleagues, but the same scanty, temporary tents were to be seen among the sprinkling of buildings standing around the inevitable parade ground at Concho—and, worse, the Carters were assigned to one of them.

An icy Texas norther was blowing that day in late November 1870 when they arrived and moved in. They affixed blankets to the north side of their tent as reinforcement against the rude wind that continued to push its way into their private quarters. Later they discovered some other inconveniences that Bourke already had seen: centipedes and scorpions that inhabited some of the permanent buildings, tarantulas that hid under shrubbery and cactus plants, rattlesnakes that idled in rock piles, dry-weather sandstorms that cut visibility to ten yards or less and deposited a gritty covering indoors on floors, tables, and desks.

Other unpleasantness lay on the far side of the river, where a young shanty-and-sod village to be known later as San Angelo—inhabited then by a hundred human snakes—enticed army personnel "Over the River," by which name the town first became known. There soldiers could escape the boredom of garrison life by drinking, gambling, quarreling, and fighting, even if poisonous whiskey did sometimes threaten to remove them permanently from all that army monotony.

Fort Concho employed no chaplain, and Sunday communion could be only with nature. But Carter would not have objected to that, anyway. He enjoyed the view toward Twin Mountains, where sometimes could be seen herds of antelope flashing their white-spotted flanks in the sun and at other times thousands of buffalo grazing in spring fields. The garrison killed buffalo only for meat at that time, even though the presence of the animals nearby caused occasional stampedes of the cavalry horse herds pastured a mile or so away from the post.

By night other animals made their presence known with melancholy calls that came at all hours—usually a bark followed by staccato yelps tumbling into each other, then a climactic, tremulous howl that seemed like a beseeching voice from some faraway spirit world. When these sounds awakened Mary Carter from deep sleep, the Lieutenant noticed, she would jerk up in bed to a sitting position, then shrink back under covers. Sometimes the wolves and coyotes ventured into the post itself, searching for food, and occasionally they upset garbage barrels standing a short distance from the Carters' tent.

Hostile Indians ventured close to the post, too, on raids. Comanches were responsible for many attacks around Fort Concho; young Quanah Parker would have led some of them from his refuge far out on the Staked Plain. Kiowas under White Bear and other leaders also raided frequently, but their strikes were aimed more often at Texans living in an area directly below the Indian Territory. These bands and others had increased their maraudings following the Medicine Lodge council and the disappointments that ensued—and in the wake of the Washita battle and the arrests of White Bear and Lone Wolf. The attempts at peace by the United States Government had left most tribes as frustrated, angry, and vengeful as ever.

Bob and Mary Carter had just settled down in their airy quarters when Indians raided a locality within sixteen miles of the post. Not even a month after that warriors ventured closer, almost into that miserable town across the river. Then came another attack—on a stagecoach bound for Fort Griffin, one hundred miles to the north.

Cavalry galloped out each time in unsuccessful pursuit. Carter went with the detachment sent out after the stagecoach raiders and received his first experience in frontier warfare. Most of the instruction came from a superior who had been an officer in the German army, a Major Rendlebrock—"Old Joe" to his colleagues. Carter recorded an early lesson learned during his first scout.

"How you put dis command in camp, eh?" Major Rendlebrock asked him one evening, at the completion of a day's march.

Carter, not knowing, bluffed. "Why, Major, I would picket the horses close to camp, with a small herd guard on to prevent surprise or stampede."

"Oh, no!" Rendlebrock roared. "What you do for de animals at night so close to camp and wid no grass, eh?"

After that Carter remembered his first lesson. Send the animals, under guard, some distance out to graze until shortly before dark, then at night bring them in around camp, for better protection, to graze on grass that would then still be available.

But the officer who gave Carter his most unforgettable lessons in

103

frontier fighting was Ranald S. Mackenzie, a thirty-year-old New York who had been brevetted through every grade from first lieutenant to brigadier general before the end of the Civil War—during which he had also been wounded several times. Mackenzie assumed command of Fort Concho in February 1871—three months after Carter's arrival. The commander's incongruous appearance struck young Carter immediately.

Judging by looks, Mackenzie could be no match for Indians. His wounds by this time had eaten into his health, and he never had been truly robust after having suffered sunstroke at the age of three.

Mackenzie stood about five feet nine inches tall and weighed around 145 pounds. He was (as Carter found) morose, introspective, fretful, irritable, irascible—a hard man indeed to serve with. Mackenzie ate little, slept little, and, because of almost constant pain brought on by the earlier wounds, usually rode poorly—although he was to command the 4th Cavalry during most of his time on the frontier. But when action forced prolonged horsemanship on Mackenzie, as Carter would soon find, the commander could outride any of his officers and men—some of whom would suffer hallucinations after remaining too long in the saddle.

Mackenzie cared nothing for neatness in dress. The one thing he did care about in 1871 was finding and fighting Indians. He had his own plan for stopping raids: leading expeditions into hostile country and attacking the warriors there. The ability and tenacity he would display in this work would win him the loyalty of his officers and men, when his personality might otherwise have antagonized them all.

Lieutenant Carter became one of the staunchest supporters of Mackenzie—as well as of the Army generally—despite the fact that Carter's chosen career soon proved to be an exceedingly arduous one. It tested the perseverance of a man who had sworn to do any job given to him, no matter how dangerous or unpopular it might become. Charles King, an author and an army officer who served at that same time, later described the Indian wars (at the twenty-first annual meeting of veterans):

A warfare in which the soldier of the United States had no hope of honors if victorious, no hope of mercy if he fell; slow death by hideous torture if taken alive; sheer abuse from press and pulpit, if, as was inevitable, Indian squaw or child was killed. A warfare that called us through the cliffs and canyons of the southwest, the lava beds and labyrinths of Modoc land, the windswept plains of Texas, the rigors of Montana winters, the blistering heat of midsummer suns, fighting oftentimes against a foe for whom we felt naught but sympathy, yet knew that the response could be but deathless hate. . . . A more thankless task, a more perilous service, a more exacting test of leadership, morale, and discipline no army . . . has ever been called upon to undertake than that which for eighty years was the lot of the little fighting force of regulars who cleared the way across the continent for the emigrant and settler.

Carter, plodding and loyal, was mentally and physically ready for the test that lay ahead of him that winter of 1870–71 as he combined conjugal happiness with Concho harshness.

10

ABILITY TO PROJECT

In masculine Arizona harshness outweighed happiness for certain. Even an effervescent like Lieutenant John Bourke would have admitted that. During the winter of 1870–71, while Lieutenant Bob Carter began learning about survival on the Texas frontier, Arizona Apaches resorted to clever tactics previously tried and proved to make Indian warfare for the United States soldier an even greater rigor. The Apaches engaged in "a number of simultaneous attacks . . . at points widely separated, thus confusing both troops and settlers, spreading a vague sense of fear over all the territory infested, and imposing upon the soldiery an exceptional amount of work of the hardest conceivable kind."

Bourke put in his share of labor, accompanying one punitive expedition after another during those months. Still the raids continued, on into spring. Apaches attacked stage stations and ranches, killed mail riders, massacred parties of travelers, then vanished.

Success inspired more boldness. The Indians sneaked up to the very fringes of Tucson, a siesta-prone town of 3,200 inhabitants now, and stole an entire cattle herd. The Lieutenant left on yet another scout, while Tucson citizens preened a paramilitary Committee of Public Safety as local protection.

Bourke's cavalry detachment had moved fifty-five miles southwestward to Tucson from old Camp Grant before that last raid and some earlier ones, to be in a more central location and nearer supplies. During the march to their new location they had traveled through the gloomy-walled Cañon del Oro, across Eight-Mile Mesa, over a lengthy expanse of sandy and hilly terrain, past miles of desert vegetation—flowering mescal, white-plumed Spanish bayonet, forbidding prickly pear, mesquite with low-hanging pods ripening in the sun, ready to provide nutrition for horses and cattle that could survive in this wasteland. They also rode past an occasional heap of loose stones that marked the grave of some Apache victim. Then, from a distance, they sighted the Tucson oasis, capital of the Territory of Arizona. A green expanse of barley land surrounded the town, and two cottonwood strips lined thirsty little Santa Cruz River, which bisected a narrow, fertile valley. Officers and troopers went into quarters at Camp Lowell, a small post on Tucson's eastern edge.

Bourke found the town to be a bustling place, certainly in comparison to Camp Grant. This paradise of the desert drew forth whistling and singing from men who entered it after passing through a surrounding purgatory—"Tucson, whose [newest wells] yielded water sweeter . . . whose maidens were more charming, whose society was more hospitable, merchants more progressive, magazines better stocked, climate more dreamy, than any town from Santa Fe to Los Angeles."

Tucson struck Bourke also as being entirely foreign (not Anglo-American like Prescott, then a rival town built amid pines and granite cliffs of a country much farther north). In Tucson most native residents spoke in lilting Spanish—although there was to be heard a sprinkling of other tongues—and their dress, religion, and customs proved utterly strange to a newcomer from the Atlantic Coast.*

A visitor soon discovered other peculiarities. The town had plenty of twenty-four-hour gambling hells and saloons, but not one hotel. Unless a traveler carried a letter of introduction to some honored citizen and might thus gain access to private bed and board for a night or two he slept as best he could in a convenient corral or some other semipublic place, to be awakened throughout

* On the other hand, in Tucson and in all Arizona at this time peace officers were Anglo-Americans, as opposed to the situation in the Territory of New Mexico, where Mexican-Americans kept the law.

the night by the barking of dogs that thrived in the town and to be roused, finally, near sunrise by countless roosters that began sounding off with the first eastern sweep of the rose-tinted brush that painted the beginning of another Arizona day. Teamsters accompanying wagon trains that arrived in town for stocking merchants' shelves usually parked their unloaded vehicles in the plaza before massive San Antonio Church—old Tucson's anchor and, through the regular ringing of bells, its clock also. The teamsters lashed their oxen and mules to wheels, then slept under bright stars and in cool comfort no matter what had been the day's temperature.

Other inconveniences proved to be less romantic. The town had no paving or street lamps and little lumber. Most houses had been made of adobe, and some "did not possess ten dollars' worth of furniture." Water had to be purchased off the cart of an old Mexican who hauled it in antique barrels from a spring nearby, or it might be obtained from a new well somewhere—but older wells became alkaline after a few months. Garbage collection was unknown; the streets "were every bit as filthy as those of New York."

Nevertheless, Bourke found the town to be fascinating, as might have been predicted. Further, scouting expeditions took him into the dangerous countryside often enough to give him inevitable pleasure upon returning to the place, even with its smelly shortcomings, after he had seen comrades die on the open desert from Apache-inflicted wounds. Those risky trips would have reminded him that Tucson was more than an oasis. It was a haven, and safety could easily be lost on the very outskirts. Subsequent events proved this to Bourke, although he was not to be a participant—just an observer.

During the spring of 1871 a Mexican-American boy looking after a herd of sheep was himself reminded of this precariousness. He sat, dozing, in the shade of a mesquite tree while his animals grazed in foothills within two miles of Tucson. As the day's heat increased, so did the boy's torpidity. He began depending more and more on the bellwether animal to do his own job. As long as the boy heard an occasional clinking from the bell fastened around the sheep's neck he assumed his flock to be grazing peacefully. His eyes began to stay shut for longer periods.

When next he forced his lids open for a look he saw an Apache warrior staring at him. The Indian was holding the wether's bell and had been ringing it, at intervals, for some time while other warriors made off with the flock. The boy screamed; the amused Apache threw the bell at the youth's head, then ran off to overtake the other warriors. Pursuers later recovered the sheep.

Two raids in April 1871 (although more distant) also demonstrated Tucson's vulnerability. On the tenth Apaches stole cattle and horses south of town. Three days later they killed four Anglo-Americans to the east. Someone said the marauders had come from a village of peaceful Apaches encamped not far from Bourke's old station of Camp Grant.

This time the Tucson Committee of Public Safety determined to retaliate, without leaving decisions to the local military force, which seemed consistently undermanned and continually reluctant to wipe out Indians in the manner that most Arizonans advocated.

That very village near Camp Grant seemed, in fact, to typify the Army's weakness. A muscular chief named Eskiminzin, weary of leading his band of 150 Aravaipa Apaches in flights from soldiers, had asked the post commander for sanctuary. The officer, a lieutenant named Royal Whitman, lacked rank and authority to render a decision, but he told Eskiminzin that if his people surrendered all their firearms they might reside near the post as prisoners of war until he could get instructions from superior officers. The Apaches agreed, planted corn, hired out for army work, and began a peaceful existence while awaiting the functioning of tedious military bureaucracy, which would be slowed further in this case by wretched communications. Meanwhile, some other Indians joined the Aravaipas.

This was the village a well-armed force of six Anglo-Americans, forty-two Mexican-Americans, and ninety-two Papago Indian mercenaries attacked, early in the morning of April 30. Army officers at Tucson sought to warn Lieutenant Whitman of the departure and purpose of the citizens' force, but the message reached Camp Grant three hours after 144 of Eskiminzin's peace seekers had been massacred and the village left ablaze.

Whitman and his surgeon described (in the 1871 *Report* of the Secretary of the Interior) the sight they beheld upon arrival.

I found quite a number of women shot while asleep beside their bundles of hay which they had collected to bring in . . . [Whitman said]. The wounded who were unable to get away had their brains beaten out with clubs or stones, while some were shot full of arrows after having been mortally wounded by gunshot. The bodies were all stripped. Of the whole number buried, one was an old man and one was a well-grown boy—all the rest women and children. . . .

I found that I should have but little use for . . . medicine [the surgeon wrote]; the work had been too thoroughly done. The camp had been fired, and the dead bodies of some twenty-one women and children were lying scattered over the ground; those who had been wounded in the first instance had their brains beaten out with stones. Two of the best-looking of the squaws were lying in such a position, and from the appearance of the genital organs and of their wounds, there can be no doubt that they were first ravished and then shot dead. Nearly all of the dead were mutilated. One infant of some ten months was shot twice, and one leg nearly hacked off.

The vicious attack dismayed many Americans—including President Grant, who called it pure murder—and it motivated Lieutenant Whitman to press for a trial of Tucson citizens responsible. But an Arizona jury acquitted all defendants after deliberating little more than a quarter of an hour (and Whitman ruined his career by his locally unpopular action; later he resigned from the Army).

At Tucson, reflective Lieutenant Bourke had kept himself informed of the Camp Grant attack and the trial, and he regarded the entire event as "one of the saddest and most terrible in our annals . . . one over which I would gladly draw a veil." His analysis of the failure—the utter impossibility—of peace in the West showed logic typical of his reasoning and exhibited none of the emotion that warped the thinking of Indian-hating frontiersmen inclined to slay any or all natives or of Indian-sympathizing idealists who gushed forth while residing safely a thousand or so miles from border violence.

To my mind [the Camp Grant massacre] indicated the weak

spot in all our dealings with the aborigines, a defective point never repaired and never likely to be. According to our system of settling up the public lands, there are no such things as colonies properly so called. Each settler is free to go where he pleases, to take up such area as the law permits, and to protect himself as best he can. The Army has always been too small to afford all the protection the frontier needed, and affairs have been permitted to drift along in a happy-go-lucky sort of way indicative rather of a sublime faith in divine providence than of common sense and good judgment.

The settlers, in all sections of the West, have been representative of the best elements of the older states from which they set forth, but it is a well-known fact that among them have been . . . more than a fair . . . share of the reckless, the idle and the dissolute. On the other hand, among the savages, there have been as many young bloods anxious to win renown in battle as there have been old wise-heads desirous of preserving the best feeling with the new neighbors. The worst members of the two races are brought into contact, and the usual results follow; trouble springs up, and it is . . . [often] the peaceably disposed on each side [who suffer].

Because of those murders of helpless Apaches, President Grant sent a personal representative, Vincent Colyer, to Arizona to make another attempt to secure a peace through negotiation. Surprisingly, most survivors of the Camp Grant massacre expressed willingness to try again, but other Apaches whose trust (if any) had vanished long ago continued to raid.

In June 1871 a new commander arrived in Tucson to take over the Department of Arizona: General George Crook, a forty-one-year-old man who had, as had most other frontier officers, served in the Civil War.

Like his subordinate, Bourke, Crook realized the cost to date of the Apache extermination war. One thousand American lives and $40 million had been devoted to failure. Apaches had not been annihilated; in fact, the hostile bands seemed as numerous as ever. Arizonans supposed, however, that Crook would continue the policy of killing.

Crook astounded and angered them by expressing some sympathy for the Apaches' problems and by announcing that he hoped to be able to save Indian lives for better things, not to snuff them out. Still, Crook was a military leader, and if raids continued, he said, a "sharp, active campaign" would become necessary. Bourke was to be a participant in many ensuing events—and perhaps the closest observer of Crook.

The Lieutenant saw and described a strong, silent man with keen, blue-gray eyes. Crook "was a little over six feet in height, straight as a lance, broad and square-shouldered, full-chested, and with an elasticity and sinewiness of limb." The new commander arrived in Tucson unannounced on the morning of June 4. He lunched with an old friend, Territorial Governor A. P. K. Safford, then assumed control in typical Crook fashion. "Before sundown every officer within the limits of what was then called the southern district of Arizona was under summons to report to him." By questioning those officers Crook acquired all information possible on such subjects as climate, geography, and Arizona grasses, as well as Apaches. Later he laid his plans, without asking for further advice.

To Bourke this new commander was ideally suited for the hard job of establishing order in the Territory of Arizona. Other leaders might boast and bluster—but not the retiring Crook, who did not drink coffee or tea, did not smoke, did not spout profanities or obscenities, did not care for military pomp or fame. Any promise Crook made to an Indian was one to be carefully kept, Bourke noted; yet the commander also learned quickly the art of survival in Indian warfare. "He became skilled in the language of 'signs' and trails, and so perfectly conversant with all that is concealed in the great book of Nature that, in the mountains at least, he might readily take rank as being fully as much Indian as the Indian himself." Crook's ability to project even extended to empathy: "There never was an officer in our military service so completely in accord with all the ideas, views, and opinions of the savages whom he had to fight or control."

Arizonans began calling Crook an Indian lover, but the man continued to set his own course. Bourke regarded his new commander as a Daniel Boone with "the advantages of the better education of his day and generation."

Bourke's admiration increased further after accompanying Crook on his first scout. The General had considered problems in advance, even those regarding pack mules and packing, and Bourke soon realized that the cavalry was moving faster, with lighter loads, and with greater precision than before, while its commander had time to show a great interest in everything—particularly in observations of nature made by the Apache scouts whom Crook employed.

Bourke discovered also that Crook's first scout was not made for the purpose of waging war, but for encouraging peace. The commander spoke with various Apache chiefs whenever he could persuade them to come and listen, and his message was the same to each one. Peace was best, Crook would say, and it was in fact becoming essential for the well-being of any Indian, with white men inexorably crowding the West. Game would soon vanish. Apaches and all other natives must go to a reservation and learn farming or ranching to survive. No matter what grievances Apaches had they must for their own sake forget them if they were to exist. If they chose to fight Crook would have to follow their lead.

Bourke listened and always marveled. Here was a military leader following orders, just as glory-bound Custer had been doing at the Washita, yet one who allowed logic and sympathy to intrude. "[Crook] wanted to treat the Apache just the same as he would treat any other man—as a man. He did not believe in one kind of treatment for the white and another for the Indian."

Convincing Apaches was another matter. Most Indians were wise judges of a man's character, but they had heard words like this earlier and had been disappointed. Might Crook be just another conniver?

Bourke never doubted his commander from the first, and his respect for such a man said something, too, about Bourke's own personality, character, and attitude. The Camp Grant massacre and a study of Apache history had begun to convince the Lieutenant of the weakness of that "good . . . dead Indian" theory of Sheridan's.

11

INSPECTION ALONG
THE BUTTERFIELD TRAIL

The same spring of 1871 that produced a massacre of Aravaipa Apaches near Camp Grant and brought General Crook to Arizona heralded another tumultuous season on the Texas frontier, where North American warfare against Indians became focalized at this time. Except for those comparatively few hostile Apaches in Arizona and a strong encampment of unpacified Sioux in the Powder River country of Montana and Wyoming, Sheridan's policy of hunting Indians during winter months had sent tribes elsewhere onto reservations.

In West and North Texas, Comanches, Plains Apaches, and Kiowas cooperated in raids usually commenced from the Indian Territory and set the border ablaze again. They even seemed to be successful in pushing it back. Around the time of full moon, especially, many Texas settlers staggered into the army posts strung out along that loosely drawn trouble line to report robberies, rapes, and murders. Many victims never ventured to return to their homes —not at this time, anyway. They chose instead to give up frontier life or to remain in the proximity of one of the forts. Only the more daring and usually better equipped settlers chose to stay on outlying farms and ranches.

Frontier people complained all the way to Washington about the deviltry of reservation Indians and about a lack of military protection, but federal officials suspected that the Texans exaggerated their plight and that the raiders were not reservation Indians anyway.

114

This angered frontiersmen even more. A newspaper correspondent reported from distant Jacksboro, Texas, to the state capital at Austin:

> I have been in this neighborhood nearly a week . . . and I can assure you that the great number of silent graves by the wayside, and all those buried in the quiet country graveyard slain by the bloody hands of the red men, fully attest to the just cause for alarm in these frontier counties. . . . Is it a wonder . . . that a bitter feeling should be engendered against the whole race of savages?

The protests eventually persuaded the nation's ranking general, William Tecumseh Sherman, who had assumed command of the Army when Grant became President, to visit Texas for a firsthand observation.

In the first few days of spring, on March 25, Lieutenant Bob Carter and his wife, now six months pregnant, heard of an impending move from their tent at Fort Concho. His E Troop, with headquarters and four other companies of the 4th Cavalry, were to move to that tumultuous frontier area around Jacksboro—to Fort Richardson, 180 straight-line miles northeast, there to relieve the 6th Cavalry for duty in Kansas. It would not be a routine trip for a woman in Mary Carter's condition.

Two days later a column of troopers, covered ambulances, and canvas-topped supply wagons splashed across the Concho, lumbered past that squalid village called "Over the River," and headed across a spring-enriched carpet of grass and flowers toward the Colorado River of Texas, thirty miles distant. Cold rain soaked them as they forded that stream, then halted for the night, but they found enough drift cottonwood for starting some luxurious camp fires.

Colonel Mackenzie, a bachelor, stared at Mary Carter and other wives of officers as they cooked dinner on mess kettles heaped with glowing embers. His face, alternately showing a slight frown and an incredulous smile, reflected his bewilderment at observing women of sensible appearance who would give up eastern refinements to accompany their men to this awful region.

On northeastward they traveled, now following the route of the old Butterfield Mail that had linked California with eastern points, by way of El Paso, during the years 1858–61. To another night halt at little Fort Chadbourne, on Oak Creek, a two-company post whose parade ground had been commandeered by prairie dogs for an unmilitary bivouac filled with "sharp, squeaking barks and comical antics." The next day, past hundreds and even thousands of buffalo grazing contentedly while their remaining months here waned. Into another chilling, soaking storm that quickly obscured a view of previously sighted Pulpit Rock and Church Mountain; then into another wet camp, this time on Bluff Creek. After another reveille and another breakfast, through shrub-lined Mountain Pass, where hostile Indians were fond of attacking mail stages, and down a slope from the mesa on which they had been traveling, to a seemingly endless prairie. On its expanse the distant brown of countless buffalo once more contrasted with the green-velvet cover of spring grass.

On to Fort Phantom Hill, built of logs and stones and garrisoned by a small, nervous detachment, and to Fort Griffin, looking down upon the countryside from a position atop an elevation; across a bad ford on the Brazos River; through the grounds of ramshackle Fort Belknap, occupied by a few jittery soldiers and squatters; across Salt Creek Prairie, a favorite area for raiders from the Indian Territory and now sprinkled with fresh graves of victims; and (on April 8, the thirteenth day out of Fort Concho) into another frontier post that sprawled around a parade ground. The post had been built near a creek called "Lost."

One-half mile north of Fort Richardson lay, leechlike, the inevitable frontier settlement, this one with that name of Jacksboro. There a soldier could rid himself of his meager pay in a hurry, and there resided a contingent of settlers who had retreated temporarily to the vicinity of the post, together with a small number of home-building citizens and a large collection of gamblers and saloon keepers "occasionally increased by a roaring . . . gang of cowboys on a spree . . . who . . . spent their time, especially at night, in riding up and down 'Jacks'' only street . . . yelling like a lot of wild Indians and firing their six-shooters at saloon windows and many other imaginary enemies."

Mary Carter had fallen ill during the last two days of the march and her condition required bed rest, but this was something Fort Richardson facilities could not provide in great comfort. The Carters moved immediately into quarters previously assigned: a one-room jacal walled with mesquite branches placed upright and chinked with red clay that had, in spots, broken and dropped to the ground. The cottage, unporched, had been roofed with material similar to that used in the walls, but the overhead had cracked, too, so that it allowed occupants to lie in the cots furnished and gaze at stars through the ceiling opening.

Some finer quarters existed on officers' row—five frame story-and-a-half residences of four rooms each, with porches in front and rear—but they were already occupied by the families of officers whose rank exceeded that of lieutenant. More austere quarters stood there, too: weathered tents, supposedly temporary, used for an "overflow" crowd. So the Carters made out as best they could in a home "a New England farmer would hardly [use to] stable his animals."

In time Bob Carter learned more about his habitation and four other "picket quarters" similarly built. Before the arrival of the 4th Cavalry and the ensuing demand for more married officers' quarters, bachelor officers of the 6th Cavalry had used the jacales for dog kennels. The animals were gone, now, and the places had been cleaned and tidied as much as possible, but a population of fleas remained, and the bites inflicted by those pests left victims covered with pits resembling smallpox.

Nor were these the only discomforts to be endured. Centipedes occasionally crawled up and down the shoddy walls and made appearances, too, from floor cracks and knotholes. Sometimes dark, hairy tarantulas wandered about the room, as did scorpions whose sting felt like a burn. By night mice and rats might be heard scampering across the floor.

Storms would deposit sand or hail or water to be removed somehow from beds and dining table before satisfactory sleeping or eating. Dried clay that dropped suddenly from chinked partitions might allow a clear view into next-door quarters—and between those two rooms a whisper could be heard almost any time anyway.

In such a residence did Mary Carter finally recover from the hard journey, with the aid of the post surgeon, and there, less than three months later (on the morning of June 21, 1871), she would give birth to a daughter at the very moment the 4th Cavalry band was thundering music for the day's parade a short distance away. Following a man to this frontier demanded the genuine devotion that already had awed such an imperturbable observer as Colonel Mackenzie.

For the soldier-husband life was made somewhat easier, if not less dangerous, by work that kept his mind occupied much of the time—and for Lieutenant Carter this meant scouting assignments. The numbers of Indian raids that spring of 1871 already were running well ahead of previous years, and sometimes warriors attacked within sight of Fort Richardson. In January raiders had killed four Negroes hauling supplies to their frontier homes. On April 19 Indians had scalped a white man on Salt Creek. The very next day they had attacked several persons within sight of the fort. The day after that they had struck again, at a location three miles from the post, and had stolen horses. By late spring fourteen settlers had been reported killed.

Other chores besides scouting assignments demanded some of Lieutenant Carter's time, too. As a junior officer newly arrived at the post—and a willing one, ready to follow orders without mulling them over much—he was given a variety of jobs deemed much too inconsequential for seniors, and he drew also the usual assignments: officer of the day, drill, boards of survey, and courts-martial.

Toward the middle of May another unsolicited job came his way. He received orders to select fifteen men from the 4th Cavalry to form an escort for General Sherman, who had left San Antonio May 2 and was expected at Fort Richardson soon on his inspection tour. Sherman's small party would be riding in after visiting forts located farther west along the old Butterfield Trail. Carter and his men were to travel westward in the direction of Indian-infested Salt Creek Prairie, to meet the General at a site called Rock Station, and to accompany him into Richardson.

Another job went with that one. Carter received orders also to select a squad to fire a smart artillery salute to the General upon his arrival at the fort—ceremonial honors common enough around headquarters of the nation's senior army officer (and at this time potential next President), but not often rendered or even practiced in Carter's part of the world. After Carter and his men had met Sherman at Rock Station they would join the General's party for the trip to Fort Richardson. Carter's approach would alert the fort to prepare its salute.

During his planning Carter decided to use for the ceremony the garrison's two three-inch guns. Required for manning them, then, would be two detachments.

Carter asked around and learned with dismay that apparently no cavalryman ever had fired one of those pieces. Then he went from company to company looking for veterans of artillery service, but first sergeants reported no such men on muster rolls.

At F Company Carter's dejection suddenly vanished. He heard the first sergeant declare, "Sergeant Foster and Corporal Charlton have both served one enlistment in Light Battery K of the 1st Artillery, sir."

Carter sought out Foster. "Have you ever served in the artillery?"

"Yes, sir! Five years in the 1st."

"Can you drill a gun detachment?"

The Sergeant stood even straighter and replied, "Yes, sir-r-rr!" adding an extra roll to the "r." "I think I *ought to know how!*"

Foster and Charlton then began drilling two gun squads until their smartness became satisfactory, and on a warm May 18 morning Carter left with his fifteen men to meet General Sherman at Rock Station, westward along the Butterfield Trail. "I had the four big black mules from the post water wagon, and my instructions were to tender these fresh mules for use on General Sherman's ambulance; also to offer the use of Mackenzie's quarters to him."

That same May 18 a powerful raiding party composed of a hundred or more Comanche, Plains Apache, and Kiowa warriors, accompanied by numerous chiefs, lay in hiding on the far side of a brushy knoll that overlooked a three-mile stretch of the Butterfield Trail twenty miles to the west of Fort Richardson, where the old highway crossed Salt Creek Prairie—that site favored by attackers.

119

The Indians were waiting to ambush any unsuspecting white men traveling along the road.

One of the chiefs with the raiders was White Bear, the great Kiowan orator who had been accused by some of his people of "acting the woman" while Sheridan's prisoner. In an attempt to regain esteem he had led several raids into Texas. Now he was carrying his bugle to direct another attack.

But White Bear was only one of several leaders present. Others included Sitting Bear, Big Tree, Eagle Heart, Big Bow, Fast Bear, Red Warbonnet, Sky Walker, and still more. The main leader of this raid actually was Sky Walker (Mamanti), a Kiowa medicine man who had won strong following among his people lately as a great seer. For the moment, however, the most important members of the party were the few warriors crouching atop the hill and watching the road from positions behind clumps of brush.

The idea for this raid had come out of a council held earlier in May forty miles north of the Red River, at a camp on rolling prairies of what is now western Oklahoma. There White Bear and other chiefs, including Sky Walker, had talked angrily of happenings since the Medicine Lodge meeting: further dwindling of buffalo and their virtual disappearance from reservations; rumored construction of tracks for another "iron horse" (the Missouri–Kansas–Texas Railroad) that would cut through their lands and probably drive off more buffalo; increased animosity of Texans, who apparently wanted to sweep all Indians off this part of the earth.

White Bear and the other chiefs reciprocated the Texans' hatred. They considered those people, more than any other whites, to have been responsible for constant encroachment on the best lands. For that reason Indians already had increased their raids. Inspired by White Bear and a few other leaders, they ignored the relentless future, refusing to admit that fate already had sealed their doom, that more and more white men would swarm over their land—white men, and not their beloved buffalo.

Now these Indians would strike into Texas again. The medicine man Sky Walker, majestic in appearance and action, proposed this particular raid and prophesied success. Because of his involvement, influence, and authority—all recently strengthened by tribal events that seemed to attest to his magical powers—he also assumed leadership of the raid, but one can imagine the egocentric White Bear as having been unable to mask his jealousy and resentment, and perhaps acting out the part of highest chief. White Bear often served himself much better than he did his fellow tribesmen.

The raiding party crossed the Red River into Texas, watching for army patrols that looked for reservation Indians sneaking away southward. The raiders cut through the center of present Wilbarger County, Texas, where for greater mobility they left behind some horses, equipment, and supplies, all in the care of a small guard. Then they went on eighty miles or more southeastward, exercising even greater caution as they neared the Texas settlements. On May 17, one day before Lieutenant Carter and his fifteen men rode out of Fort Richardson to meet Sherman, the war party edged into present Young County and on toward Salt Creek Prairie, that area already specked with stones that marked the graves of earlier victims. On the following morning they went into position on the far side of the brushy hill overlooking Salt Creek Prairie. This location was a few miles south of the present town of Loving and not far west of Rock Station, where Carter would meet General Sherman.

White Bear, still leaderlike, would have made a point of surveying the landscape again, although he had seen it many times before. Peering from behind scrub vegetation atop the knoll, he could see off to his left, almost due east of his vantage point, Cox Mountain— as it was called, but actually just another hill in comparison to respectable mountains. The road from Fort Richardson, old Butterfield Trail, came into view after rounding the north side of Cox Mountain: a ribbon of earth curling through thin foliage of light green. The trail continued on southwestward for three miles before crossing the north branch of a usually dry creek named Flint at a position some distance in front of, and below, White Bear's hill. From there the road ran on westward, out of sight of White Bear's gaze, toward distant, ramshackle Fort Belknap.

The land between the hill on which White Bear stood and Cox Mountain over to his left especially interested him. There, where the road crossed grave-specked Salt Creek Prairie (so-named, although Salt Creek itself lay eight miles farther west), travelers could be seen and ambushed most easily. They would have no refuge immediately available in that area. Only a sprinkling of mesquite trees provided so much shelter as scattered shade, and little of that. Eastward, around Cox Mountain, scrub-oak thickets bounded a more heavily forested area beyond; and at the bottom of the hill where White Bear stood, the now dry extension of Flint Creek (which the road crossed there) nurtured a line of trees along each bank. But let travelers get a mile or so onto the plain from either wooded area and they would be easy victims for a powerful war party attacking from the very hill where White Bear and the other Indians waited, hour after hour, that sunny morning of May 18.

About midday warriors still watching from behind shrubbery atop the hill saw a group of blue-uniformed horsemen emerge from trees lining the creek. They were traveling eastward. Behind them lumbered a mule-drawn vehicle of some sort—not an ordinary wagon, not a stagecoach.

The Indians this time turned to Sky Walker, not to White Bear, for guidance. Many warriors wanted to attack, but the medicine man refused to approve, apparently because he prophesied the arrival of a larger wagon train that would afford much more plunder—perhaps including weapons and ammunition. Sky Walker's prestige restrained the Indians while the small detachment of mounted soldiers and the mule-drawn vehicle crossed Salt Creek Prairie under an afternoon sky that was now becoming covered with puffy clouds scudding in from the south. A hundred pairs of dark eyes stared as the miniature caravan rounded Cox Mountain and disappeared.

Sky Walker, for all his magical powers, never realized that his people might have captured and held for ransom the general-in-chief who commanded all of the Great Father's soldiers everywhere —William Tecumseh Sherman.

East of Salt Creek Prairie, at the site known as Rock Station, Lieutenant Carter, his men, water wagon, and mules awaited Sherman's arrival. The troopers had dismounted and were temporarily at ease—or at least as much so as was possible for extreme juniors about to greet the ranking general of the United States Army.

Carter heard Sherman's cavalry escort clattering along the road "at a spanking pace" before he saw the horsemen come into view.

White Bear

Sitting Bear

Quanah

Cynthia Ann Parker

Old Camp Grant, Arizona, in 1871. Lieutenant John Bourke reported for duty there the year before — in March 1870 — on a chilly, windy day.

Hostile Sioux encamped in South Dakota. Horses and stolen baggage wagons are seen ready to move quickly in the event of U. S. Army approach.

Pack train in Arizona. The Army usually relied on this cumbersome method for transporting supplies, while most Indians rode unburdened.

Emigrant train attacked by hostile Indians on the prairie. The wagons probably would have circled, as would have the attackers.

Buffalo herd on the move. The animals afforded Plains Indians plentiful food and clothing before white hunters slaughtered herds to get the hides.

Plains railroad depot scene. The "iron horse" meant doom for Indians by bringing more white settlers, splitting the Great Plains, and affording easy transportation to eastern markets for buffalo hides.

An army ambulance followed. Immediately Carter ordered his men to mount, to be ready to render the usual military honors.

After salutes Carter was shown to the ambulance and introduced to Sherman, who greeted the Lieutenant warmly and presented four companions riding with him—one general and three colonels. Carter proffered the mules and Colonel Mackenzie's quarters at Fort Richardson as instructed, but he heard polite refusal: "That is kind in Mackenzie to tender the use of his quarters," Sherman replied, "but I have got plenty of canvas and we will pitch our tents right behind and close to him."

The General continued. "Your horses look warm. It would be too hard on them to try and keep up with us. If you will put us on the right road, you had better come in at your leisure."

Sherman was a most thoughtful man, Carter reflected, but what about advance warning to the fort for the gun salute? This disturbed him. Then he heard the General conclude, with finality that comes from rank. "I will thank Mackenzie personally for his kindness in sending you and such a fine-looking detachment out to insure my safety."

Sherman's escort and ambulance moved on toward Fort Richardson, for further inspection along the Butterfield Trail. Carter heard later they arrived about sunset, unheralded and unsaluted by the newly trained three-inch gun squads—a neglect the General seemed not to mind or even notice. Carter followed him in at a respectful distance and arrived at a cloud-darkened dusk, "crestfallen."

On a hill overlooking Salt Creek Prairie, Sky Walker's patience and prophecy had been rewarded, finally, in the face of growing unrest among young warriors who had begun to regret their failure to attack the soldiers. While Sherman and his troopers were nearing unsuspecting Fort Richardson to the eastward, the waiting Indians glimpsed a canvas-covered wagon emerge into view along the road leading west from Cox Mountain. A second wagon appeared, then another. Eventually the silent watchers saw a total of ten wagons lumbering along on Salt Creek Prairie toward the creek crossing, still far ahead of the caravan. When the train had reached the utter openness of midprairie Sky Walker signaled White Bear to sound

123

"Charge!" on his bugle. The old chief, thus reduced to following another leader, raised the instrument to his lips, but even before he could blow the first note many Indians, long before mounted and ready, raced downhill toward the prairie and the slowly moving wagon train in a wild contest for first coup. Then the great leader White Bear rode off behind them, carrying the bugle apparently for blasting forth more unheeded orders.

When the raiders saw teamsters begin to circle their wagons for defense they loosed a din of shouts, shrieks, and shots—while, overhead, clouds now dark and lowering curtained the sunlight.

12

PRIDE BEFORE DESTRUCTION

That evening at Fort Richardson enlisted men working against a threat of rain hurriedly erected General Sherman's canvas tents. The General enjoyed a late supper, then received garrison officers who called to pay respects.

A delegation of citizens also appeared, eager to present their argument about lack of protection to a general they knew already to be dubious in regard to their claim. The day before, in Austin, the *Daily Journal* had carried a report from Jacksboro:

> In anticipation of the arrival of General Sherman at Fort Richardson, the citizens of Jack County held a meeting at Jacksboro to obtain the material for an authentic statement of Indian murders and [other] outrages. The data obtained show that since 1859, in Jack County alone, about one hundred murders have been committed . . . besides the wounded and captives. Hundreds of other settlers have vacated their homes through fear. This destruction in a county never numbering over six hundred souls speaks for itself of the direful need of protection.

The correspondent then listed raids, houses burned, and names of victims—occasionally encompassing entire families. Among the slain were "George Hampton, a crazy man, tied to a tree and stoned to death" eighteen miles east of Fort Richardson.

Now Jack County citizens would have an opportunity to per-

125

suade General Sherman, through a delegation of six men ushered into his presence on the evening of May 18. After introductions the Texans commenced their testimony, reciting details of suffering endured by themselves and others, and accusing Fort Sill agency officials of giving Indians weapons and of allowing them to bring onto the reservation numbers of cattle and horses stolen in Texas. They showed the General a collection of scalps, a number of them from women, that had been taken from Kiowas and Comanches living on the reservation. They pleaded with Sherman to punish these people and to help recover stolen stock.

Sherman listened politely but still doubtfully. The stories seemed exaggerated, but he promised to investigate further at Fort Sill, which he planned to visit after leaving Fort Richardson.

The delegation of citizens left in great dejection, and Sherman went to bed. A patter of raindrops on the canvas roof made sleep more sweet and snug for the occupant.

The General did not know until later that about midnight a wounded man limped into the fort and to its hospital, asked for medical attention, and reported another tragedy on Salt Creek Prairie. A ten-wagon train owned by a man named Henry Warren had been carrying corn under government contract to Fort Griffin when Indians attacked. Of the twelve teamsters with the train, five (including the man who had hobbled into Fort Richardson) had escaped—by dashing for the nearest thickets around Cox Mountain while attackers tore into wagons hoping to find weapons and ammunition instead of the vast store of corn they eventually uncovered.

This calamity brought still another unsolicited chore to Lieutenant Carter. Before the hour of sunrise on a rain-swept May 19 an orderly awakened him and told him Colonel Mackenzie desired his presence. The Lieutenant, as post adjutant, was directed "to take down from dictation some letters and dispatches . . . General Sherman wished to rush off without delay."

Sherman, upon rising, had heard of the wounded teamster's arrival during the night and had rushed to the hospital without waiting for breakfast to hear the man's story. Thus far on Sherman's inspection trip the frontier had appeared so peaceful to him that he could not believe all those horror tales he had been hearing.

Might this be another exaggeration by a man who hoped to corroborate the claims of the Jack County delegation? Might it actually be only coincidence that the teamster had told his story within a few hours of the visit to Sherman of the other six Texans who sought to influence frontier military policy?

Carter and an accompanying sergeant found the General impatient to have more information. Carter's own emotion bordered on trepidation. Never before had he been called upon to record dictation. Now he was a beginner at the very top, striving to record the words of the senior general himself, one who spoke with the rapidity of a six-shooter—but without having to stop and reload.

> All sorts of dashes, signs, abbreviations were made, which the sergeant . . . and [I] in trying to transcribe later could hardly decipher. . . . The substance was as follows: [Colonel Mackenzie] was directed to send out a strong force at once to the scene of the massacre and ascertain the truth or falsity of the man's story. If it proved true, [Mackenzie] was to send couriers through to Fort Griffin, and with the two companies there to cut the trail, and to prepare to move out with his entire command upon it, and to meet [General Sherman] later at Fort Sill. . . . Letters were also rushed out to Dept. Headquarters, and to Fort Sill, all by runners, couriers, or mounted messengers, as we had no other means of communication.

That work as general's secretary ended, but what Carter had done led now to still another job for him. His Company E was one of four troops ordered out by Mackenzie for the Colonel's march to the site of alleged massacre.

Rain that had reached storm proportion soaked them and their animals; it had flooded the post parade ground. Still it poured down. Horses sloshed through half a foot of water.

When Carter came upon the Salt Creek Prairie scene he felt sick. "The . . . victims were stripped, scalped, and . . . mutilated; several were beheaded and their brains scooped out."

He could only gape at the sight. "Fingers, toes, and private parts had been cut off and stuck in . . . mouths, and . . . bodies, now lying in several inches of water and . . . bloated beyond all chance of recognition, were filled full of arrows which made them resemble porcupines." Carter saw that one man had been chained to a wagon wheel and roasted alive—a horror indicated by his contracted, contorted arms and legs. Littering the flooded area were five dead mules, scores of slashed grain sacks, piles of soaked corn, waterlogged debris from wagons, torn harnesses, and sloshy pieces of cloth.

Troopers buried the seven bodies in mud near the road and marked the burial site with two small stones. Colonel Mackenzie rushed dispatches to two forts, Richardson and Griffin, then sought to follow the Indians' trail—an impossibility, everyone soon saw, because of the deluge. Few would have doubted, however, that the track led to Fort Sill.

White Bear had lost none of his egotism lately. Sky Walker might have envisioned and led the raid on Henry Warren's wagon train, but the great-mouthed chief still claimed pre-eminence, as always.

Much earlier White Bear had convinced his white enemies of his ultimate leadership. Every time a bugle blew directing Indians to an attack somewhere some surviving victim would declare later that White Bear had been there, even though the notorious chief might truthfully have been hundreds of miles away and in ignorance of the raid. Bugle notes sounded by an Indian during a skirmish had become his trademark, through original usage. Now White Bear had plenty of tribal competition in that area, too.

The bugler-orator-fighter was no reader of the Bible, of course, but he was on the verge of proving the truthfulness of Proverbs 16:18, "Pride *goeth* before destruction, and an haughty spirit before a fall." After the latest sweep onto Salt Creek Prairie had ended in fresh victory he and other raiders had collected animals uninjured in the fight (including forty-one mules belonging to the wagon train), had put their own wounded companions on horses, and had commenced a withdrawal, in blinding rain, toward the place where they had left those other animals and supplies in care of a small guard. Then they had crossed the Red River and returned to their reservation near Fort Sill.

Unknown to White Bear and his companions, some changes had occurred at their agency. The Quaker agent there, Lawrie Tatum, called Bald Head by his Indians, had begun to doubt the wisdom of remaining pacificatory while, as he now felt certain, his charges sneaked away southward into Texas from time to time to loot and kill. When General Sherman arrived at Fort Sill on May 23 from Fort Richardson he reported the newest atrocity to Tatum, at the agency nearby. Tatum promised to ask White Bear and other Kiowas where they had been on the day of the wagon-train attack. He said he would do this the next time the Kiowas came in to draw rations.

Four days after Sherman had reached Fort Sill, White Bear and the Kiowas appeared at the agency for their supplies—about four o'clock on a Saturday afternoon, May 27. White Bear, like all the others, wanted to get his allotment of coffee, sugar, flour, and bacon at once. He knew that Tatum and his assistants would not work on Sunday—they would only preach to Indians that day—and White Bear had no desire to wait around until Monday. But when he appeared at the commissary he heard the clerk say that Tatum wanted to talk with him.

To White Bear this would not have been objectionable at all. He certainly had no fear of Bald Head or of anything he might have to say on any subject. White Bear's attitude toward the agent was one of scorn. The chief believed that Tatum's patience and placidity indicated cowardice. A talk with the man—an argument, it almost certainly would be—would even be good. It would give White Bear a chance to smother an opponent with oratory again.

The chief's dark, squinty eyes would have been flashing a challenge as he entered the agent's office along with (as it had developed) other chiefs: Sitting Bear, Big Tree, Kicking Bird, and Lone Wolf. White Bear quietly accepted Bald Head's hand and shook it, as did the other Indians. Then he and the rest waited to hear what the agent had to say.

Tatum told the story he had heard from Sherman about the attack on Henry Warren's wagon train, and he asked if any of the chiefs knew who might have been responsible.

No one replied immediately. For a few seconds even the talkative White Bear stayed silent. Then, with an air of great importance, he pointed a finger at himself and declared, "Yes, I led in that raid."

129

I have repeatedly asked for arms and ammunition, which have not been furnished. I have made many other requests which have not been granted. You do not listen to my talk. The white people are preparing to build a railroad through our country, which will not be permitted. Some years ago they took us by the hair and pulled us here close to Texas where we have to fight them. More recently I was arrested by the soldiers and kept in confinement several days. . . . There [will] never . . . be any more Kiowa Indians arrested. I want you to remember that. On account of these grievances, a short time ago I took about one hundred of my warriors . . . whom I wished to teach how to fight [to Texas]. I also took the chiefs [Sitting Bear], Eagle Heart, Big Bow, Big Tree, and Fast Bear.

Sitting Bear, a withered old chief with an Oriental look that extended even to a dropping mustache, angrily interrupted the freely speaking White Bear and told him in Kiowan not to mention any more names. But White Bear would not be completely silenced. He noticed that his talk so far had magnetized Tatum—and White Bear loved to enthrall a listener. He believed he could talk his way to supremacy and victory in any council, and he continued:

We found a mule train, which we captured, and killed seven of the men. Three of our men got killed, but we are willing to call it even. It is all over now, and it is not necessary to say much more about it. We don't expect to do any raiding around here this summer; but we expect to raid in Texas. If any other Indian claims the honor of leading that party he will be lying to you. I led it myself.

When White Bear had finished talking the other chiefs nodded agreement—White Bear had indeed led that raiding party; they had not. Nor was Sky Walker's name mentioned. White Bear surely would not have included it.

The great Kiowan orator probably believed now that Bald Head Tatum was quaking behind his desk, appropriate to the religion he professed, and White Bear went on to demand arms and ammunition. Tatum replied that he had no authority to issue such items, but that White Bear might discuss the subject with an important soldier chief who happened to be visiting Fort Sill at this very moment.

White Bear could not have suspected that Tatum would send a note within minutes to Fort Sill meant for the eyes of the post commander and for General Sherman. In it he paraphrased the story White Bear had just told, and he asked the Army to arrest the chiefs involved.

13

SENTENCE OF DEATH

Lieutenant Carter rode into Fort Sill with Colonel Mackenzie's mud-splashed command on June 4. The 4th Cavalry had not overtaken the raiding party; the recent deluge had swept away the Indians' trail. Marches had been wet, monotonous, and exhausting.

But now, riding into Fort Sill, Carter was favorably impressed by what he saw. The post had been built on a plateau, near the junction of deliciously clear Cache and Medicine Bluff creeks, from where the land sloped gently in every direction. To the west and northwest, twenty or thirty miles distant, rose the Wichita Mountains, imparting "savage grandeur and beauty to the entire country about."

Fort Sill had been located in an area watered by many streams whose origins lay in those mountains. The flow nurtured grass and trees—oak, hackberry, mesquite; numerous animals—buffalo, elk, bear, antelope, deer, panthers, wolves, rabbits, raccoons; a variety of game birds—quail, highland plover; and, of course, fish—mostly trout and bass.

No giant walls enclosed the fort. Like Camp Grant and many other posts, Sill consisted of a group of buildings—stone and frame—erected around the usual parade ground. Some distance away lay a corral and a clutter of tents, jacales, and dugouts where resided laundry women, their ragged children, and scores of hungry pets. Compared to Carter's former station at Concho and his current one at Richardson, Fort Sill presented a scrubbed, manicured appear-

132

ance, with the exception of the laundresses' quarters. But Fort Sill lacked Mary Carter, and the Lieutenant would have been anxious about returning to Richardson.

After Carter arrived at Fort Sill and talked with some of the officers, however, his thoughts might have been diverted from his wife for a while by details of some recent excitement. He learned that Sherman had arrested the very culprits Mackenzie had been trying to track down, and that chiefs White Bear, Sitting Bear, and Big Tree were being held for transfer to Jacksboro and trial in a civilian court for the murders of the teamsters. As far as Carter knew, this would be the first formal trial for Indians under the whites' judicial system.

Carter listened to all the details. White Bear and other chiefs had been summoned by Sherman to a council on the porch of the Fort Sill commanding officer's quarters. Armed cavalrymen of the 10th Regiment, a Negro unit, had been hidden around the porch, for just such a possibility as ensued.

Sherman asked for information about the raid. White Bear, still certain of his speaking prowess and apparently unwilling yet to let go of tribal reins, again boasted of his own leadership. Then he elaborated, in contradiction of his oration at Medicine Lodge:

> This is our country. We have always lived in it. We always had plenty to eat because the land was full of buffalo. We were happy. We got along with each other. When we felt the need of horses we raided the Utes, or the Navahos. When they needed horses they raided us. . . . It was fair.
>
> We did not farm the land. That is woman's work. . . . Men need to hunt.
>
> Then you came. First the traders. That is all right, for we were in need of blankets and kettles. . . . Then . . . farmers [came]. . . . That is not all right. . . . This is good land, but it is our land. . . . You kill the land by taking things out of it. . . . When you work the land the buffalo will leave and never return. Then we have nothing to eat. . . . We have to protect ourselves. . . . We have to fight for what is ours. . . . We have to kill those men who drive away our buffalo. . . . We kill them to save what is ours so that we

might live. Now you ask who killed those men. Now I tell you. I did.

Sherman listened, then told White Bear he would be arrested and sent to Texas for trial. The Kiowa chief grabbed for his revolver. At that instant Sherman shouted a command, and Negro cavalrymen appeared instantly with weapons aimed at White Bear and the other chiefs.

"Don't shoot," White Bear reportedly yelled. Afterward he sought to backtrack, denying that he really had led the recent raid in Texas. He claimed instead that he had watched other warriors pounce upon the wagon train. But no white man believed his denial now.

So when Carter arrived at Fort Sill he heard that White Bear, Sitting Bear, and Big Tree were being held in double irons in the post guardhouse. Sherman had left for Fort Gibson.

Four days after Carter's arrival the 4th Cavalry, following orders left for Mackenzie by Sherman, commenced a march to Jacksboro and Fort Richardson with the three chiefs in custody. Carter would return, too.

Sitting Bear, the withered old chief with an Oriental look, rode in the first of two rumbling, creaking army wagons that rolled along between two dusty columns of mounted men wearing blue blouses. On each side of him sat a soldier guard. Sitting Bear had not climbed voluntarily into the wagon, which had been filled with shelled corn to feed the animals along the way. Four men had taken him by hands and feet and had tossed him in.

White Bear and Big Tree, with trooper escorts, rode in the second wagon. All three chiefs had been handcuffed and leg-chained for the journey.

Sitting Bear had thrown a blanket about his body, despite early-morning heat generated by summerlike sunshine. As cavalrymen and wagons lumbered down the road to Texas, Sitting Bear began complaining of his treatment. Then he commenced singing a shrill, sad chant that amused some soldiers of the guard nearby. His wail was an echo from that dark, nebulous cave where lie unrecorded, and presently beyond reach of human knowledge, thousands of years of history. Possibly it was an echo from prehistoric Asia, where (many authorities say) the old man's ancestors lived before they used steppingstones around the Bering Strait for their passage into North America.

To some curious soldiers the Indian's voice might have seemed to quiver as he worked his lips. The shakiness would have been caused by high pitch or old age, however, and not by fear; for the man had been recognized long ago as a great fighting chief of the Kiowas, ranking with or ahead of White Bear himself.

As Sitting Bear continued his song some of the soldiers tried to mimic him, but this was not true of the Indians (on U. S. Army payroll) who also comprised part of the escort. They remained silent while the chief shrilled his personal lament.

Kaitsenko ana obahema haa ipai degi o ba ika;
Kaitsenko ana oba hemo hadamagagi o ba ika.

The white soldiers probably neither understood nor cared that "Kaitsenko" referred to an elite Kiowa society composed of the ten or so bravest warriors—including, of course, Sitting Bear. Nor would the soldiers have understood the old man's announcement, spoken in Comanche for every Indian present to hear and to comprehend. "Take this message to my people," he said. "Tell them I died beside the road. My bones will be found there."

Minutes later he added, "See that tree? When I reach that tree I will be dead."

Then Sitting Bear lapsed into silence while his wagon creaked and rumbled on toward the tree through the day's heat and dust, which had returned after the recent rains. No longer did he sing his death song, which had said (translated into English):

Oh, sun, you remain forever, but we Kaitsenko must die;
Oh, earth, you remain forever, but we Kaitsenko must die.

The Fort Sill interpreter, Horace Jones, had heard Sitting Bear's song and had realized its meaning. He called out a warning to the corporal of the guard before the soldiers and their three prisoners had passed out of earshot: "You had better watch that old Indian. He means trouble."

But the soldiers continued smirking. Those irons would keep all three chiefs peaceful.

Unknown to his guards, Sitting Bear had used his blanket as a shield for some incredible activity. He had torn loose from the handcuffs, shredding and cutting his flesh in the process. He seized a scalping knife secreted earlier in his breechclout (said an Indian— or in one of his leggings, said Lieutenant Carter) and attacked a guard sitting beside him. The man tumbled from the wagon, leaving his carbine to Sitting Bear. But then a quick shot from another soldier hit the chief. White Bear and Big Tree, riding in the last wagon, immediately raised their hands to show nonresistance. In the lead wagon, Sitting Bear fell wounded, then raised himself and threatened other guards with the carbine. More shooting flattened him again.

Colonel Mackenzie rode up and asked what had caused the firing. He saw Sitting Bear dying in the wagon and ordered him removed. The chief was left beside the road, just as he had foreseen, while the march continued. Not only was guarding the prisoners themselves a concern; Mackenzie worried also that Kiowas might try to free the chiefs, and he wanted no delay in transporting them to Texas.

Examination showed that Sitting Bear had been hit in the head, lungs, and right wrist, but he lived, hopelessly, for a few minutes more, squatting in roadside dust while blood spurted from his mouth. No Kiowa dared to claim his body from the Army; most of the tribe had, in fact, fled the reservation when the chiefs were arrested. Sitting Bear's bony remains were buried in the post cemetery.

On June 15 the 4th Cavalry and the army-paid Indian scouts arrived at Fort Richardson with their prisoners, who had been given ponies to ride during the latter part of the journey. Members of the garrison and the post band turned out to welcome their long-absent comrades.

Carter peered at the crowd that had gathered in fine, sunny weather to stare at the notorious chiefs. Many of those persons had lost relatives or friends to Indian attacks and were in a mood for revenge.

Next, Carter turned his attention to White Bear, the focus of most interest, and described the Indian as he saw him that day.

He was over six feet in his moccasins, and, mounted upon a small pony, he seemed to be even taller than he really was. He was stark naked, except for a breechclout and pair of bead-embroidered moccasins. Owing to the intense heat he had allowed his blanket to slip to his saddle and about his loins. His coarse, jet black hair, now thickly powdered with dust, hung tangled about his neck except [for] a single braided scalp lock with but one long eagle feather to adorn it. His immense shoulders, broad back, deep chest, powerful hips and thighs, contrasted singularly with the slight forms of the [Tonkawas] grouped about him. The muscles stood out on his gigantic frame like knots of whip cord, and his form proud and erect in the saddle, his perfectly immobile face and motionless body, gave him the appearance of polished mahogany. . . . Nothing but his intensely black, glittering eyes and a slight motion of the eye lids betokened any life in that figure. [But] . . . his proud face bespoke the disdain with which he regarded the curiosity of the crowd—the despised white race—now gathered about [him].

Carter saw that Big Tree, mounted on a pony nearby, lacked White Bear's impressiveness in many ways, although he, too, was naked except for breechclout and a single feather to ornament his scalp lock. Big Tree, lighter in color and smaller in size, showed interest in the activity around him. When the band broke into brassy music he turned his head and watched the musicians, while White Bear never moved so much as a muscle. Both chiefs were handcuffed and tied to their ponies; their feet were lashed together under the animals' bellies with rawhide lariats.

After completion of the welcoming ceremony the Fort Richardson officer of the day took custody of both Indians and put them in a post guardhouse watched over by many armed sentinels stationed there to prevent two more murders. Later the chiefs would be moved to the Jack County Courthouse—a log building standing in the center of the town square.

At Richardson, Carter rejoined his wife, now only days away from giving birth to their first child, but soon he was forced to devote his time to those many tasks given him because of his low rank and his unquestioning devotion to duty. Among the most interesting assignments were his tasks as post adjutant of looking after the safety of White Bear and Big Tree and of arranging certain trial preliminaries. Six days after his return from Fort Sill, however, that long-expected event competed for attention: the arrival of a baby (daughter), with Mary Carter still quartered in that pest-ridden one-room shack. When the trial of White Bear and Big Tree opened on July 5, 1871, Lieutenant Carter was surviving the second week of fatherhood along with all those other vicissitudes.

Proud, haughty White Bear was imprisoned with Big Tree in the small guardhouse at Fort Richardson for three weeks. Although he left no written account of his experience, of course, that time would have seemed interminable to the free-ranging Kiowa chief and to his companion.

White Bear would have been much aware during that period of the possibility that some frontiersmen might decide against waiting for a formal jury verdict to eliminate him and his cellmate from the earth. This would have caused him worry. As the past had shown, White Bear was not absolutely fearless and resolute when scales of strength tipped against him. But he always seemed to think that his powerful and persuasive oratory could eventually extricate him from all threatening situations—not realizing that recent stance changes had created doubters not only among white men but among his own people, too. Nevertheless, he thought he knew what white men and women wanted to hear, and soon he would let them hear it.

Lieutenant Carter also realized the threat of mob justice and was responsible for taking care to prevent it. Carter never slighted any army duty, even though he could work up scant sympathy for murderers like White Bear and Big Tree. He had seen ghastly results of their so-called leadership.

The guardhouse location worried Carter. It had been built adjacent to Lost Creek; and on the opposite side of that inconsistent stream lay a dense thicket where one or two vengeful frontiersmen could hide until guards brought the two chiefs from their cell. Then a few carefully aimed shots would obviate the necessity of wasting time and money on a trial.

Lieutenant Carter conferred with the Jack County sheriff and with District Attorney S. W. T. Lanham, later congressman and Texas governor. Both officials were sufficiently sensitive of potential eastern reaction to insist that the Indians be shielded from violence and to seek a trial that would show supposed impartiality—an actual impossibility, however, in that venue. As a result of the Lieutenant's suggestions, a screen of twenty or more men protected the prisoners when they left the guardhouse, in irons, for Jack County's wood courthouse and their trial.

Having transported his charges safely, Carter became mostly an observer, and his writing at this point indicated some loss of enthusiasm for what he saw and heard about.

All men within riding distance seemed to have converged on the ragged village of Jacksboro. Most of them had lost wives, children, friends, or stock to plundering Indians. Armed and angry, they were "intent upon seeing *justice* done." Carter, as a Civil War veteran and an aspiring Indian fighter, had experienced plenty of unpleasantness during his still-young life, but his eastern sensibilities seemed to have been repelled by the sight and smell of an aroused frontier: "every man armed to the teeth" and chewing wads of tobacco, spitting, whittling, waiting with little patience. When the courtroom door opened to admit spectators they all sought to push in, but most of them could not squeeze into the small space. The overflow surrounded the courthouse and stared through windows left open against the day's heat. Lieutenant Carter, inside, enjoyed a better view.

White Bear and Big Tree already had been led into the courtroom. Clanking chains had announced their arrival. Blanketed, they sat now near the front of the twenty-by-thirty-foot chamber and again monopolized attention.

> Two long, dingy, wooden benches, well whittled and worn, held the jurors, who, in their shirt sleeves and with [pistols] in their belts, nervously hitched about in their seats, and uneasily regarded the extreme novelty of their situation. Inside the prisoners' railing sat the stolid chiefs, closely wrapped in

139

their blankets. The charge was . . . read . . . [and] "not guilty" [pleaded] for the prisoners.

Then the lawyers took the stage. Spectators heard District Attorney Lanham's castigation of eastern "Indian lovers" and his denunciation of the two chiefs.

"[White Bear], the veteran consul chief of the Kiowas—the orator, diplomat, the counselor of his tribe—the pulse of his race. Big Tree, the young war chief, who leads in the thickest of the fight, and follows no one in the chase—the mighty warrior athlete, with the speed of the deer and the eye of the eagle, are before this bar, in the charge of the law!" So they would be described by Indian admirers, who live in more secure and favored lands, remote from the frontier—where "distance lends enchantment" to the imagination—where the story of Pocahontas and the speech of Logan, the Mingo, are read, and the dread sound of the war whoop is not heard. We who see them today, disrobed of all their fancied graces, exposed in the light of reality, behold them through far different lenses! We recognize in [White Bear] the arch fiend of treachery and blood—the cunning Catiline—the promoter of strife—the breaker of treaties signed by his own hand—the inciter of his fellow to rapine and murder—the artful dealer in bravado while in the powwow, and the most abject coward in the field, as well as the most canting and double-tongued hypocrite when detected and overcome! In Big Tree we perceive the tiger-demon, who has tasted blood and loves it as his food.

The district attorney's eloquence impressed Carter and it magnetized the jurors. When Lanham described the recent scene on Salt Creek Prairie in trial lawyer's language—re-creating the death of the teamster who had been roasted alive—the Lieutenant noted that "every brow on that jury grew black, every juryman settled himself in his seat, gave an extra hitch to the gun on his belt, and . . . [showed] the verdict plainly written on [his face]."

Real doubt about a verdict, however, never infiltrated the courtroom. If two defendants ever needed a change of venue White Bear and Big Tree did; but perhaps those frontier officials could have been called generous for allowing the defense counsel, a man named Thomas Ball, even to speak as he did. Ball referred to the Indian as "my brother" and depicted his suffering as he had been "cheated and cheated and despoiled of his lands, driven westward, westward until it seemed as though there was no limit to the greed of his white brothers."

Ball's eloquence also attracted Carter.

Warming up to his task, [Ball] now threw off his coat, as it was an intensely hot day, and . . . [talked about the human instinct of retaliation against aggressors]. But when he spoke of the majestic bird, the eagle, that emblem of our national freedom, and urged that the great chiefs be allowed to "fly away as free and unhampered," we turned quickly to watch the jury. Every cowboy juror had been industriously whittling the bench with his hunting knife and squirting tobacco juice at a crack. . . . [When] the words of the counsel [had] been interpreted to the chiefs, their frequent grunts of approval and delight at what they supposed meant immediate release . . . sounded loudly over the courtroom, [and] we noted an immediate change. [The jurors] all hitched [to the front] the "shootin' irons" . . . strapped to their hips . . . rolled their shirt sleeves a little higher, immediately ceased [carving on] . . . the jury bench, and now closely watched for further developments and more oratory.

Carter recorded developments himself—for three days altogether, while, outside the courtroom, the overflow crowd stared through those open windows. After the trial had ended the Lieutenant would remark that it "was one of the most impressive and picturesque—yet most ludicrous—acts of legal jurisdiction ever witnessed."

White Bear, listening from his position inside the prisoners' railing, could have understood little of what was happening. Anglo-Americans who knew him always claimed that the crafty old Kiowan understood much more English than he ever acknowledged, but this situation was unique. White Bear could only have been confused by legal proceedings, even though the Fort Sill interpreter,

141

Horace Jones (the same man who had warned the corporal of the guard about Sitting Bear's death chant), had been sent from Fort Sill to assist him and Big Tree.

White Bear would have known this much: he had not been given an opportunity to talk. Now the chance came. Judge Charles Soward would allow him to speak in his own defense. Interpreter Jones passed along the information to White Bear.

That once-great Kiowa chief might have used the opportunity to make an exit with some dignity and nobility before the pressures of the oncoming white race. He might have spoken (as he could, with feeling) of the Indians' prior claim to this part of the earth; of the free life they had enjoyed on it, taking only what was necessary for their own existence but leaving productivity unhampered for future generations; of the sweet grasses and pure streams that nurtured all life before white men came along with their plows, guns, railroads, and their selfish search for personal wealth, to be reaped at the expense of Indians and even other white men. For those reasons White Bear and his tribesmen had fought back, had killed the same as white men had killed, considering the finality of death.

The chief, with his oratorical power, could have made a majestic departure, one that might have been quoted for centuries by students of history. Instead, he did not make even much of a fighting exit. White Bear obviously mused over what he thought would best serve his momentary purpose; overrated his speaking ability and underrated the fire of these frontiersmen, who were nothing like those Quaker agents on Indian reservations; substituted supposed craftiness for sincerity; and vanished into historical mists with this ignominy, translated into English by interpreter Jones:

> I cannot speak with these things upon my wrists: you make me a squaw. . . . I have never been so near the Tehannas [Texans] before. I look around me and see your braves, squaws, and papooses, and I have said in my heart that if I ever get back to my people I will never wage war upon you again. I have always been a friend of the white man. My tribe has taunted me and called me a squaw because I have been the friend of the Tehannas. I am suffering now for the crimes of

bad Indians—of [Sitting Bear], Lone Wolf, and Kicking Bird, and Big Bow and Fast Bear and Eagle Heart—and if you will let me go I will kill the three latter with my own hands. If you will let me go I will withdraw my warriors from Tehanna. I will wash out the stain of blood and make it a white land, and there shall be peace and the Tehannas may plow and drive their oxen to the river. But if you kill me it will be a spark on the prairie—make big fire burn heap!

White Bear waited, then, for his magic to work. But he had used similar orations before: on Winfield Scott Hancock before attacking Hancock's post while wearing the very uniform the General had given him in appreciation for his kind words, and later at Medicine Lodge, where he had spoken feelingly of his desire for peace. Too many Texans knew about those orations and the bloody contradictions that followed.

After making his big plea White Bear returned to his seat next to Big Tree, and the two chiefs watched developments with no show of emotion or understanding. They stared at the judge delivering his charge, then at the twelve jurors who huddled briefly in a courtroom corner especially cleared for their consultation. The jurors returned to their "well-whittled benches" in a very short time and let their decision be known to the judge, to the wondering Indians, and to the armed frontiersmen still standing outside the building peering through windows. When Judge Soward asked the foreman about the verdict, that juror (a man named T. W. Williams) startled everyone in the room by shouting so that the crowd outside could hear: "They are [guilty]! We figger 'em guilty!"

White Bear watched while his companion stood before the judge and received a sentence of death by hanging—a manner of execution abhorred by any Indian, who would have preferred to let his life be ended by almost any other method.

Then came White Bear's turn to stand before the bar of justice. The judge's words would have been translated for him: "It is . . . ordered, adjudged, and decreed by the Court, that the said Defendant [White Bear], be taken by the Sheriff of Jack County, and hanged until he is dead, dead, dead, and Lord have mercy upon his soul."

White Bear said nothing. For a few seconds the spectators behind him and at the windows remained silent, too. Then White Bear heard them erupt in a din of yells, cheers, and shouts. Possibly he expected pistol shots to follow—with some of them aimed his way.

White Bear and Big Tree had been eliminated. Sitting Bear was already dead. Trials loomed for other Kiowa chiefs implicated by White Bear: Big Bow, Fast Bear, and Eagle Heart.

Many Jack County citizens believed their security from Indians had been assured. But in their rejoicing they overlooked another threat: Comanche Indians, equally implacable, who liked to strike Texas from refuges on the Staked Plain under chiefs like Quanah, the son of that white woman, then vanish northwestward again.

14

TRIUMPH AND SUFFERING

The Army did not share the momentary civilian complacency. Colonel Mackenzie was directed to assemble the entire 4th Cavalry for a climactic campaign to end the Indian threat on the Texas frontier. He ordered detachments previously stationed at San Antonio, at various locations in the Rio Grande Valley, and elsewhere to join the main body. Together this large force would search for "hostiles," whether Kiowas, Plains Apaches, Comanches, or others, and terminate their troublemaking.

Preparations for the expedition again compounded Lieutenant Carter's work load. Still worried about the health of his wife, who never seemed to flourish on the hard frontier, and for good reasons, Carter nevertheless was forced to devote himself to other concerns that demanded a schedule of very-late-to-bed and up-at-reveille. "Boards, courts, papers galore" competed for attention. "Hobbles, sidelines, picket pins, packs, panniers, saddles, bridles, carbines, pistols, lariats, ordnance and . . . stores . . . had to be looked after, besides . . . other details in an expedition of this kind."

Once more he told his ailing wife good-bye—and this time an infant daughter, too—then he left Fort Richardson on August 2, 1871, with Mackenzie's headquarters company for a scheduled rendezvous with Troop L that night on the West Fork of the Trinity River—toward Red River and the Indian Territory. (Troop L and all other companies had left Richardson earlier under various orders.)

Carter found the march much different from the one made in pursuit of those Kiowas following the wagon-train raid. No rain had fallen since the day that other march had begun—on May 19, a period of two and a half months now. Earth had dried and cracked under the hammerlike rays of a Texas summer sun. Grass had thinned and browned, balding the prairies. Water holes had disappeared or had been contaminated with putrid carcasses of animals— victims of the drought. Midday sunshine drew out a man's sweat and moistened the dust that already powdered him, transferring the dirty layer into a maddening paste. But dusk brought relief from the heat, at least; then evening provided some cooling as the men "rode through . . . bright moonlight, across . . . silent prairies, under . . . brilliant stars."

About 8:45 P.M. the men of headquarters company came upon the bivouac of Troop L. Camp fires still flickered among the pecan trees and post oaks selected for shelter, but most of the L troopers were already asleep. Carter and the others lay down, rolled up in blankets, and quietly joined them in slumber. Tents were not to be pitched during the expedition unless weather made them essential. "Such [was] the sudden transition from affluence to poverty—or . . . from a good bed in a picket house to a soldier's couch upon Mother Earth."

For a month thereafter Carter, as field adjutant, acted almost as Colonel Mackenzie's shadow, ready to take orders, while troopers of the 4th Cavalry combed a wasteland in the vicinity of the Red River. They suffered from heat, became sick on bad water, ate austere rations without much pleasure, stumbled through and up and down ravines and dry creek beds—all in a futile search for hostile Indians and especially for a village of Kiowa Indians whose chief was Kicking Bird. The cavalrymen accomplished nothing, although the Kiowas and Kicking Bird (who in time became such a friend of white men that some of his own people would poison him) did return to the reservation where they belonged, possibly because of the proximity of the 4th. Carter and his commander and an escort returned to Fort Richardson the first of September after being soaked during the final march by a drought-breaking thunderstorm.

At Richardson, Carter greeted his wife and child, compiled reports from the recent trip, and drew accompanying maps; then on

September 19 he left again with Mackenzie and six hundred troopers—this time in the direction of the Staked Plain, where roamed those wild Comanches led by unpacified chiefs like Quanah.

That remote country had not yet become even a frontier. It was an unsettled wilderness, almost treeless, inhabited by Indians, buffalo, antelope, wolves, coyotes, jackrabbits, prairie dogs, and rattlesnakes. Neither railroad nor telegraph had poked in fingers seeking to extend progress and civilization. In canyons and on streams of what is now the Texas Panhandle area lived Quanah's roving band of Quohada Indians, those people who never had considered signing the Medicine Lodge treaty and whose hostility had not lessened since. By this time they had become known as the most consistent raiders on the Texas border.

October had begun adding a chill to ever-lengthening nights when the 4th Cavalry neared Indian country, having tarried a short time at a temporary post for field training and reorganization. Mackenzie ordered his scouts—Tonkawa Indians—to keep an even more careful watch for signs of hostile Indians. They returned one day and reported Quohadas encamped some miles ahead in Blanco Canyon—a break in the Staked Plain threaded by what is now known as White River. Mackenzie, fearing Quohada scouts had in turn sighted his column, ordered horses to be double hobbled at night and guarded by a strong picket.

Carter, relieved of duties as field adjutant, rode now with a cavalry troop and contemplated action soon. But when it came it surprised the Lieutenant. The 4th Cavalry had encamped along a narrow strip of Blanco Canyon, hemmed in by the river on one side and a line of small bluffs on the other, when Comanches struck the first blow—in midnight darkness October 9—by stampeding cavalry horses and mules, just as Mackenzie had feared. The Indians ran some animals beyond reach before troopers could leap from their blankets and drive off the attackers. A quick count showed seventy horses and mules gone; the Indians would be trying to round them up and herd them away.

"We had found [the hostiles] at last!" Carter exulted. "Or, at least, they had found us."

Any further sleep vanished with the stampede. Detachments of

147

men who had been able to retrieve their horses galloped off, seeking the trail of the stampeded animals and of the Indians who had scared them. Carter rode away in predawn gloom to examine picket outposts around camp to learn whether they, too, might have become casualties, or, if safe, whether they had seen the direction taken by Indians and stampeding animals. He held a pistol in one hand and his horse's reins in the other, wary about being ambushed by lurking Indians, but he stumbled upon no hidden enemies, and he found the nearest posts intact.

Despite the murkiness Carter made out the trail of the stampeded horses when he came across it. Still, he continued on to the farthest outpost—one located atop a hill overlooking camp and, in the opposite direction, a descending slope largely enveloped in early-morning darkness.

Carter was preparing to question pickets there when he heard a shot from somewhere nearby and a shout from the slope below. Two detachments of troopers galloped up; a sergeant in one of them had fired at what he thought to be Indians. The shout seemed to confirm his suspicion.

Carter and everyone else stared into the gloom from atop their hill, and Carter discerned the dark, distant forms of a dozen or more mounted Indians "making off with as many of our horses." He and the troopers dashed away in pursuit and closed the distance rapidly, until the Indians abandoned their captured animals, galloped into a ravine, and vanished from view momentarily before emerging on the other side. Then they raced on across an ascending prairie toward a butte ahead—Mount Blanco—which had been gradually painted into the scene by approaching sunrise.

Carter and Captain E. M. Heyl, commander of one of the two detachments that had galloped up to the hill outpost, and a dozen troopers spurred their horses into the same ravine. Other pursuers, fearing a fall, halted at the edge; the ditch looked dangerously steep.

Up a gentle slope the twelve undaunted men and their officers rode, gaining again on the Indians, toward a ridge that momentarily cut from view both their fleeing enemy, who had vanished beyond it, and the base of the butte farther on. When they reached the summit themselves and scanned the area ahead they were astounded to see, around the foot of the butte, a swarm of Indians—hundreds of them—"all mounted and galloping toward us with whoops and . . . yells that, for the moment, seemed to take the breath completely from our bodies." Carter realized then that he and the others had been led deliberately into an ambush.

Carter and Heyl and the vastly outnumbered troopers halted their horses atop the ridge and stared in awe for a moment. Carter heard his fellow officer mutter, "Just look at the Indians!" As for himself, he could not speak—only gape at the scene. Then he realized an extra predicament. He was riding a borrowed horse, one much less reliable than his own mount. Even at that moment he felt the horse trembling beneath him from the recent effort.

"The supreme moment in a soldier's life" for which he had studied at West Point and had trained during the rest of his short military career had arrived with suddenness that required immediate decision and action. Could they race back to the ravine? Probably not, judging by the debilitation shown by his own horse. They could only hope to hold off the attackers here until Mackenzie, in camp more than two miles distant, might hear the shots and send help.

The Lieutenant turned to Captain Heyl, waiting silently some distance off to the right, and was shocked at what he saw: the man "mounted on a large, powerful, and speedy black horse, full of fire and go, [waiting] for some word of command. [Heyl] seemed . . . momentarily paralyzed. . . . He gave no commands, but simply stared."

Within seconds Carter shouted to the Captain that they ought to try to repulse the attack here and hope for quick aid. "Yes, that is right!" he heard Heyl answer, then yell, "Deploy out on the run, men, and give them your carbines!" Heyl added instructions to dismount after deploying right and left, and to fall back slowly toward the recently crossed ravine. Then Heyl took the seven men present from his own troop, all recruits, far off to the right, to a point beyond easy voice communication, and opened a steady fire with Spencer carbines. Carter, left with five men from the other detachment, moved in the opposite direction and commenced shooting, too. The Lieutenant saw that the attackers were "moving like a cloud upon us, spreading out in fan shape, . . . evidently intent upon outflanking us, thus cutting off our only hope . . . of escape to the camp." Obviously the Indians hoped to finish the job before help could arrive, but the troopers' fire proved effective and caused them to slow and scatter. Then Carter saw them begin another favorite maneuver: circling.

The Lieutenant looked on in awe, thinking not of proper ownership of this land or of his duty to win the West, but only of the "most terrifying spectacle" he was witnessing and of somehow surviving it through the deliberate shots he and his men continued to deliver as they fell back slowly toward the ravine.

The Indians were Comanches of Quanah's Quohada band.

> They were naked to the waist; were arrayed in all their war paint and trinkets, with headdresses . . . of fur or feathers fantastically ornamented. Their ponies . . . were . . . painted and decorated with gaudy stripes of flannel and colored calico. Bells were jingling, feathers waving. . . . Mingled with the shouts, whoops, and yells of the warriors could be . . . heard the . . . screeching and . . . [screaming] of the squaws, far in the rear. . . . In the midst of the circling ponies we could see what appeared to be two standard bearers, but upon their nearer approach we discovered them to be two . . . poles gaily decorated with long scalp locks, probably of women, with feathers and pieces of bright metal attached [that] flashed in the morning light. There were . . . other flashes . . . along their line [that] I afterwards ascertained were [from] small pieces of mirrors held in the [hands of principal warriors] and used as signals in the alternate advances and retreats, deployments and concentrations.

A shout from a trooper nearby distracted Carter from his methodical shooting. "Lieutenant, look over there, quick!" the man called. "They are running out!"

Carter glanced over to his right and saw, a hundred or more yards distant, Captain Heyl and his seven troopers, mounted now, spurring their horses away from the fight. Carter and his men shouted pleas and curses, but without effect. The Lieutenant heard Comanches yell, too—in jubilation—and saw them concentrate their attack upon himself and the few soldiers left around him.

He saw also that the ravine lay only a hundred yards away now.

A panicky run for it would prove fatal, Carter knew; so he ordered his men to keep well deployed, to mount, and—bending low on horses—to move slowly toward the rear, firing well-aimed single shots at the Indians and thus perhaps keep them at a distance until the hoped-for sight of army reinforcements would send the enemy racing away.

Still no help came into view; but the Spencer carbines did their part, and the Comanches obviously feared them. The Indians' own muzzle-loading rifles and pistols lacked Spencer accuracy, although their arrows occasionally thumped into horseflesh, but without felling any animals.

Carter had taken his men nearly to the ravine before suffering his first casualty: a trooper struck in the hand by a shot. The man continued firing.

Near the ravine Carter shouted, "Bunch your shots—pump it into them, and make a dash for your lives." A quick fusillade sent the Comanches reeling; Carter and his men galloped for the ravine, but one of them—a private who had been riding to the right of Carter— never reached the shelter.

"Lieutenant," he shouted, "my horse is giving out." Carter looked back and saw that it was true. The animal had begun to sway in utter exhaustion. Comanches saw this, too, and swarmed near the rider.

Carter and the remaining four men, still retreating, sought to help their struggling companion with another fusillade—a counterattack would have been suicidal—but the shots (which killed five Comanches) only delayed the inevitable. Carter himself never expected to survive the next few minutes, either.

One Indian boring in caught the Lieutenant's attention. Carter recalled his appearance afterward and identified the warrior as Quanah.

> A large and powerfully built chief led the bunch, on a coal-black racing pony. Leaning forward upon his mane, his heels nervously working in the animal's side, with six-shooter poised in air, he seemed the incarnation of savage . . . joy. His face was smeared with war paint, which gave his features a satanic look. A large, cruel mouth added to his ferocious appearance.

A full-length headdress . . . of eagle's feathers [spread] out as he rode. . . . Large brass hoops were in his ears, and he was naked to his waist, wearing simply leggings, moccasins, and a breechclout. A necklace of bear's claws hung about his neck. His scalp lock was carefully braided in with . . . fur, and tied with bright red flannel. His horse's bridle was . . . ornamented with bits of silver. . . . Bells jingled as he rode.

Carter said he saw the chief come up and fire his pistol into the skull of the straggling private, who then fell to earth. The man's horse, relieved of his weight, dashed off.

Incredibly, the attackers themselves galloped away moments later. Carter soon saw the reason for their flight: blue-clad troopers and Tonkawa scouts riding toward them from the direction of camp. They were led by Lieutenant P. M. Boehm, who had heard the firing, gathered men, and rushed out to investigate.

Boehm had encountered the seven fleeing troopers and had forced them to accompany him. Their captain, Heyl, had quietly fallen in line, too (according to Carter), but despite his seniority he gave no commands, and Boehm continued to lead the rescuers.

At the ravine Carter, who had been expecting death minutes earlier, realized, "We were saved!"

Quanah, now withdrawing with his Comanches, had tricked Colonel Ranald Mackenzie himself. During the stampede Quanah had even succeeded in stealing a fine gray pacer prized by the Colonel. That feat alone should have been worth a coup. On the other hand, the fact that Mackenzie and his troopers were here in this country should have seemed ominous to Quanah.

The Quohadas, joined by disaffected remnants of other Comanche bands, had done most of their raiding until now in the Texas settlements, from where they always hurried back to the safety of these remote haunts on the Staked Plain. Now here were soldiers searching for them in their very hiding places.

Just as Mackenzie had feared, their scouts had seen the army column approaching Blanco Canyon and had alerted the village, which had been set up in the canyon several miles away. That evening when the 4th Cavalry encamped in the narrow strip of canyon

Quanah had planned the attack that stampeded Mackenzie's horses and mules—despite all the Colonel's precautions—and that led to Lieutenant Carter's fighting retreat in front of the ravine.

A Comanche participant many years later was to recall the skirmish and to give Carter credit for effective defense. "The bullets," he would remember, "came toward us like the roar of a sling whirling through the air." The Indian also recalled something that Carter did not report—or perhaps did not see in all the excitement: One Comanche succeeded in scalping the private whose horse had given out. The scalp proved to be "no good," said the Indian eyewitness (possibly because of the pistol shot aimed at the owner's head), but it later sparked a celebration anyway.

That joyful event, however, lay in the Comanches' future. The Battle of Blanco Canyon remained undecided temporarily. Quanah, who had wisely separated his warriors into smaller fighting units, faced the necessity now of escaping from Mackenzie's 4th Cavalry doubly angered by the stampede and the attack that had inflicted casualties.

About the same time that Lieutenant Boehm and his hurriedly collected group of rescuers saved Carter and the four surviving enlisted men, Mackenzie and five hundred mounted troopers, raising dust, moved out of camp and up the canyon in pursuit of the Comanches. Boehm, Carter, and their men kept in front of the advance. "With our skirmish line well deployed we moved forward steadily toward the butte of the Cañon Blanco," Carter said later.

The Lieutenant could see, far ahead, Indian women to the rear of the warriors' lines frantically herding ponies, and he could hear their distant screeching and screaming while their men, mounted and spread out, circled "like a swarm of angry bees" at the base of the butte, waiting to protect the women and ponies during a fighting retreat up the sides of the mountain. To get at their enemy the cavalrymen apparently would have to climb the height, too. Carter saw that the uppermost reaches became steep after a gentle initial ascent.

As the skirmishers in blue drew closer, the warriors moved up the mountain, "gliding from rock to rock." Shots that dug into earth nearby told the wary troopers that Comanche marksmen were covering the retreat from the summit. Behind the skirmishers came Mackenzie's large force, hastening the Indians' retreat up the height.

Carter heard Boehm shout a suggestion that they spur their horses up the incline and try to eliminate the sharpshooters at the summit. The two officers collected a handful of men and started up, following a steep, narrow, zigzag path and expecting to be stopped at any time by a shower of shot. Carter spurred his tired horse into greater effort seconds before he saw, ahead, a sharp rock jutting out into the trail. He sought to avoid a collision, but his left leg struck the boulder with a noise that seemed to him almost like "the crack of a pistol."

> I was almost lifted out of my saddle. . . . I grasped the pommel, for it made me sick, and all was dark and swimming before my blurred eyes. I felt myself sway and stagger, then apparently fall down an interminable distance. . . . Cold sweat came from every pore, and I became unconscious, but dropped myself forward upon the horse's neck as I lurched. It has always been a puzzle how I got up the side of the butte. My horse had carried my dead weight, and my arms were still tightly clasped about his neck, with the reins loosely dangling. Luckily, the Indians . . . had hastily galloped off, abandoning the position, and scattering in every direction. I remember the cheering, seeing the big column come up, with Mackenzie at its head . . . —and then all is blank.

The Comanches continued their retreat while someone revived Carter with a dash of water to his face. Then the man gave him a drink.

Pain became more intense, but a surgeon's examination later showed that Carter's leg had not been broken, although it was blood-covered, swollen, and stiff: "black and blue." With no adequate medical facilities Carter could only endure the agony and stay with the command, riding with his battered leg reinforced with splints and wrapped in thick bandages.

Later he witnessed the burial of the private killed during the retreat to the ravine. The man's body was placed in a lonely grave at the southeast foot of Mount Blanco, then covered with earth and stones. After that Carter, still a cripple and in much pain, accompanied Mackenzie's column during further pursuit of the Quohadas. Bad weather and exhaustion eventually persuaded Mackenzie to give up and return to base—but not before Indians, during a brief fight, had buried a spiked arrow in the Colonel's upper leg, missing Carter, only a few feet away.

Mackenzie, whose health never had been radiant, "came in from that campaign a sick and very much disappointed man," Carter said. The Lieutenant's description might easily have been applied to himself, too.

The Colonel questioned Carter about rumors he had heard regarding the conduct of Captain Heyl in the skirmish around the ravine, but he deliberately discouraged Carter from making a charge of cowardice against the officer, who happened to be a favorite of Mackenzie's. Carter agreed not to raise the issue. Then the Colonel, in his official report of the Blanco Canyon action, ignored the valor of both Carter and his rescuer, Boehm, and for some reason mentioned neither officer, although Carter later was brevetted first lieutenant for his conduct—recognition that fell far below his expectation.

Such a slight left Carter dismayed, but (typical of his almost blind loyalty and devotion) he never ceased to regard the Colonel with something akin to hero worship. Carter blamed everything on a lapse of memory by Mackenzie, and he implied that it was due to the most recent of the Colonel's wounds and to the man's generally precarious health.

So Carter's personal triumph and suffering at Blanco Canyon went into nothing more than an overall failure of Mackenzie's 1871 campaign—and the Lieutenant's valor at the ravine went officially unrecognized, as far as the Army was concerned. Further, for many months after Carter's feat Quanah and his Quohadas would remain as much of a threat as ever.

15

LIKE FIGHTING WILD ANIMALS
IN A TRAP

In another area of major violence, the Territory of Arizona, un-
manageable bands of Apaches remained as much of a threat to
white settlers as did the Staked Plain Comanches.

General George Crook's plans for peace and President Grant's
search for solutions, conducted by his representative Vincent
Colyer, had not proved successful. Memories of the recent massacre at Camp Grant and an antipathy to being caged on a reservation
governed emotions of these Apaches, who actually increased their
attacks about this time. Accordingly, Crook—pursuant to his professionalism and to his promise to subdue "hostiles"—determined to
commence in waning 1872 a campaign to punish the Apaches and
to force them onto reservations, where he hoped to make peaceful
farmers of them.

The military operations would be conducted with the efficiency
that Lieutenant John Bourke had noticed as characterizing this
commander. One of Crook's earliest and, for his purposes, wisest
decisions was to rely completely on friendly Apaches as scouts for
finding hostile Apaches. In other geographical areas some white
men had been able (through close contacts like marriage or com-
mercial trading) to become sufficiently familiar with the thinking
and the habits of Indians to serve capably as army scouts, but this
was not generally true in regard to Apaches, whose mentalities and
mores would remain (because of their inherent secrecy) relatively
unknown to whites even into the twentieth century. "Only an

Apache can catch an Apache" went the talk among settlers in the Arizona Territory, and Crook, whom the Apaches came to call "Gray Wolf," had realized the truth of it; so he hired Apaches willing to work against their own kin.

Crook decided, too, on a winter campaign, as had proved effective against Plains Indians earlier. Such an operation would force the small bands of Apaches higher and deeper into mountains, compounding the misery brought by cold weather, and might make the work of spotting them easier—through smoke from camp fires the chilly weather would force upon them.

The General had transferred his headquarters to a new location—one that, incidentally, helped to acclimatize his troopers for hard winter marches. He had moved from Tucson to Fort Whipple, within one mile of Prescott, the thoroughly Anglo-American town that might have been "transplanted bodily from the center of the Delaware, the Mohawk, or the Connecticut valley" and built amid pine trees in the higher elevation and cooler temperature of central Arizona. In spring and summer meadows of luxurious grass replaced the prickly cactus plants of southern Arizona as major vegetation. Water from wells and mountain streams delighted a man with its cool purity. Mountain peaks nearby rarely doffed their caps of snow during the year. Neat residences and barns constructed of wood or stone speckled the landscape and provided relief from those dreary adobes of the southern country.

The fort itself, however, made a less favorable impression—at least on Lieutenant Bourke, who accompanied Crook as newly appointed aide-de-camp. Bourke peered around his new station and saw a collection of disintegrating, unbarked, pine-log houses that seemed ready to collapse with every wind gust. Only one structure differed in appearance: an unpainted one-room shanty produced from unseasoned pine planks, sitting atop a hill nearest the town. In this hut the General made his headquarters and formulated his plans for the campaign.

On November 15, 1872, Crook was ready to move out with Bourke as aide and with the rest of his force—the 5th Cavalry, units from the 3rd and 1st Cavalry, and the 21st and 23rd Infantry. Every man had been trained recently in Apache fighting. With the expedition went only essential supplies, to allow faster traveling.

The first few marches traversed picturesque country. Bourke, a military man with something of a poet's soul, marveled at the scenery: forests of towering pines and, not far away, snow-blanketed peaks. Wintry weather already gripped the lofty Colorado Plateau across which they traveled, leaving a thick layer of ice over springs and creeks and making difficult the watering of stock.

Bourke also saw scenes that saddened him: men at work felling trees for the money they would bring. Someday the earth that had nourished those natural beauties might be barren of them, for all the tree choppers seemed to care. Earlier, around Flagstaff, the Lieutenant had been aghast at the wantonness. A large firm had built a great saw and planing mill there, "equipped with every modern appliance for the destruction of the old giants whose heads had nodded in the breezes of centuries," and men were cutting a giant swath through the timber belt. Bourke reflected:

> Man's inhumanity to man is an awful thing. His inhumanity to God's beautiful trees is scarcely inferior to it. Trees are nearly human; they used to console man with their oracles, and I must confess my regret that the Christian dispensation has so changed the opinions of the world that the soughing of the evening wind through their branches is no longer a message of hope or a solace to sorrow. Reflection tells me that without the use of this great belt of timber the construction of the railroad from El Paso to the City of Mexico would have been attended with increased expense and enhanced difficulty—perhaps postponed for a generation—but, for all that, I cannot repress a sentiment of regret that the demands of civilization have caused the denudation of so many square miles of our forests in all parts of the timbered West.

Bourke found Crook's marches to be long and hard. Reveille came during the cold depth of night—at 2 A.M. Men moved out before four o'clock, not to stop again until late afternoon. The schedule reflected Spartanism almost worthy of Apaches themselves. Two hundred and fifty miles separated Crook's immediate destination, Camp Apache (in the eastern part of the Territory), from Fort Whipple, but the column arrived at the very time Crook had planned.

At the camp more Apache scouts were enlisted for the campaign before the column moved on, in further exhausting marches, one hundred miles to old Camp Grant, Bourke's recent station. From there the real work would begin: a sweep of the Tonto Basin, a large area to the north of Camp Grant where hostile Apaches liked to hide.

Crook's force was to be split up into half a dozen units, each one to have its own commander operating under the General's direction, and each—as an entity—to have its own Apache scouts and pack train of supplies. The units would enter Tonto Basin from different directions, meet at the center, and exit in different directions. If a unit encountered Apaches the commander was under orders from Crook to give the Indians a chance to surrender and to take as scouts any warriors who volunteered. In event of Apache refusal the commander would attack until the last hostile warrior surrendered or died; but women and children were to be spared. If cavalry horses gave out during a pursuit, the determined General ordered, Apaches were to be followed on foot.

For this part of the campaign Lieutenant Bourke was attached to a veteran unit commanded by Major W. H. Brown that would depart for the Tonto Basin from Camp Grant, reconnoiter the Mescal, Pinal, Superstition, and Mazatzal ranges, generally east of present Phoenix, and proceed to Camp McDowell, twenty-five miles northeast of Phoenix, for further orders. In December they set out northward along the dry bottom of the San Pedro, traversed an area filled with thickets of mesquite and sage, then crossed over to another dusty stream called Deer Creek. They forded the Gila River and entered a broken foothill area of rough, rocky trails that provided a narrow passage through scrub oak, mescal, Spanish bayonet, and other plants generally regarded as inhospitable, into a higher region—the Pinal range—where snow covered the ground and where grew junipers, pines, and cedars.

To Bourke the abrupt change of temperature seemed almost like going from summer to winter. It was an unpleasantness common to Arizona scouting, which often required leaving warm valleys in the morning and ascending mountain heights in the afternoon, then encamping on summits in deep snow. The Apache scouts—eagerly sniffing for a fight, even against other Indians—stayed twelve or more hours ahead of the main body of troops, but in frequent communication.

Whenever Bourke had an opportunity to observe these army Apaches he was constantly amazed at their ability to derive maximum utility and comfort from the environment. They wore footgear that made no noise as they climbed over rocks and descended slippery trails—and after listening to scouts' persuasions most of the officers and enlisted men changed to moccasins, too. The Indians used wads of dry grass stuffed into moccasins for more comfortable walking, and they used grass, too, under blankets for soft beds at night; while a strategically arranged windbreak of stones provided warmth for the two or three Apaches invariably huddled together. When fires were allowed scouts would make small ones, then hover over the yellow-red embers for warmth. They slept with feet close to the coals—and they laughed at the white man's fire, which usually was so large that it created consternation around the countryside among both friends and enemies who sighted it, yet threw out so much heat no one could get near it for greatest warmth.

Christmas Day brought more marching, but a festive break in the routine of Bourke's detachment occurred when G Troop of the 5th Cavalry, accompanied by nearly one hundred friendly Pima Indians, joined it after having crossed over the Mazatzal Range. During the journey they killed six hostile Apaches.

A day or two later Major Brown called Bourke and all other officers together for a talk. What the Lieutenant heard presaged a battle.

Brown told his officers that a scout who had been reared in a Salt River Canyon cave nearby had offered to lead them there. They would surely find Apache holdouts—plenty of them—living in the hideaway. Terrain would require, however, that the soldiers leave their horses behind; and a danger lay in the troopers' being discovered on the tortuous, narrow trail leading over mountains to the canyon and the cave. If Apaches caught men in the act of negotiating that rugged pathway, the scout had warned, they could kill every man.

The advance, then, would be made on foot and in darkness, Major Brown said, and anyone who felt physically incapable of completing such a march should remain behind with the horses, mules, and pack train—to guard against possible plunderers.

Officers and men chosen for the attack checked weapons and filled belts with cartridges. Each also took a blanket and packed into it twenty more cartridges, some bread, bacon, and coffee, and a canteen of water, slung it across his shoulders, and commenced the march before 8 P.M. The scout who had volunteered the information led the way—up a twisting trail, toward the summit of mesas that surrounded the Apaches' canyon and protected its remote cave.

The temperature seemed to drop much more swiftly than the hours passed. Bourke, thoroughly chilled, was glad enough to be climbing; and he heard with regret a whispered command to halt and to lie down passed from ahead. Major Brown had given the order so that scouts might creep on farther to investigate what appeared to be illuminations in the distance, possibly Apache fires, and to allow the rear guard to close up.

Bourke, like the rest, lay on freezing earth, not daring to whisper. When others around him were forced to cough they wrapped their heads in blankets or coats to muffle the sound.

A search ahead disclosed four empty wickiups, only recently vacated, and a dozen or so horses and mules apparently stolen from whites or Pima Indians in Gila Valley settlements. No lurking enemies had been detected, however, and the column moved again —with increasing uneasiness—after a few scouts and fifteen of the best marksmen from among the troopers had been sent far in the lead, under the command of a Lieutenant William Ross.

Predawn gloom began bringing immediate surroundings into view and giving everything a ghostly tinge—rocks, canyon walls, the slim, slippery, descending trail ahead.

Bourke was moved to think of the "valley of the shadow of death." He crept along the trail not far behind Major Brown, and he heard Brown whisper, "They ought to be very near here," just before a series of thunderlike claps startled everyone.

"What was that?" Bourke heard Brown exclaim. Then, without waiting for an explanation from messengers sure to appear soon from the position ahead, Brown ordered Bourke to take command of the first forty men in the column and to reinforce Ross and the sharpshooters.

Down into the canyon Bourke clambered, risking his footing on the thin path and a fall into the river hundreds of feet below. As he made a sharp turn in the trail he saw the outline of the cave. It was located behind a rocky, platform-like natural shelf jutting from the lower part of an awesome canyon wall hundreds of feet high. Giant boulders lying around the cave entrance formed a rampart. Bourke realized how secure the Indians must have regarded themselves in this refuge—safety "such as only the eagle or the vulture can feel in the seclusion of the ice-covered . . . pinnacles of the Andes." The Lieutenant knew that other army units had probed the canyon previously by struggling along the banks of the stream. Now he could visualize the Apaches silently watching those troopers from behind rocks that seemed to form a stone curtain for their abode.

Bourke hurried farther along the trail and encountered Lieutenant Ross, who explained the thunderclaps. In the early-morning gloom Ross had come upon a group of warriors dancing near a small fire burning on an open space near the cave, apparently in celebration of a recent victory. Ross and his marksmen had commenced shooting. The shots had killed six Indians and had reverberated "from peak to peak and from crag to crag." Survivors had scrambled for the cave and were now inside there, with an undetermined number of others.

Bourke gave a few quiet orders, then surveyed the situation, which happened to be surprisingly good for the troopers. His and Ross's detachments, numbering between fifty and sixty men, "had secured positions [on the canyon floor] within thirty yards of the other, and each man [had been] posted behind rocks in such a manner that he might . . . as well [have been] in a rifle pit." They intended to wait for Major Brown's arrival with the main body of soldiers before opening fire, but one of the Pima Indians, disregarding orders, maneuvered for a better position, drew a fusillade from the hidden Indians, and fell dead.

An Apache soon became another victim. Using a screen of rocks to sneak out of the cave, he crawled along the lower canyon wall to a point beyond the troopers' right flank, then ascended a precipice—apparently intending to summon assistance from somewhere nearby.

Overconfidence ruined his plan. Some distance down the canyon he climbed to the top of a high rock and paused to give the surprised besiegers a yell of defiance, considering himself beyond the range of their weapons. But the silhouette of his body against the lightened sky made a fine target for one of the sharpshooters, who dropped the Apache from his wild perch.

When Major Brown arrived he positioned the rest of his men, placing some in locations that served to imprison the Indians in their cave and others in a reserve force ordered to crouch and wait behind the front line. Then, through an interpreter, he called for surrender.

Angry yells and shouts and a few random shots gave him a negative answer—twice. After the second summons Brown asked the warriors at least to send their women and children out of the cave, promising them safety, but he heard only jeers in reply to that suggestion.

For a while the potential battleground lay enveloped in strange silence, with the exception of a few scattered shots occasionally fired from one side or the other at bodies seen moving behind rocks. Sometimes a flurry of arrows swished from the canyon—aimed high with the hope of falling straight down and finding victims among men snuggled behind boulders.

Bourke saw that Major Brown himself did little other than encourage his men to crouch low for safety. An assault obviously would prove too costly—especially without ladders: "The great rock wall in front of the cave was not . . . less than ten feet in height at its lowest point, and smooth as the palm of the hand. It would be madness to attempt to climb it." Apaches shooting from behind rocks above could annihilate attackers.

After some reflection Brown devised a way to get at the Indians. He ordered men nearest the entrance to fire rapidly at the cave roof, to see what damage ricocheting bullets might do.

A long, shattering rumble worse than terrible thunder reverberated throughout the canyon. During slackened periods of fire sounds coming from inside the cave told Lieutenant Bourke of the effectiveness of the Major's plan. He could hear "a wail from a squaw, and the feeble cry of a [child]." He felt certain that warriors among them were taking casualties, too, but they would have been enduring their pain in silence, as was their custom.

Bourke heard the Major yell for cease-fire and once more call for surrender. This time the reply came in the form of a weird chant—

163

"half wail and half exultation," so it sounded to Bourke—"the frenzy of despair and the wild cry for revenge." Then the shouts of Indian guides and translators told Bourke and his commander the meaning. "Look out!" someone yelled. "There goes the death song. They are going to charge!" Almost immediately came another warning: "Look out! Here they come!"

An awed Bourke saw about twenty "superb-looking" warriors appear in front of the cave. Half of them halted near the edge of the rocky rampart and, deliberately aiming arrows or rifles at bodies below now more clearly exposed to them, sent a rapid covering fire while the others clambered down from the stone shelf and sought to sneak around the soldiers' right flank—as that overconfident Apache had done earlier. Furious volleys sent the Indians plunging earthward in bloody heaps or retreating toward the cave. Inside again, the survivors joined other Apaches there in a continuation of that ghastly death chant.

Major Brown determined to end the battle. He ordered men to pour more long, rapid fire onto the roof of the cave, then to charge by way of that rough passage around the right flank that the Indians themselves had sought to use.

Once more a din rocked the canyon, but during a brief lull Bourke saw an Apache boy three or four years old appear where the warriors had stood earlier. The child stared out at the soldiers while he sucked on a thumb. A bullet knocked him down, but one of the Apache army scouts leaped from behind a rock, grabbed the injured boy, and carried him to safety—while troopers paused to cheer.

Bourke later heard about (rather than participated in) an event that proved climactic in the fight.

The latest fusillade brought to a canyon rim nearby a small group of Brown's troopers who had been left behind earlier. They had heard the noise of battle and had hurried to see if they might help.

Their leader, a Captain James Burns, peered down from above. He saw soldiers firing from behind rocks and, from his position, he could see some distance inside the cave into which they were shooting.

He saw a group of Apaches crouched close behind the stone-protected rampart at the entrance. There they were as safe as possible from the bullets showering down from the cave roof farther back.

Burns ordered his men to fire at the Apaches; then he thought of an even deadlier attack. From his position he could send boulders crashing into the huddled group.

He had his men start giant rocks rolling caveward. They crushed bodies before smashing into fragments. From in front of the entrance troopers continued their fusillades.

Bourke looked on in wonder and remarked, "No human voice could be heard in such a cyclone of wrath; the volume of dust was so dense that no eye could pierce it."

Major Brown's location, however, enabled him to see Captain Burns and to signal him to stop sending down the boulders. Brown intended now to charge the cave. Exactly at noon, Bourke noted, the advance began. A trooper from G Company became the first man to climb the natural parapet and to offer himself as a target for vengeful warriors, if any remained alive. Nothing happened to the soldier.

Surprisingly (as Bourke said later), some thirty Apaches had survived, by shielding themselves with stones or piles of dead bodies, but some of those survivors died afterward. Resistance had been beaten out of them, however, and for good reason, as Bourke saw. Sixty or more Apaches had been killed. "There were men and women dead or writhing in the agonies of death and with them several babies killed by our glancing bullets or by the storm of rocks and stones that had descended from above."

Major Brown hurried his men away, leaving dead Apaches where they had fallen. The Major had learned from a few women survivors that other Apaches lived nearby and might be expected to attack. He wanted to get out of the canyon and onto more favorable ground before that happened.

But Brown had another reason for his quick departure. He wanted to go on to Camp McDowell, as previously ordered. More work remained to be done, and he would learn the details there.

Lieutenant Bourke mused over the recent battle, which would remain vivid in his memory. He thought "it was . . . like fighting . . . wild animals in a trap. The Apaches had made up their minds to die if relief did not reach them."

16

OLD ENEMIES

After several other fights like the one at the cave many hostile Apaches indicated willingness by 1873 to settle for peace. With the assistance of another general—O. O. Howard, one-armed since a Civil War battle in Virginia—Crook enticed most of these people onto reservations, there to try farming—the future life he had wanted for them.

General Howard, another emissary sent by President Grant, succeeded in talking with (and even winning the friendship of) two Chiricahua Apache chiefs whose names alone instilled fear among Arizona settlers—Cochise and Geronimo (who had continued to concentrate on raiding in Mexico, where his family had been massacred). Howard persuaded them to go to reservations.

Violence still flared occasionally, but compared to earlier years the Territory of Arizona seemed peaceful—temporarily at least.

The recent experiences of Crook's aide, Lieutenant Bourke, had heightened his sympathy for these erstwhile enemies. He had observed with something akin to awe and even admiration their courage and resolution as exhibited at the cave, and he liked certain other characteristics, which he wrote about often. His ranging mind afforded some understanding of Apaches and an empathy with them that were closed to less thoughtful, or more selfish, white men. Years later he would mean to include Apaches specifically when he wrote:

> The American Indian, born free as the eagle, would not tol-

erate restraint, would not brook injustice; therefore, the restraint imposed must be manifestly for his benefit, and the government to which he was subjected must be eminently one of kindness, mercy, and absolute justice, without necessarily degenerating into weakness.

The American Indian despises a liar. The American Indian is the most generous of mortals: at all his dances and feasts the widow and the orphan are the first to be remembered. Therefore, when he meets with an agent who is "on the make," that agent's influence goes below zero at once; and when he enters the trader's store and finds that he is charged three dollars and a half for a miserable wool hat [that] during his last trip to Washington, Albuquerque, Omaha, or Santa Fe . . . he has seen offered for a quarter, he feels that there is something wrong, and he does not like it any too well.

"Absolute justice" proved never to have been forthcoming for the Indians Bourke fought, and it saddened him. When reservation Apaches were moved from a satisfactory location on the Verde River to share with other tribes some poor land at the mouth of the "sickly" San Carlos, Bourke remarked, "I should . . . blush had I not long since gotten over blushing for anything that the United States Government did in Indian matters."

Bourke would have heard of another case of injustice that occurred elsewhere during the same period (1872–73) while he was engaged in quelling Apaches. On the Pacific Coast, which had escaped most of the violence that characterized these last years of warfare on the Plains and in the Southwest (largely because of the peacefulness of California Indians), a tiny rebellion by Modocs flared. The war theater comprised a small area where the Indians had established positions: seventy square miles of California lava beds located near the Oregon border. The resisters numbered only seventy-five warriors and one hundred fifty women and children. But their subjugation required a thousand troops and volunteers, six months of bloody work, and more government money, proportionately, than was expended in any other area of fighting.

The trouble stemmed largely from more apparent injustice—certainly ineptness. The Modocs, after fighting Oregon settlers for possession of their dwindling homeland, had agreed to share a reservation with their more numerous rivals, the Klamath Indians, but the Klamaths had forced the Modocs out. An Indian agent told the Modocs to return. They refused. The agent then asked General E. R. S. Canby, military commander of the area, for help, but Canby (and some other officials) merely suggested the Modocs be given a reservation of their own—a reasonableness opposed by white settlers nearby. The agent persisted elsewhere with his demand, and eventually orders arrived from Washington for Canby to use troops to force the Modocs back to the unsatisfactory reservation.

Fighting broke out, and the well-meaning Canby later was killed by a Modoc during negotiations being carried out under a truce. Not until June 1, 1873, did the last resistance end—after governmental expenditure of half a million dollars and after many deaths that could have been avoided by the gift of several thousand acres of land, as General Canby had suggested.

So by 1873 Modocs had been persuaded into peacefulness, as had been most Apaches that same year—and by the same methods.

Even the Sioux who lived around their sacred Black Hills, in the Dakotas, seemed tranquil—at least when compared to what they had been in the past. But the degree of their placidity always could be traced to the extent white men left those proud people to themselves. The situation would change during that very year, 1873, with the spread of rumors of a gold strike in the Black Hills and an ensuing flood of fortune seekers.

In Texas, too, raids continued, although in 1872 Colonel Mackenzie had led a punitive expedition against Staked Plain Indians and had pursued one band as far westward as the site of Alamagordo, New Mexico. Later, in the spring of 1873 (under orders from General Sherman), he had taken his men into Mexico, an action protested without consequence by that nation, to seek out bands of Indians who made a practice of crossing the Rio Grande, raiding Texas, then fleeing across that international boundary to safety.

Before all that activity occurred a quiet move had been made to bring peace to the Texas frontier. Through the persuasion of Washington officials the death sentences of those two Kiowa chiefs convicted of murder—White Bear and Big Tree—had been commuted to life imprisonment, in an effort to placate tribesmen and to influence them against seeking revenge.

Still the raids continued.

Lieutenant Bob Carter's leg wound continued to trouble him, but it had not resulted in his discharge from the Army. He accompanied Mackenzie into Mexico in 1873.

The year before that Carter had added two other memorable experiences to a young life already crowded with drama. He had become the father of a second daughter, and he had commanded a detachment that had escorted convicts White Bear and Big Tree northward to a meeting with other Indian chiefs, in accordance with a request made by the tribe. Officials had approved the trip with the hope of encouraging peace.

Carter still had been stationed at Fort Richardson when those events occurred, but he and his family had moved from the miserable jacal into a comparative mansion—one made of canvas. He had put up as a sort of parlor a large, framed hospital tent, with flooring underfoot. To the rear of that he had placed two smaller tents, also framed and floored. One became a bedroom, the other a combination dining and storage room. The two were separated by a narrow passageway that allowed rear exit to a small cook tent. Behind that shelter he had thrown up still another tent to serve as a servant's sleeping quarters.

Colonel Mackenzie chided the Lieutenant about what he liked to call "Carter's Village," and the Colonel sometimes stopped in to joke with Mary Carter, too. "Look here," Mackenzie would say, "I told Carter he could put up some tents . . . but I didn't intend that he should use . . . all the canvas in the Army."

The Carters' new home certainly afforded pleasant relief from the pest-plagued jacal. A black-and-red wool rug in the parlor added color and luxury. Underneath it, as protection and insulation, Carter had tacked a covering of canvas to the board floor, which stood elevated on blocks. A wood stove provided warmth on cold nights, and other furniture, although primitive, afforded more comfort throughout the house: a center table with oil lamp and five fold-up chairs, a rocker, chintz-covered chest, shelves for books and other articles, washstand and towel rack, knocked-down bedstead, barrel chiffonier, and a few other useful pieces. Chintz drapes and pictures pinned to canvas walls provided decor.

Finding reliable domestics became an immediate problem for Carter, as for all other officers on the masculine Texas border, and he never would solve it to any satisfaction. Some other officers brought maids and cooks from the East, but many of the servants—white or black—soon found suitors waiting in line and succumbed to marriage not long afterward. Any junior officer drawing no more pay than Carter did eventually relied on discharged soldiers who "floated about from one garrison to another"—chewers and spitters of tobacco and guzzlers of red-eye whiskey or cheap wine who might, when sober and watched carefully, perform the most fundamental duties—such as broiling a steak, boiling coffee, and baking "dobe" biscuits in a Dutch oven—without making off with too many household possessions.

One cook known only by the name "Jim" proved a particular risk. The man would commence drinking at any time of day or night, Carter said, "and when bringing in the coffee or the biscuits to the table, we never knew whether he was going to pour the scalding beverage down our backs or slip the plate of hot . . . biscuits into our laps."

But almost any kind of domestic could help the Carters—because of Mary's lingering poor health and, during the fall of 1872, because of her second pregnancy. For this delivery she escaped from the dreadful jacal, but the devilish Texas climate happened to make the event another remarkable ordeal.

As the hour approached (on November 14, 1872) a giant norther howled into the area, pushing clouds of sand and dust before it. Cold wind sifted into every corner of "Carter's Village." "The guy ropes strained, the tent frame shrieked and groaned, the canvas lifted and filled like the mainsail of a ship at sea; the rug rose from the floor in great waves . . . until it made one dizzy and sick as [though] one were really upon the ocean." Carter summoned a detail of men to hang on to the guy ropes and to keep his bedroom tent from flying away. Inside, Mary Carter and her second daughter survived.

Carter's experience in escorting White Bear and Big Tree actually had come before the birth of the second daughter. During the

Major General Custer (left), his brother, Tom, and his wife, Libbie. Later Tom Custer would die with the General in the Sunday fight on the Little Big Horn.

Custer's Black Hills Expedition of 1874, photographed about July 28 in Castle Creek Valley. Twelve hundred soldiers and scientists entered sacred lands of the Sioux, reported gold, and brought hordes of white fortune seekers (and eventually fierce fighting).

Sod house in Nebraska and the family that occupied it. Early white settlers on the windblown Plains wanted room, free land, or opportunity (or all three) and not great comfort, which they rarely found.

Black Hawk City, Colorado Territory. Some western towns never left planners' imaginations. Some prospered and became great cities; others became ghost towns. Black Hawk did much of its growing about the time this photograph was made in 1864.

Winter camp. Cold weather forced Indians who moved continually in warm months to stop in some favored location, there to live on supplies gathered in advance.

United States cavalryman. Eventually troopers like this one (painted by Frederic Remington), aided by Indian scouts, ended the Plains wars, largely through winter campaigns.

Geronimo, Naiche

Geronimo at surrender

Bourke, Crook

Robert G. Carter

summer of 1872, with those Comanche and Kiowa raids continuing, government officials had determined to try another method of stopping them—one used often before, with some degree of success. They planned to transport a delegation of chiefs to Washington, D.C., to give the Indian leaders a chance to see the true power and potential of white civilization. Presumably, then, the chiefs would return to their people and urge peaceful cooperation rather than war, which could only destroy them.

But the Kiowas refused to consider any proposal until White Bear and Big Tree were released—or at least were brought to the Fort Sill agency so that doubting Kiowas could see for themselves whether their two tribesmen were alive and well. Further, the other chiefs wanted to confer with them.

Necessary arrangements were made. Lieutenant Carter and his E Troop received orders to go to Dallas, there to pick up White Bear and Big Tree and to take them in double irons to Fort Sill.

Ironically, White Bear (who had become convict No. 2107 in the state penitentiary), and Big Tree (No. 2108), had been helping to build a railroad—something they surely never would have anticipated as free men—when plans for conveying them to Fort Still were completed. A builder for the Houston and Texas Central had contracted with the state of Texas for the labor of one hundred penitentiary inmates, and the two Indians, weary of close confinement, had been happy enough to be included in the work force. Now they were separated from it.

Carter and his troopers left Fort Richardson on September 4, 1872, traveling southeast. They took four days to complete the trip of ninety straight-line miles, marching across what is now the densely populated Fort Worth–Dallas area, but what was then little more than empty countryside. On the night of the fourth they camped at Crawford's Ranch; on the fifth, near Weatherford; and on the sixth, near Johnson's Station. At Dallas on the seventh they camped in the vicinity of the railroad depot, and a curious crowd gathered to gawk.

Carter had been told that the two chiefs would arrive by train sometime after midnight that evening. He marched his company over to the depot in time to receive them, then waited—and waited. Again a crowd gathered, but no chiefs appeared. The soldiers returned to their bivouac, and Carter telegraphed an inquiry to state prison officials. A reply assured him the chiefs would arrive sometime around the following midnight.

Again he and his troops went to the depot and waited. Finally the Indians arrived on a train that chugged in at eight o'clock on the morning of September 9.

"We saw through the windows [White Bear's] stalwart and familiar form," Carter said, "heard the clanking . . . of leg irons, and very soon we had encircled them with our armed troopers, pressed back the crowd, and had them secure in tents under heavy guard."

Still, Carter worried about the safety of his charges. Armed men loitered constantly in the vicinity of the camp. No one attempted to harm the prisoners, however, and on the following day Carter commenced the march to Fort Sill.

That night they camped on Denton Creek. Owl screeches, coyote yelps, and prisoners jangling chains kept them awake for a while, but with commencement of a slow rain quiet returned. A gentle patter of drops against canvas tents helped to lull occupants to sleep. As the rain increased so did the dry comfort inside.

About midnight Carter heard the drumbeats of a galloping horse, then a shouted challenge. Immediately afterward one of the sentinels brought to the Lieutenant's tent a boyish-looking Fort Sill scout named Jack Stillwell, who was carrying a message that read something like this (as Carter remembered later):

To the Officer Commanding Escort of Kiowa Chiefs:
This is to inform you that there are 3,000 or more Confederated Indians . . . about the Fort Sill Reservation today, or will be by the time you are expected to arrive with the prisoners . . . They are all well armed and are sullen, ugly, and warlike. I have five troops of Cavalry [10th] aggregating nearly 300 men; with your troop here [there] would be about 360. To bring [White Bear] . . . here in irons and expect to take him back to the State Penitentiary . . . would be almost impossible. . . . I beg, therefore, in spite of your positive orders to the contrary, [that you] not . . . bring them here . . . but . . . take them to the present terminal of the [Missouri-Kansas-Texas Railroad], where the Commissioners

172

. . . will meet you . . . with . . . Indians . . . destined for Washington.

The message was signed "G. W. Schofield, Major, 10th U. S. Cavalry, Commanding Post."

Carter mused over the request for some time. He knew the risk of disobeying orders, no matter for what reason, and his instructions from the departmental commander had been to escort White Bear and Big Tree to Fort Sill. Any mere lieutenant who assumed the responsibility of changing a departmental commander's order would have to give unassailable reasons for doing so; and Carter was not known as a daring thinker.

The Lieutenant sought the advice of the scout who had just come from Fort Sill. Stillwell was no army man, but he was plentifully experienced with Indians (although Carter did not know this at the time; he simply wanted firsthand information about Fort Sill). In 1868, while still in his teens, Stillwell had used the cover of darkness to slip through lines of Indian besiegers and had traveled 125 miles to get help for a surrounded force commanded by Major George Forsyth at a location on the Arickaree River (in Colorado) later called Beecher Island—in honor of a lieutenant who died there.*

"What is your judgment on the conditions at Fort Sill?" Carter asked the scout.

Stillwell answered softly, and with a slight drawl, "I ain't no soldier, but I have been in some pretty tight spots in my life. As sure as you take these chiefs into the . . . reservation you will be taking very big chances on getting them out again. . . . My . . . advice would be . . . not to take them there."

That helped to sway Carter, but (typically) he even asked the advice of a newspaper correspondent accompanying his detachment. The man, who might have been expected to urge going on to Sill with the hope of getting a dramatic story, voted with Stillwell.

Lieutenant Carter mused over the two suggestions while rain continued to patter against his tent and decided then to disobey his previous orders. But as soon as he was able (at Gainesville, Texas)

* In that same fight Chief Roman Nose of the Cheyennes was killed.

173

he telegraphed the departmental commander for approval, which he received.

Carter headed for Atoka, the railroad terminus at that time, located in the southern part of the Indian Territory, but far to the east of Fort Sill.

When Carter left the Fort Sill trail he studied the faces of the two chiefs, who said nothing and seemed to try to remain as inscrutable as ever. Nevertheless, Carter thought he detected a flicker of surprise and chagrin. Later Carter noticed that White Bear became animated again, occasionally pointing out some landmark to Big Tree and talking in Kiowa—no doubt in recollection of an occurrence from grand days past when the two led raiding parties through the region.

On September 14 they forded the Red River and went on northward—through land occupied by Cherokees and other peaceful tribes, across the Blue River, on to the railroad terminus. Upon arrival that same day, while waiting to transfer his prisoners, Carter indulged himself in a restaurant meal at the only hotel around, and he was introduced to a "fine-looking man with a handsome daughter" who proved to be Cherokee Indians. The man, a minister, surprised Carter with his excellent English usage and his conversational ability; and the girl, recently returned from school in the East, amazed him by a ladylike air.

Carter listened, looked, and quietly reflected—not how other tribes might be influenced to adopt a similar life to their advantage someday, but (typical of him) how "these Indians were direct descendants of the wild tribes that once infested the Atlantic border states . . . and [were] drenched with the blood of our best officers and soldiers, [and cost] the government millions of dollars to subjugate them and remove them."

Continuing to muse, Carter gave the credit for removal to "the bravery and peace-producing influence of our little Regular Army, wholesome force and restraint, with, it is true, some bloodshed, and the . . . wisdom of a great soldier, General Andrew Jackson."

> It was a task accomplished with very great difficulty, having been most strenuously opposed by all of the superfine humanitarians of that period, including Clay, Webster, Calhoun, by

the entire Whig Party, and even by the Supreme Court of the United States, which rendered a decision in favor of the treaty rights of these Indians.

Jackson, nothing daunted, stood by his policy, because he fully understood the necessity for such a step to the country and more thoroughly understood the Indian character than any other man. John Marshall said: "He has rendered his decision, now let him enforce it!" Jackson, however, was so strong . . . that he was able to carry out his policy. . . .

It was one of the best and most farsighted strokes of practical statesmanship that the country ever experienced. There were no more Indian troubles east of the Mississippi. . . .

The little Regular Army proved to be the greatest conservator of peace and practically the best friends these savage warriors ever had.

Carter was a thinker typical of many white Americans of his time, despite his occasional deviations. He could completely ignore the question of prior occupation of land—probably never thought of it—and (deliberately erring or not) could twist facts around to support his argument. It was President Jackson, not Chief Justice Marshall, who spoke of the other man's rendering a difficult-to-enforce decision. Jackson had been speaking of a Supreme Court ruling in favor of eastern Indians. "Let him enforce it" referred to the Chief Justice's inability to do so without help from the Chief Executive—help that did not come.

Carter roused himself from his musings and took his leave. Later he conducted his prisoners to the Atoka depot, but commissioners who were to accompany the other Indian chiefs to Washington intercepted him with a plea not to bring in White Bear and Big Tree wearing those ugly double irons—and, in fact, to remain completely out of sight for a while. The commissioners wanted to prepare their Indian guests for the meeting—especially for the word that the two Kiowas would not be accompanying them to Washington and, further, would not be freed. They still trembled over what the Indian reaction might be.

For one more night the responsibility of guarding White Bear and Big Tree fell to Lieutenant Carter. He remembered it more than half a century later. "It proved to be a most bitter . . . night . . . with no tents and the two prisoners short of blankets for such weather. . . . The loud grunts—'ug-gh-h-s'—of [White Bear] sounded . . . on the . . . frosty . . . air. . . . We lay curled up and huddled until daybreak."

Then Carter, acting under further orders just received, put the chiefs on a train bound for St. Louis. The other chiefs had been spirited away earlier by the commissioners, bound for the same destination. In the Missouri city White Bear and Big Tree enjoyed a brief, happy reunion with the other tribal leaders before the two convicts were returned to the state penitentiary at Huntsville, and the other chiefs went to Washington, where they were feted and shown white power. During their visit they met the Commissioner of Indian Affairs, who blundered into promising unrestricted release of White Bear and Big Tree provided the Indians would stop all raiding. Since the Kiowa chiefs were prisoners of the state of Texas, a federal commissioner had no authority to make such a promise, but Washington pressure later exerted on the Texas governor eventually enabled fulfillment during the following year, 1873.

Still the raids in Texas did not slacken after the goodwill gesture. They multiplied. Once more Colonel Mackenzie would be forced to lead troopers out to subdue or destroy.

His former adjutant, Lieutenant Carter, would serve on the Texas frontier a while longer, but Carter's old injury sustained during the Blanco Canyon fight never ceased to pain him. The leg damage resulted in varicose veins, an ailment that surgery could not then correct, and eventually in Carter's release from duty as "permanently disqualified," on June 28, 1876.

But the Army would hear from Carter again one day—and in years ahead the Lieutenant would have occasion to be reminded at least once more of his two old enemies, White Bear and the halfbreed Comanche chief, Quanah.

176

17

A DAKOTA BLIZZARD

Rumors of gold existing in those Black Hills so sacred to Sioux Indians resulted in army orders for George Armstrong Custer to return to frontier duty with his 7th Cavalry. Custer would investigate the rumors and would seek to police the area, supposedly protecting whites and Indians from each other.

Custer's regiment had been split after its removal from Kansas to Kentucky several years earlier, and it had inherited some disagreeable duties. The primary responsibility of several detachments sent farthest south was to suppress Ku Klux Klan activities. Other units concentrated on searching southern mountains for "illicit distilleries"—bootleggers' stills. The General himself had escaped much close work with either inglorious activity. He and his wife had resided in the quiet village of Elizabethtown, Kentucky, where Custer maintained a relatively pleasant headquarters and devoted much of his time to writing about earlier experiences.

Young Mrs. Custer, thirty-one now, probably enjoyed the interlude more than did her restless husband, especially after the first few blissful months. The Indians that once had made Kentucky a "dark and bloody ground" had vanished westward into the area that the Custers had only recently left, and Libbie Custer would have been elated (even if she had hidden her feeling from her husband) that the General was not expected to risk his life daily by saddling up and leading troops against Cheyennes or Arapahos or Comanches or Kiowas.

But when orders arrived in early spring of 1873, Custer—always a boy on such exciting occasions—bubbled with ecstasy. Libbie had learned to let his enthusiasm boil over before it could cool sufficiently to allow rational planning for the move. She knew from experience what to expect.

Custer would celebrate first by smashing a chair to pieces and throwing the debris into the kitchen—to inform the Negro cook of the arrival of good news. Libbie would be watching him from a safe position atop a table or desk, having retreated there earlier. "We had so few household effects," she said once, "that it was something of a loss when we chanced to be in a country where they could not be replaced."

Her safe position would be secure for only a short time. After Custer had finished with the chair he would grab Libbie and toss her around the room, laughing, yelling, and joking. Eventually calm would return to the household, but not before the cook would have reproved Custer with great disgust: "Chairs don't grow on trees in these yere parts, Gen'l."

After this latest explosion Libbie took the family atlas to a quiet corner and examined their destination. Her finger traced a route from Kentucky almost up to the Canadian border.

She and her husband began packing. Within an hour their quarters appeared storm-struck—partly from Custer's joyful rampage, but mostly because the Custers and their cook already had commenced gathering up possessions. Army life had brought proficiency to the chore. Even Libbie said it was "short work to move."

Troopers would bring in from the stables a supply of gunnysacks and hay. The Custers would secure all the "old traps" for transferral. Kitchen utensils went into barrels. Bedding and rugs were rolled and wrapped in waterproof canvas, then tied with rope for easy handling. Pictures and books went into chests and boxes. Troopers loaded all these possessions on a wagon and put the cook's things on top: a roll of bedding and a few personal possessions tied up in a fiery red quilt. Before leaving, the cook would make a methodical final search, examining now empty rooms for small articles left behind. These she would put in a bag improvised from a bandana, ignoring an empty satchel that she carried around for some purpose unknown.

Then they were ready. Custer never cared to linger on such an occasion as this, and Libbie had a reason for hurrying, too: "Had I dared to stop . . . that hurried day and think of myself all the courage would have gone out of me. This removal to Dakota meant to my husband a reunion with his regiment and summer campaigns against Indians; to me it meant months of loneliness, anxiety, and terror."

The regiment assembled at Memphis, where old friends met and talked for the first time in many months. Then they embarked for Cairo, Illinois, on three steamboats that also carried horses, luggage, supplies, and ordnance up the wide Mississippi.

At Cairo the regiment transferred to trains for a slow trip into Dakota—more than a week en route, with frequent stops to water and to exercise the horses. The railroad then had been built as far west as Yankton, located on the Missouri River in the southeastern corner of present South Dakota. On a sunny morning in mid-April 1873 trains carrying the 7th Cavalry chugged across the last few miles of finished track and ground to a halt on a mostly open plain about one mile from the town. Only a few frame cabins could be seen in the vicinity.

Soon the plain swarmed with troopers and horses. Piles of equipment unloaded alongside freight cars mounted and multiplied. Libbie Custer was "helped down from the Pullman car, where inlaid woods, mirrors, and plush surrounded us, to the ground, perfectly bare of earthly comfort." Other officers' wives went on into Yankton, where rooms in a frontier hotel awaited them. The General urged his wife to go, too, but Libbie chose as usual to stay with her husband, who alone could give her any comfort in these unpleasant surroundings. Further, he had been unwell lately, and she probably wanted to look after him.

When Libbie left the train she watched as her household goods were unloaded and assembled inside a sort of stockade made of trunks and chests. With that completed, she waited. Her husband and some enlisted men from headquarters company had left to supervise erection of the main camp, and Libbie could do nothing more until the General returned.

She sat on a chest and observed a blanket of clouds smother the sun. A chill in the air quickly followed, and a light sprinkle began to fall. The increasing cold this time of year surprised her after living in a more southerly latitude.

As the weather worsened she looked with envy at a partly finished, two-story frame hut standing empty some distance from the railroad. Experience on the Plains had shown her the fragility of an army tent during high wind, and the vacant shack looked substantial. While Custer continued to supervise camp layout Libbie (planning for herself for once, as she said) sought the aid of some "kind-hearted soldiers" in locating the shack's owner.

They found the man in another cabin nearby. With Custer's approval Libbie rented the cabin, which had begun to look more and more like a palace to her. "There was no plastering, and the house seemed hardly weatherproof. It had a floor, however, and an upper story divided off by beams; over these [the cook] Mary and I stretched blankets and shawls and so made two rooms."

On this trip the Custers also had brought a manservant, Ham, and he helped to transfer the household belongings into the cabin. After wood and water had been brought in the place seemed ready to be lived in—except for the absence of a stove. Libbie sent Mary, with money, the mile into Yankton to buy a small cookstove. Mary found one there, but could not persuade the merchant to make his delivery until the following morning; so she bought a few staples and returned while a young snowstorm blew.

Libbie had seen the falling snow and had begun to worry about her absent cook; but another anxiety also troubled her. Custer had returned from work around camp "exhausted and very ill." She put him in bed upstairs under sheets and blankets, then sent for the regimental surgeon, who brought medicine and a suggestion that the General stay where Libbie had put him. By that time—and as Mary returned—darkness had begun to obscure the dismal landscape, and the advance fringes of a genuine Dakota blizzard had struck. Weather thickened quickly.

> The snow was so fine [Libbie said] that it penetrated the smallest cracks, and soon we found white lines appearing all around us, where the roof joined the walls, on the windows

and under the doors. Outside the air was so thick with the whirling, tiny particles that it was almost impossible to see one's hand held out. . . . The snow was fluffy . . . like wool, and fell so rapidly, and seemingly from all directions, that it gave me a feeling of suffocation as I stood outside. Mary was not easily discouraged, and piling a few . . . faggots outside the door, she tried to light a fire. The wind and the muffling snow put out every little blaze that started, however, and so, giving it up, she went into the house and found the luncheon basket we had brought from the car, in which remained some sandwiches, and these composed our supper.

Custer's adjutant appeared at the door for orders. Concern for the horses and a lack of fuel moved the General to tell his aide that camp must be broken at once. Troopers were to take their horses into town and seek shelter anywhere—in homes, sheds, stables. Officers should try the hotel.

Libbie heard countless snow-muffled hoofbeats drum past their cold cabin; then silence returned. The once-bustling camp lay nearly deserted—only the laundresses and a few officers and enlisted men remained—and the blackness of a wintry Dakota evening engulfed them like the dark waters of a night flood. Only the faint flickers of a candle placed near one window provided any light at all —and that faded into darkness before reaching far corners of the house.

In town (as the Custers would learn later) citizens provided havens for chilled and weary men and their animals, but on the deserted prairie scant comfort was available. The wind moaned, howled, and then shrieked as it pounded the cabin with increasing power. The little house rocked and groaned in the storm and seemed to Libbie on the verge of losing its roof or of capsizing like a boat caught in tempestuous seas.

She had changed into her heaviest nightgown, then had put on a jacket over that, and had gone to bed beside her husband under a heavy pile of blankets. But still she shivered, and snow continued to sift in. Occasionally she rose to shake small, icy drifts off the "counterpain"—bedspread—where snow collected after gaining windy entrance into the room between roof and clapboards. In the down-

181

stairs room Mary and Ham barricaded the door and sought to stuff all cracks that allowed freezing drafts to penetrate.

Despite the extreme discomfort Libbie never let her thoughts stray for long from the health of her husband, who lay silently beside her, too ill to talk. Ordinarily the mere sound of his voice would give her confidence, but now she was acting entirely on her own, and what she did might mean life or death to him and to others, too. The surgeon had said before leaving that he would return soon, but his reappearance on a night like this, Libbie knew, was impossible. She might as well have been on an island in a river, or even in some distant ocean, as in a cabin only one mile from Yankton.

Libbie guessed at the importance of the medicine the surgeon had left. The doctor's serious mien had indicated to her that the continuity of her husband's life depended on the regularity with which the dosage was given. "I hardly dared take the little phial in my benumbed fingers to [administer] the precious medicine," she said, "for fear it would fall." Between those dosages and the shakings of the counterpane she would wriggle back under the weight of all that cold bedding and wonder if the ordeal would ever end.

She was lying sleepless in bed when a rumbling noise from below startled her. She leaped from the covers, dashed down the stairs, and saw Mary and Ham prying open the frozen front door to admit half a dozen soldiers who had become lost while en route to town. The weak flickers of that dim light in the window had brought them (and, later, several others) to the cabin, but not to much comfort. Libbie desperately thought over alternatives, but could offer no warmth—no fire, not even whiskey, which the Custers did not use or have.

Then she remembered the rugs, still rolled up and tied. They had been stacked in a corner of the cabin. She opened them and counted out enough to go around. The servants helped her to spread the coverings on the cold floor and to roll each frozen man in a mat of his own.

Still the soldiers suffered. Their groans and haggard faces put her in agony. Worse, she saw "symptoms of that deadly stupor [that] is the sure precursor of freezing."

She remembered another possible aid: a jar of alcohol brought along to fuel the "spirit lamps." She knew men could drink the stuff without harm, and it might help them. Despite the objections of Mary, who wanted to save the alcohol as the only way of brewing coffee or other hot drinks or heating food when morning came, Libbie divided it among her freezing guests, and she saw them revive somewhat "under the influence of the fiery liquid."*

The hour of dawn brought no brilliant sunrise—only a glimmer like twilight as wind-whipped snow continued to fall. Glances outside showed that huge drifts had piled up against three sides of the house. Libbie's terror did not subside. She realized that they were as helpless, as desolate, and as isolated as ever. "The long hours dragged themselves away, leaving the General too weak to rise, and in great need of hot, nourishing food."

Night came again, and with it even colder temperatures. Libbie believed they would all die. The cook seemed beyond caring. She had given out and now lay sleeping in a corner of the room.

Lying again in bed upstairs, Libbie cleared a spot on the frozen windowpane, peered out, and saw that the drifts had reached nearly to the level of the window itself. Only the front door remained clear. Wind had swept snow away there.

For Libbie the horror of the second night actually exceeded the first, partly because of the plight of some animals caught outside. She first became aware of their presence when she heard over the storm's roar "the tramping of many feet."

A great drove of mules rushed up to the sheltered side of the house. Their brays had a sound of terror as they pushed, kicked, and crowded themselves against our little cabin. For a time they huddled together, hoping for warmth, and then despairing, they made a mad rush away, and were soon lost in the white wall of snow beyond.

All night long the neigh of a distressed horse, almost human in its appeal, came to us at intervals. The door was pried open once [with the thought that] it might be some suffering [human being] in distress. The strange, wild eyes of the horse peering in for help haunted me long afterwards.

Occasionally a lost dog lifted up a howl . . . under our win-

* Later, however, some soldiers lost feet or fingers to amputations.

dow, but before the door could be opened to admit him he had disappeared in the darkness.

When the night was nearly spent I sprang again to the window with a new horror. . . . A drove of hogs, squealing and grunting, were pushing against the house, and the door [that] had withstood so much had to be held to keep it from being broken in.

Sounds inside were no more bearable: groans from men whose swollen feet pained them more and more. Finally, however, Libbie fell asleep, from sheer exhaustion. When she awoke she saw Mary standing over their bed holding a tray of hot food. The cook, though still complaining about the vanished alcohol, had improvised a stove from a number of large candles found among the luggage. She had arranged them to make a fire hot enough to fry bits of steak and small slices of potatoes. Libbie was delighted soon after that to see that the meal and its warmth revived her husband somewhat. Strength began to return to him.

All this heralded better fortune outside the house, too. That same morning the snow stopped falling; then help came to them from Yankton.

18

STRONGER MEDICINE

In Texas, the release of White Bear and Big Tree still had brought no peace to that long-troubled frontier. The treaty agreed to at Medicine Lodge had proved to be about as worthless as any other scrap of paper. White men and women of good intent and honesty had reason to complain, but that was true also of victimized Indians. During the years 1873–76 groups of white outlaws dressed like Indians sometimes attacked settlements for plunder. A few raiders died of the ensuing gunfire, and their impersonations were thus revealed. In 1874 white-skinned thieves stole an estimated two thousand horses from the Kiowa-Comanche reservation in the Indian Territory. Some of those culprits boasted of their deeds, or at least excused them, by declaring they were only retrieving animals previously stolen in Texas.

But the Indians' greatest grievance lay in the increasingly swift disappearance of buffalo. During a two-year period, 1872–74, nearly four million of those animals were killed in the West. Of that total the Indians (who wasted no part of any carcass) accounted for only 150,000 head. White hunters killed all the rest, for sport or for skins that could bring three dollars each on the current market, and they left each rotting carcass to add more stench to fouled Plains air.

The slaughter reached such heights that concerned Texas legislators contemplated halting it by a law that, if passed, might have prevented the near-extinction of those animals, but General Sherman persuaded them against it. Extermination of the buffalo—thus eliminating food and clothing supply—had become a war necessity, Sherman said, and it would be the "only way to bring lasting peace and allow civilization to advance."

Even the other major Indian complaint, railroad extension, became secondary to their bitterness over the buffalo slaughter, although rails actually helped to contribute to the waste. In addition to altering those animals' ranging habits, the tracks abetted their destruction by providing transportation of skins eastward to markets. Some freight trains originating in the West carried no other cargo than buffalo skins, and in one year alone, 1874, the Santa Fe Railroad transported an estimated 750,000 hides.

So the Indians who had been promised at Medicine Lodge hunting privileges south of the Arkansas River for "so long as the buffalo may range" observed the swift disappearance with alarm and anger. They knew who was responsible—those white hunters—and they determined to do some exterminating of their own. This feeling was not limited to the still-free groups like Quanah's roaming Quohadas. It included also reservation Comanches—and Kiowas, Arapahos, and Southern Cheyennes.

War against buffalo hunters was first proposed in Quanah's band, apparently by a medicine man whose Indian name, Isatai, has been rendered into English as "Rear End of a Wolf" by some, as "Coyote Droppings" by others, and "Little Wolf" by still others.

Clever as a wolf Isatai was. He had lost an uncle to soldiers' gunfire, and now he apparently determined to have revenge, using other Indians for his purpose. He urged Quohadas to make war against white men responsible for killing the buffalo, and he convinced them that his medicine would provide protection in battle. Buffalo would return in glorious numbers, Isatai said, and Indian life would revert to the old ways.

Quanah believed in Isatai's magic, and he wanted to enlist it in exterminating those hunters before they killed off all the buffalo. At a sun dance held in what is now southwestern Oklahoma, at the location where Elk Creek flows into the North Fork of the Red River, Quanah and Isatai planned their campaign as warm spring days of 1874 approached the sizzle of summer heat.

Comanches had never given a sun dance before. Now they welcomed as guests the Kiowas—old sun dancers themselves—along with some Arapahos and Cheyennes angered by recent losses of horses to white thieves. Some chiefs, like the Kiowan Kicking Bird, had foreseen the trouble that would ensue from all this Quohada conniving and refused to bring their people to the sun dance. Other leaders who came realized the intent of Quanah and Isatai, and they tried to leave, sharing Kicking Bird's opinion that more war could only go against Indians, but persuasion and pressure kept them there.

Quanah and his magical colleague agreed on specifics. The Comanches knew that a party of buffalo hunters was working out of a camp erected near Adobe Walls, the name for ruins of an old trading post built in 1843 by William Bent on the South Canadian River in the present Texas Panhandle county of Hutchinson. This buffalo camp—some 130 miles northwest of where the sun dance was being held—would be the first target of the warriors, who numbered seven hundred. (Coincidentally, they would be fighting near the site of an earlier battle, in 1864, in which Colonel Kit Carson, leading a force of four hundred soldiers and Indian scouts against Comanche and Kiowa winter quarters, used Bent's old adobe ruins as a defensive position against several thousand aroused Indians before finally withdrawing.) After ridding the land of these hunters, the Indians decided, they would then ride northward, before word of the attack could be relayed elsewhere, and destroy other camps.

Summer had truly begun baking the Southwest when Quanah and Isatai and their warriors rode northwestward toward the place on the Canadian River known as Adobe Walls. Isatai reassured them all. "Those white men can't shoot you," he declared. "With my medicine I will stop all their guns. . . . You will wipe them all out."

Quanah listened and believed. It was right. The treaties those white men had enticed other tribes to sign, Quanah knew, had assured Indians use of the buffalo in exchange for many other privileges given up. Quanah, although half white himself and knowing it, never believed in the good intent of those hated intruders, and now their dishonesty had been proved by men who slaughtered buffalo by the thousands simply to get skins for coats to be worn by faraway people who had a choice of other equally warm material for winter apparel. If the Great Father would not see to it that promises were kept the Indians would do it for him.

In early-morning darkness of June 27 seven hundred warriors quietly approached the hunters' camp. They halted a mile or so away and waited. Young Chief Quanah whispered to eager men some final words that they all hoped would result in a slaughter at sunrise of sleeping buffalo killers. The charge would come at that time.

Isatai, painted yellow for the sun and mounted on a white horse, ascended a hill and prepared to watch his prophecies unfold from a distance.

Present in the hunters' camp was the same West Virginian who, as a boy, had seen and described White Bear before the Medicine Lodge Peace Council seven years earlier and who had recorded his recollections of the awesome sight of mounted and armed Cheyennes racing toward the council site, terrifying everybody before they eventually showed their peacefulness.

Billy Dixon—that was his name—recalled later that the evening of June 26 in the hunters' camp had been sultry and that stars had glimmered from a cloudless night sky upon the crude village, which centered on three rough adobe buildings erected with low overhead and high dollar-earning in mind: two mercantile stores and a saloon, separated from each other by distances of up to fifty yards. Eight or nine men made up the permanent population of this outpost of civilization, but on the evening of the twenty-sixth, twenty-nine persons were present—including one woman who had come to open a restaurant in the rear of one of the stores.

The people were sheltered in or near the three buildings. Doors lay open because of the heat; any puff of air could bring some relief. For a while Billy Dixon watched the drinkers frolicking in their frontier way at the saloon, run by a man named Jim Hanrahan. In their hilarity the happy men ignored a hazard of the place: the weight of the heavy earthen roof was sustained only by a large cottonwood ridgepole braced underneath.

Dixon headed for a bed under the stars. He spread blankets on ground near his wagon, which had been brought to a stop near a small blacksmith's shop. Carefully he placed his powerful 50-caliber Sharps rifle within easy reach between two blankets, to protect the weapon from possible dew. Then he lay down.

Before he slept he heard familiar, peaceful sounds: stock somewhere in the vicinity "moving and stumbling around"; his saddle horse, retrieved earlier that night from Adobe Walls Creek and now tethered nearby, "shaking himself" as he paused in his search for young grass; owls hooting in the darkness along the creek, which lay some distance to the east. He saw flickering lights around camp wink a final time and go out, one by one, until the place lay in darkness. Dixon fell asleep.

About two o'clock a loud snap like that of a distant rifle shot startled sleepers. The ridgepole holding up the earthen saloon roof had cracked, as Dixon soon learned. Two men asleep in the building leaped from their beds, saw the danger, and roused others to help them repair the support before the roof fell in. The noise of this labor awakened every last sleeper in Adobe Walls while, some distance away, Quanah was whispering those final words to his warriors.

Like everyone else, Dixon investigated the disturbance. By the time repair work had been completed a predawn glow had begun illuminating camp. Some men crawled back into their covers, however, while others went after their horses to prepare for another day's hunt. Dixon rolled up his blankets and tossed the soft bundle into his wagon; a young man in this country could enjoy very little sleep if he meant to compete. He turned then to pick up his rifle, still lying on the ground, and at the same time he happened to glance at a distant tree grove. Near it the hunters had left the bulk of their horses, in a close herd.

Dixon saw the horses and, farther on, at the edge of the wood, other objects not immediately identifiable to him in the morning light. He squinted and stared, but for a few more seconds he could not make out the odd sight. It appeared to him to be a dark blob in motion, moving slowly toward the horses. Entranced, he forgot about the rifle momentarily.

Then he felt thunderstruck. "The black body of moving objects suddenly spread out like a fan and gave out a single, solid yell." The long war whoop seemed to Dixon to "shake the very air of early morning," and he heard a distant rumble of galloping horses. A thought flashed through his mind: the Indians were aiming to take the stock, not to attack the camp.

Acting more in accord with mechanical reflex than conscious reflection (as Dixon realized later), he sought first to save his saddle horse—one of his two most precious possessions (next to life itself) on these vast Plains. By this time the horse had become frightened and was tugging furiously on his rope, but Dixon managed to secure it to the wagon with a firmer hold that would prevent the animal's escape. Then he reached for the second precious possession, his rifle, and fired a quick shot at the Indians "before [they] could run away." The rifle report performed double duty, serving also to warn every person in camp of danger. (Some persons later reported hearing also a series of bugle calls coming from the Indians' direction.)

Dixon saw immediately that the warriors were not attempting to flee after stealing stock. They were instead bound directly for him and for the camp. He could see—or imagined he could see—Indians and horses painted in a variety of wild colors, with red and ocher predominating. On they came, shielded in part by the radiance now of a blinding sunrise behind them.

He fired another shot and ran for the nearest building—Jim Hanrahan's saloon. He found the door already barred, but a shouted entreaty gave him quick entrance.

Soon afterward the Indians had this building and the others surrounded. Inside, besieged men—some barefoot and dressed only in undershirts and drawers—commenced firing at their attackers, who rode recklessly up to the very doors and sought to smash an entrance with gun butts and clubs. Quanah was one of these intrepid warriors, but no one inside recognized him.

Dixon still had time for a brief moment of meditation. Except for the cracked ridgepole, he mused, he and everyone else at Adobe Walls probably would have been asleep when the charge came.

Before the attack had commenced and before Isatai had gone to his vantage point on the hill he had added another prophecy to his earlier declaration, "You will wipe them all out." He had told the warriors that all white men in camp would be found asleep and could be killed with clubs.

After that Quanah had led the charge that Dixon had noticed accidentally. While still some distance away the Indians had come upon two hunters who had been sleeping under the heavens in comfortable isolation and had killed them as the surprised pair were trying to escape in a wagon. Then the Indians had ridden on, aiming for further vengeance and leaving puffballs of Texas dust billowing behind them (as Quanah remembered later).

During their charge they encountered an area pocked with holes left by prairie dogs. Some ponies tripped and tumbled, tossing their whooping riders earthward, but the surge continued.

Quanah, bolstered by Isatai's prophecies, took his men into the heart of camp instead of relying on the usual Indian tactic of circling. Once there they sought to smash in doors and windows to get at the occupants Isatai had said could be clubbed to death. But these enemies were wide awake and shooting not only energetically but accurately, Quanah found.

He and another Comanche scrambled atop one adobe building and tried to poke holes through the roof, in order to fire into the men below. They failed. Elsewhere, other raiders realized that their enemy possessed more powerful and accurate rifles—heavy, large-bore weapons made especially for killing buffalo. Still, they hoped that the hunters might soon use up all their ammunition in excited defense.

Instead, the hunters' fire dropped several attackers and forced the others to retire temporarily. The Indians retreated, reorganized, and charged again—several times.

During one attack Quanah heard a bullet plop into the flesh of his horse. The animal staggered and fell, throwing its rider. Quanah struck the ground heavily, but he ran for cover just as another shot creased his shoulder, giving him a vicious blow. He slithered through weeds into a brush thicket nearby, out of action temporarily. Later a mounted warrior dashed up and rescued him. Quanah fled the scene gladly, if ignominiously—riding double on a pony and probably thinking bad thoughts about the prophecies of that supposed all-wise medicine man.

Inside the saloon Dixon and several other hunters (including young Bat Masterson, who would later enter legend as a United States marshal) had been shooting so constantly that their ammunition was running low. Replenishment was becoming essential, but that would mean risking death in a dash to one of the two stores nearby. For a while they put it off.

All morning long the men in the saloon had been amazed to hear more bugle calls directing Indian movements—though not very precisely, because the attack had been poorly coordinated and had relied largely on individual effort, as was typical of Indian warfare. Two of the hunters, army veterans, realized that the calls were the same as those used in United States military service, and they were able to warn others in the saloon of what impended.

Those tense morning hours had contributed further to Dixon's practical education. Although still a young man (not yet twenty-five) his risks in the West already had far exceeded those of most men during a lifetime. This fight had made him remember once more that "to be nervous or fearful of death is no sign of weakness; staying and doing is what counts"—a comment also made by many professional soldiers of renown, then and later.* At the height of the morning attacks—while Indians repeatedly charged the three buildings, shooting into windows and trying to smash doors—Dixon had returned the fire steadily, along with his companions, and had silently thanked whatever sustainer it was who looked after wayward West Virginians for putting him and all the others behind thick sod walls rather than in frame buildings, which would not have provided protection against such a shower of missiles. After a lengthy period devoted to shooting back at Indians who galloped past the saloon with remarkable impunity he noticed that his mouth had become "dry"—his saliva felt almost like glue as a result of the excitement—and the thought plagued him that if he fell in this fight his death would likely be one of torture, unless he were instantly killed.

Outside, an Indian occasionally fell wounded or dead—victim of those shattering buffalo rifles—but other warriors usually dashed to make a rescue or to retrieve the body, sometimes galloping up to

* World War II General George Patton, for one.

the saloon walls. Inside, a crow that must have flown through a broken window called out, "Caw! Caw! Caw!" between thunderclaps of rifle fire. The miserable bird seemed like an omen of death; so during a lull someone chased it out.

By noon the furious charges had slackened and ceased. After a delay to ascertain the Indians' intentions Dixon and Jim Hanrahan, still holding their rifles, flung the saloon door open and sprinted for the nearest store—one owned by a man named Charles Rath—to get more ammunition. Dixon recalled later that a fusillade from the distant, hidden enemy sent a shower of bullets "like hail" toward them and the door of Rath's store; those clever aborigines had guessed immediately where the two men were headed and for what purpose. (Some other hunters later remembered no shots, but they had not been under fire.)

Amazingly, Dixon and Hanrahan made it unscathed, even though the men in Rath's store were slow to open the door. Later Hanrahan ran back to his saloon with the ammunition, but Dixon stayed behind.

Quanah had recalled his warriors from the intermittent attacks. Fifteen of his men had been killed and many more wounded by those rifles. He determined now to starve out the enemy and to keep his men out of further reach of the hunters' deadly weapons, but within sight of the camp. Meanwhile, the Indians continued to send forth sporadic fire for a time.

Soon after the lack of success had become evident angry warriors confronted Isatai, the medicine man. A Cheyenne lashed him with a quirt, and others prepared to join in the whipping when Quanah stopped them all. Isatai's embarrassment was punishment enough, Quanah said—but the shaman himself blamed the fiasco on a broken taboo. Quanah apparently did not believe the alibi (whether or not other Indians did), because he never again would trust a medicine man.

More than half a century later a Comanche participant described the attack on Adobe Walls and how the surprised warriors fared that morning. "The buffalo hunters were too much for us. They had telescopes on their guns. Sometimes we would be standing 'way off, resting and hardly thinking of the fight, and they would kill our horses."

Such success did not appear so immediately obvious to the hunters surrounded in their camp. They could see most of their own horses lying dead—Dixon's among them, still roped to the wagon—and they knew they could only stay and hope to survive by fighting. Three of their number had been killed—the two men who had sought to escape in the wagon and another man slain during one of the morning charges. (A fourth, husband of the only white woman present, later would lose his life when his rifle discharged accidentally.)

That evening the hunters ventured out of their adobe buildings, found they drew no fire, cautiously buried their dead, then retreated inside again. During the night no noise disturbed the unusual silence—but no one slept soundly. When Dixon did sleep, he dreamed bloody scenes. When he awoke, he realized with what must have been alarm that somewhere in the distance many pairs of Indian eyes were squinting to survey the vicinity of the darkened camp.

By morning the stench from dead horses and Indians still lying where they had fallen had become overpowering. Men risked the outdoors again and, finding it safe, cautiously began digging holes for dumping the nauseating remains of battle. Pulling a dead horse required the combined muscle of three or four hunters, but, in addition to helping rid the air of an awful stench, it gave them something to do. Still the Indians stayed out of reach of the deadly buffalo rifles, with the exception of a group of horsemen who appeared briefly on a bluff to eastward.

Hunters seized their weapons and fired. The warriors sent back a few desultory shots, then vanished.

Later that day a hunter previously unaware of the Indian attack and siege came racing into camp with two wagon teams, having somehow eluded warriors who surprised him. The animals he brought sparked hope that a man might use darkness to ride out and summon help.

That night Henry Lease took a horse and disappeared into the black gloom—bound northeastward for Dodge City, almost two hundred miles away. No one (including Dixon) expected to see him again. Two other men also sneaked out, hoping to reach other hunting camps nearby with calls for assistance.

Another grim morning dawned. Soon after that more mounted Indians reappeared—a mile away, at the edge of a high mesa east of the creek. Without much hope, considering the range, Dixon seized his Sharps rifle, aimed at one rider, and squeezed the trigger. He was astounded to see the warrior fall from his horse. Other Indians nearby fled behind a clump of trees; then two of them, on foot, dashed out and pulled their fallen companion to safety.

Later Dixon measured the exact distance of his hit: 1,538 yards.

Dixon's amazing shot showed the besiegers which side truly possessed the stronger medicine. Isatai, already despised, became mostly a joke. If any one bullet did more than others to end the southwestern buffalo war it was the one fired from Dixon's rifle—and nearly spent when it hit and stunned its victim.

Quanah gave up the siege and led his warriors away from Adobe Walls. He and the Quohadas vanished onto the Staked Plain, where they held out for a while longer. Within five days of the initial attack a hundred hunters summoned by Henry Lease and the other two men who had risked their lives to go for help had gathered at Adobe Walls. There they found only dwindling numbers of buffalo to kill.

Fighting had not ended permanently. Sporadic raids on hunters and settlers continued for a time, but the Army, following its new tactic of sending large numbers of troopers deep into Indian refuges to attack there, dispatched four strong columns onto the Staked Plain to end all resistance. In September 1874 Colonel Mackenzie (leader of one column) defeated Indians at Palo Duro Canyon in the Texas Panhandle, shot three thousand captured ponies, and made the area generally safe for white settlement. His success also ended conclusively an illicit activity known as the Comanchero trade (conducted between New Mexicans and Plains Indians), which not only had supplied Comanches and other tribes with alcohol and firearms and other flammables, but also had resulted in such desecrations as the sale of captives into slavery and prostitution.

By the mid-1870's the advancing frontier had overtaken Southern Plains Indians in their farthest retreats, and in June 1875 Quanah led onto the Fort Sill reservation his band of holdout Quohadas, who were hungry, sick, discouraged, and frightened.

Quanah had realized the impossibility of continuing to live his free-ranging life. The only hope for his people's survival on the face of this earth they once called their own, he saw, lay in submission to white demands that they live peacefully on a reservation.

Dixon's lengthy shot at Adobe Walls and Mackenzie's follow-through in force at Palo Duro Canyon cleared the way for establishment in 1876 of the first cattle ranch in the Texas Panhandle—the J A, founded by Charles Goodnight, who excelled in turning into a personal fortune lands that once had provided life's necessities for many individuals. That was the most important result of the 1874 fighting.

Another consequence was the return of White Bear to the Texas penitentiary.

Reports of bugle calls directing those Indian attackers at Adobe Walls inevitably cast suspicion on him. Probably he was present, as angry Texans claimed, although he did none of the bugle blowing. Either a Negro army deserter or a Mexican did that, according to subsequent accounts. Further, White Bear did none of the leading; Quanah did. If White Bear was there it would have been largely in the capacity of eager onlooker; but—to continue the argument—Quakers at the Fort Sill agency declared he could not have been present, because they had seen him around Sill at the time. Everyone believed the Quakers were continually alibiing for their charges, however, and few persons paid much attention to them.

Three days after his latest surrender—in October 1874—White Bear was on his way back to prison in South Texas, and his free days, like Quanah's, had truly come to an end.

19

INEXORABILITY

No white settlers had wanted any part of the Texas Panhandle until they had examined it carefully and had realized its ranching potential; then Charles Goodnight and other cattle kings moved in quickly. That followed the old pattern of take-over. Similarly, white settlers had shown scant interest in the forbidding Black Hills much farther north. Those mountains had seemed useless, and for that reason they had been left by treaty to Indians.

The locality meant much more to Sioux who knew it. Beginning in present northeastern Wyoming and extending into western South Dakota, a total length of one hundred miles, the Black Hills abruptly sent rocky, craggy heights soaring above a surrounding semiarid plain. Sufficient amounts of rain fell in this mountainous area to form a sort of oasis. Deep forests of dark green contrasted with barren backgrounds of sandstone, shale, and limestone. Tumbling streams ran pure and cold. Of greater importance to the Sioux, however, was the sacredness of these mountains.

Rumors of gold had brought white prospectors poking around the vicinity, disturbing gods and most of all the Sioux. General Custer, ordered out with his 7th Cavalry to guard railroad builders and, incidentally, to ascertain the truth of the gold rumors, trod over the holy hills and sent back an emphatic "yes" in 1874, thus starting new races for personal fortunes. The United States Government, realizing that another treaty was on the verge of being trampled underfoot by restless citizens, sought to slow the rampage

197

until it could buy the six-thousand-square-mile Black Hills area, for $6 million. A few tribes willing to sell thought $30 million a more appropriate asking price, but still others argued that no sum could compensate for land inhabited by gods. Indians previously pacified left reservations and prepared to fight, along with others who had never really come in.

But there was another reason for the mass departure. An extraordinarily hard winter had brought the specter of starvation to Sioux country, where no winter ever could be called easy. Bitter cold made hunting less productive, and increased rations became necessary to save reservation Indians from dying of hunger. As usual, however, Washington walked on slow bureaucratic feet, and a supplemental appropriation was not to be voted until the following spring. Meanwhile, some of the helpless red people indeed starved to death.

Others determined to help themselves. They left reservations for unceded lands, where game in more plentiful quantity could be found. Some sympathetic agents gave approval.

This move conflicted with military plans. Despite governmental failure to buy the Black Hills, the Army had decided on a way to protect white citizens flocking to the area of the gold strike—which was, after all, an army responsibility, and sometimes a more diligently pursued one than another duty: protection of Indians.

The Army had laid plans for eliminating all "wild" Indians occupying unceded lands as the best way of protecting Black Hills gold seekers from attack. Military officials wanted the Indian Bureau to advise tribes to return to the reservation. Otherwise they would be considered "hostile," for whatever reasons they were absent.

This time the Indian Bureau agreed with the Army. Bureau officials—at least the ones with integrity—had begun to worry about the welfare of those starving wanderers. The Bureau agreed to send an order (on December 6, 1875) to agents saying that any Sioux or Northern Cheyenne off the reservation by the following January 31 would be considered an enemy. Agents were expected to get the word to the Indians.

How they would do this in a remarkably bitter Dakota winter was left up to them. Some agents tried and were successful, but numbers of Indians never heard the warning. Many who did refused to move until spring. Caught in extreme discomfort as the Custers once had been, they felt unable to venture out—and they could not see the importance of it anyway. Why not wait until spring, when travel would be easier?

A small number of Indians who did return before the deadline were immediately disarmed to protect the gold seekers. These law abiders truly placed themselves at the white man's mercy. The last opportunity to hunt for game thus vanished; and they could easily become victims of another massacre—as some of them realized and feared.

On February 7, 1876, General Sheridan received approval to move against all "hostiles." For the campaign the Indian Bureau surrendered to the United States Army jurisdiction over all Sioux and Cheyennes absent from their reservations.

Custer was to have another chance to get his name before the public in a glorious way, and he was ready. Since the Battle of the Washita he had been able to add nothing really exciting to his list of military exploits, although he had been heard from. During this period he had written many articles and a book based on his army experiences, always with wife Libbie sitting nearby. He seemed unable to write without her presence.

Now, with war against the Sioux and the Northern Cheyennes looming, Custer appeared to be destined for new glory, and Libbie for further depression and worry.

Possibly Custer intended to use the opportunity as a lever into politics. As President, for instance, he would possess power that could be used against civil officials and military superiors he had come to despise for one reason or another. Largely because of his juvenile temper the list was lengthy. At the top stood Ulysses Grant, a general whose military renown had won him the highest office in the land—and perhaps had suggested something to Custer himself. Not far below stood Secretary of War W. W. Belknap, who had incurred Custer's wrath by supporting a post trader in a dispute brought on by Custer's charge (apparently correct and proper, this time) that the merchant had overpriced goods offered for sale to soldiers. Many other men of lesser stations were included. If Custer could gain enough influence and power he would fix them all.

Further, he was ready for the exhilaration of another campaign—

not that he had failed to enjoy the much more comfortable other-life existence, but that the restlessness in him always welcomed something new and exciting. After he and Libbie had survived the 1873 blizzard near Yankton, life even on the Plains had been largely routine—or at least without the stimulation that continued open warfare could bring to Custer.

From Yankton that year the Custers had traveled northwestward along the brush-cluttered banks of the Missouri River to Fort Rice, in present North Dakota, where three dismaying events were recorded by Libbie (who, typically, had ridden horseback along with her husband and his soldiers rather than enjoy comforts aboard a steamer that transported other wives, baggage, and supplies).

First, as she described it, they had come upon a warning sign left by the Sioux for their civilized eyes to see: a pole planted firmly in the ground and, atop it, a red flag and locks of hair attached—meaning that the troopers should come no farther or they would meet death dealt by mighty warriors who had remained mostly peaceful in recent years.

Second, after the steamer had arrived at the Fort Rice landing and had unloaded, she discovered that their baggage had been left uncovered on a Yankton wharf, and almost everything inside—wedding dress, uniforms, other clothing, linen—had mildewed and ruined.

Third, and worst of all, she learned that at Fort Rice no quarters were available for her to occupy while her husband and his regiment rode out to guard railroad engineers on the verge of offering another insult to the self-respecting Sioux by surveying a route that would run from Bismarck to the Yellowstone River. She and other officers' wives would have to go home and wait out the long months there, not knowing when a messenger might arrive with an army communication abruptly declaring a loved one nonreturnable as a result of damaged Indian pride. Libbie and the other women were put aboard a steamer, and in her wrath she said, "I hated Dakota, the ugly river, and even my native land." She threw herself on a bunk in her tiny stateroom and sobbed, while other officers' wives sought to comfort her. "Grief is so selfish," she admitted later, but at the time she wallowed in the consolations.

After the 1873 work Custer had rejoined her in Monroe,

Michigan; then they both traveled to Dakota again—to newly built Fort Lincoln, erected farther up the Missouri from Fort Rice around another parade ground marked out on a previously empty plain southwest of Bismarck. In the summer of 1874 Custer had led his 7th Cavalry into those sacred Black Hills under army orders to map and examine them, and thus, with treatment similar to that accorded the Medicine Lodge agreement earlier, he helped to shred the Laramie treaty, which had declared that the Black Hills and other areas of present South Dakota west of the Missouri River be "set apart for the absolute and undisturbed use and occupation of the Indians."

The expedition had departed Fort Lincoln July 2 to the music of "The Girl I Left Behind Me": ten troops of the 7th Cavalry, two companies of infantry, one hundred Indian scouts, and geologists, miners, a photographer, and a zoologist—supplied with a three-inch fieldpiece, three Gatling guns, more than a hundred wagons, and three hundred cattle to provide beef rations. Distant signal smokes began puffing skyward almost as soon as Custer and his men had left the fort, and a few skirmishes later ensued, but expedition members put their footprints all over the sacred area without encountering great interference.

Even the summer of 1875 and a fresh flood of gold seekers had brought little retaliation—such scant notice, in fact, that Custer soon began to tire of his current existence, although he did enjoy reading of the corruption back East attributed to the administration of that army man he considered no good—U. S. Grant. Custer asked for and received a two-month leave, later extended to five months, and traveled to the Atlantic Coast with Libbie to indulge in civilization's comforts. A contract for a series of lectures and a whirl around the exciting New York circuit of restaurants and theaters induced the General to ask for still another extension of three months, but his old enemy, Secretary of War Belknap, refused the request and piled more logs on Custer's inner fire. Soon after that, to the General's glee, a vindictive informant implicated Belknap in a scheme of profit sharing with civilian army-post traders. Belknap, admitting guilt, resigned as Secretary (on March 2, 1876), but Congress moved to impeach him anyway—and Custer, in ecstasy, wrote a letter before he and Libbie returned to Dakota offering to testify.

By that time all Sioux and Northern Cheyennes who had left reservations to hunt, to assemble for Black Hills defense, or for any other purpose had been ordered back by January 31 at the hazard of being considered hostile; and by that time, also, General Sheridan had, on February 7, been given approval to move against the absentees, who were reportedly gathered in the valley of the Big Horn River, a favorite haunt of theirs. Sheridan planned to attack with three large columns—one commanded by General Crook (of Arizona Territory experience), marching northward from Fort Fetterman, Wyoming; another commanded by General John Gibbon, moving eastward from Montana; and a third (which would link up with Gibbon), commanded by General Alfred Terry, who was to work southwestward from Fort Lincoln.

When Custer returned to Fort Lincoln he was elated to find that General Terry had determined to entrust him with the column and the fighting, since Terry himself was no veteran Indian campaigner. But within a week of Custer's return to Dakota came a summons for him to testify at Belknap's impeachment proceedings in Washington. Custer sought to avoid the trip, now that he had new purpose and probably fresh glory within reach. He offered instead to answer questions by mail. Congressional committeemen refused the suggestion. After all, they had a letter from the volatile Custer generously volunteering to present important testimony. So Custer left Fort Lincoln for Washington on March 24, and General Terry determined to wait for him. Congress had in effect set Custer up for demolition by Indians.

In Washington, Custer offered poor testimony, and nothing that, by itself, damaged Belknap very much. In frustration, then, Custer turned on the President himself, voicing some allegations against Grant in regard to Indian profits, but offering no proof and succeeding only in making Grant furious enough to remark that perhaps another officer should lead the Fort Lincoln column against the Sioux. Custer wanted to get back to Dakota immediately, was told to stay in Washington for a while, tried unsuccessfully to call on Grant twice at the White House, finally left for Fort Lincoln on his own, was halted at the Chicago railroad depot by an aide of General Sheridan's acting on orders from General Sherman himself, and received firm orders not to go further. A frantic appeal to Terry (probably the only officer in the Army who wanted anything to do with Custer at this juncture) brought a suggestion: telegraph through channels an appeal to old military man Grant "as a soldier to spare me the humiliation of seeing my regiment march to meet the enemy and I not to share its dangers."

That persuaded Grant, along with some base remarks by newspaper editors who had heard of his refusal to receive Custer at the White House and had turned the slight into a political issue. The President told Chief of Staff Sherman of his approval, and Sherman telegraphed Terry that he could have Custer back if he wanted him. But Sherman, in obvious exasperation, added this suggestion: "Advise Custer to be prudent, not to take along any newspapermen, who always make mischief, and to abstain from personalities in the future."

The Washington misadventure resulted in Custer's loss of column command; he would lead only his regiment. But (as a biographer, Frederic F. Van de Water, stated in *Glory-Hunter*, 1934) Custer told a friend he intended to cut his regiment loose from Terry as soon as he could—and later, when he would indeed do this, he also would have with him a newspaperman, Mark Kellogg. In that operation against Indians Custer seemed to have his mind on the possibility of an entirely different campaign in the future, one that might win him enough votes to enable him to get revenge against those many enemies.

Along with her husband, Libbie Custer had endured all the slights and insults thrown at the General. She had been with him for three years now, excepting summer campaigns and that trip back to Washington for testimony against Belknap.

She had endured physical hardship, too. The trip to Fort Lincoln that March (before Custer received the summons to return to Washington to testify) had been torturous—and possible at all only because railroad officials esteemed Custer after his earlier work of protecting their surveyors. They sought to return favors.

Railroad tracks had been laid from St. Paul, Minnesota, to the vicinity of Fort Lincoln, near Bismarck, but officials did not dare operate trains during the long winters. The first cold locomotive usually chugged out of St. Paul no earlier than April, and even then it risked being turned back by walls of snow.

When the Custers arrived at St. Paul en route to Fort Lincoln, however, railroad executives determined to try to send them through on a special train that would also carry other passengers—a huge undertaking that awed Libbie and no doubt evoked pride that her husband was the reason for all the trouble.

> There were two snow-plows and three enormous engines [Libbie wrote]; freight cars with coal supplies and baggage; several cattle cars, with stock belonging to the Black Hills miners who filled the passenger coaches. There was an eating house looming . . . above everything, built on a flat car. In this car the forty employees of the road, who were taken to shovel snow, etc., were fed. There were several day coaches, with army recruits and a few passengers, and last of all the paymaster's car, which my husband and I occupied. This had a kitchen and a sitting room.

The early miles were comfortable enough in the privacy of their car. A cook regularly served hot meals, well prepared. A small sitting-room stove provided warmth. Sleep came easily, especially with the realization of what a stark contrast lay only a few feet outside the protective car walls.

Farther on across the ice blanket that covered the country, however, luxury waned. "Sometimes we came to drifts, and the train would stop with a violent jerk, start again, and once more come to a standstill, with such force that the dishes would fall from the table."

After that the train crew would bundle up, seize shovels, tumble out, dig the tracks clear while blowing puffs of breath fog into the air, and clamber back aboard, stiff with cold despite the exertion—only to be turned out again for the same routine at the next icy barricade. On one occasion the snowplows and steam engines, all detached from cars and working as a great iron team to ram a clearing through a huge drift, became embedded in snow and ice and had to be shoveled free by groups of men that included army recruits and passenger volunteers. "The impenetrable bank of snow was the accumulation of the whole winter, first snowing, then freezing, until there were successive layers of ice and snow."

After several days Libbie gave up hope of extrication from the predicament, although she did not bare her feelings to anyone. Hours seemed to become as endless as the white wilderness that extended to the horizon. Insistent wind moaned and prowled outside, and occasionally huge gusts rocked the car in which she rode. As the train inched forward between drift stops, food supplies dwindled fearfully. But too many miles for any other kind of travel still separated them from their destination.

Eventually the railroad officials on board for the trip determined to ask for help. Someone found a telegraph unit among stowed equipment, and a man with experience in telegraphy affixed it to the storm-battered main wire running alongside the track. In a short time communication was established with Fort Lincoln, and Tom Custer, the General's officer-brother stationed at that post, sent an inquiry: "Shall I come out for you? You say nothing of the old lady; is she with you?"

Libbie "dared to assume a show of authority" and insisted on answering the message herself. She believed a one-man relief expedition could only end in disaster and wired back a firm "no."

As it developed, Tom Custer came anyway, after hiring the best stage driver in Bismarck to handle a large sleigh. Along the route they used a fresh team of mules kept at an isolated station for use by the mail sleigh.

From subfreezing darkness outside the train a great whoop announced Tom Custer's arrival to those inside, and the General answered with a boyish shout of his own—a family code used since youth.

Tom Custer predicted the arrival of even worse weather, and he wanted to start back at once. The General promised the people staying with the train that he would send help from Bismarck, then he carried his heavily wrapped wife over the snow to the waiting vehicle, straw-packed and already loaded with three hounds brought along on the outbound trip. Libbie made herself as comfortable as possible in the seat, although the dogs growled at her intrusion; then the brothers crowded in after her. The driver yelled at his mule team, passengers cheered, and a terrible journey through moonlight began for Libbie, although she managed to maintain a composed silence.

205

With each plunge "into what appeared to be a bottomless white abyss" she expected to be buried alive. "And so we would have been, I firmly believe, had it not been for the experience . . . [of] the old driver. He had a peculiar yell that he reserved for supreme moments, and that always incited the floundering mules to new efforts. The sleigh was [often] covered, but I could look out in front and see the plucky creatures scrambling up a bank."

Sometimes clouds veiled the moon, extinguishing the dim light thus provided and, meanwhile, sending down more snow. With no trail visible—not even the railroad tracks, which were deeply buried now—they had only the tops of telegraph poles to guide them. Occasionally great drifts made it necessary to leave even that austerity—and for long periods, during which Libbie doubted she would ever sight the markers again. Throughout the journey she remembered the blizzard at Yankton and expected wind and snow to "settle into that driving, blinding, whirling atmosphere through which no eyes can penetrate and no foot progress."

Then the ordeal ended. Lights of Fort Lincoln winked from ahead, promising warmth that quickly applied the balm of forgetfulness. Assistance went out to the still-marooned passengers. Rescuers even saved the cattle.

When within a week came that summons for General Custer to return to Washington to testify against Belknap, Libbie began packing to go with him, but he refused to allow it. This time the entire trip would have to be made in a sleigh. He left her with his usual admonition, "Be sure, Libbie, it's all for the best; you know we always find it so in the end," and "stepped into the sleigh—which he knew well might be his tomb."

For days thereafter Libbie lived in torture, until word came of her husband's safe arrival to eastward. But even that relief did not end her worry. Later, as snows melted, nature announced the inexorability of another spring—presaging another summer, which now could mean only more Indian fighting.

She always feared that thought. "When I spied the first tiny blade of grass," she said once, years later, "I used to find myself acting like a child and grinding the innocent green with my heel, back from where it sprang."

20

A GOOD DAY TO DIE

The likelihood of Sioux fighting had brought Lieutenant John Bourke and his esteemed commander, General Crook, to the Northern Plains from Arizona.

After Crook had introduced peace to the Southwest in his military way he had received orders, in March of 1875, transferring him to command of the Department of the Platte, an area extending from the Missouri River westward to the Salt Lake and including the territories of Wyoming, Utah, and part of Idaho, and the state of Nebraska. Crook's headquarters would be at Omaha, but most of his work would be done elsewhere—specifically, in the approaches to the Black Hills. The General and his staff, including Bourke, left Arizona on the twenty-fifth of the same month he received his orders.

Not until one year later, however, did Crook's army really move against the Indians. In March of 1876 (after General Sheridan had received approval on February 7 to punish all "hostiles" off the reservation) Crook had led ten companies of cavalry, two companies of infantry, and a band of Indian scouts out of isolated Fort Fetterman, located on the right bank of the North Platte River.

Bourke traveled with Crook and devoted himself to learning everything possible about the northwestern wilderness, which seemed as endless as Arizona's, although the two climates contrasted remarkably. The Indian scouts in particular fascinated Bourke, and he spent much time conversing with them.

His favorite scout happened not to be an Indian, although he looked like one and he could speak the Sioux language. The man's purported background amused Bourke.

> Frank Grouard, a native of the Sandwich Islands, was for some years a mail-rider in northern Montana, and was there captured by the [Sioux]; his dark skin and general appearance gave his captors the impression that [he] was a native Indian whom they had recaptured from the whites; consequently, they did not kill him, but kept him a prisoner until he could recover what they believed to be his native language—the Sioux.

Grouard never did "recover" his native language, but he had learned to speak Sioux. For several years he had lived in the household of the great Sioux war chief Crazy Horse, and Grouard also knew intimately the noted Sioux medicine man Sitting Bull.

Further, Grouard was a remarkable woodsman. "No Indian could surpass him in . . . acquaintance with all that pertained to the topography, animal life, and other particulars of [this] great region. . . . No question could be asked . . . that he could not answer at once."

Bourke spent much time listening to Grouard and recording conversations; but the expedition of March 1876 was not a pleasant one. From its very commencement it proved to be a severe physical trial, and it ended in failure. The journey northward from Fort Fetterman to Fort Reno, then to the Powder River—all in search of important Sioux villages to destroy—was ruined by wintry weather.

Despairing troopers often suffered from thirst not much different from that of an Arizona summer because of the difficulty of finding available water. Layers of ice two feet thick covered streams. To get meat cooks hacked with hatchets and axes at bacon frozen by temperatures as low as thirty degrees below zero. Thick flakes of blowing snow encrusted the wool and fur wrappings that covered most men from head to toe and hid any hint of army uniforms. Frozen, glasslike trails proved dangerous to men and animals.

On March 17 came ultimate disappointment. A cavalry detachment that included Lieutenant Bourke attacked a large Sioux village, but an Indian youth's shouted warning combined with other factors—an insufficiency of troopers and Indian accuracy at hitting cavalry horses (which took rider as well as his mount out of the fight)—resulted in an ignominious withdrawal and rumored abandonment of a wounded trooper by soldiers now dispirited by both failure and the ever-lingering Dakota winter. Still, they had captured several hundred Indian ponies, and these they throat-slashed during their retreat southward.

The animals' death sounds saturated Bourke with gloom: "It was pathetic to hear the dismal trumpeting of the dying creatures, as the breath of life rushed through several windpipes."

Hiding in distant hills, the victimized Sioux also heard the death cries of their ponies. No Indians risked an appearance to save the animals, but one faraway warrior yelled a defiant challenge that reached Bourke's ears with cold clarity. A volley of shots fired from the hills followed, all apparently with the aim of telling soldiers what to expect at the next meeting.

Thus it was that the momentous summer of 1876 came to Dakota. Despite Crook's setback (eventually blamed on a subordinate, who was court-martialed) General Sheridan still planned to have those three strong columns converge on hostile Indians—the first led by Crook, moving up again from the south; the second commanded by Gibbon, marching eastward from Montana; and the third led by Terry (to be assisted by Custer), traveling southwestward from Fort Lincoln. According to Sheridan's plan, the columns would split the thousands of "hostiles" and prevent their massing for common defense.

This seemed vital indeed while Crook and his aide Bourke worked at Fort Fetterman to prepare another expedition. Friendly Crow scouts began reporting to Crook that the hostile Indians were assembling a mighty army around the headwaters of the Rosebud River, near the Wyoming-Montana border, and that reservation tribesmen were augmenting their numbers. But as Crook realized (and Bourke recorded), poor communications or indifference, or both, began to hamper the military plan. As time approached for the march virtually nothing had been heard at Fetterman from commanders of the other columns—and, as it developed, the others heard nothing from Crook.

Crook waited for the appearance of new grass and for spring thaws to dry. Then in late May he took his army northward again. It included the inevitable Indian scouts, more than a thousand mounted troopers and infantrymen soon to be joined by two or three hundred Sioux-hating Crows and Shoshones, and a large supply train manned by teamsters and packers. "The long . . . line of mounted men stretched for more than a mile with nothing to break the somberness of color save the flashing of the sun's rays back from carbines and bridles."

Lieutenant Bourke thought that summer finally had arrived, but on the first day of June—just as the column sighted the white-peaked Big Horn Mountains, another snowstorm hit almost with the suddenness of an Indian attack. Cooking water froze in kettles. Then the storm passed on as quickly as it had come. On the following day, sunny and cloudless, meadowlarks rippled their yellow breasts in song. Grasshoppers chirped. Wagons rumbled along the road with creaking, cracking sounds. Surely this must have been the last wintry blast.

But other forebodings came. Plentiful Sioux trails confirmed the reports, all denied by agents, that reservation Indians had joined their kinsmen for war. "There were many pony, but few lodge-pole, tracks, a sure indication that the men were slipping out from Red Cloud and Spotted Tail agencies and uniting with the hostiles, but leaving their families at home, under the protection of the reservations."

More thought and care went into making camp. Entire companies, mounted, stood guard a mile or two away, to prevent a surprise attack and an ensuing stampede that would leave cavalrymen practically helpless. The precautions were wisely taken; for as the expedition approached the Tongue River a courier from Crazy Horse and Sitting Bull appeared with a warning to Crook: cross the stream and take the consequences. Soon afterward—on June 9, as the soldiers made camp upon that very river—an assault came, but prompt reaction drove it back with an army loss of only two men slightly wounded.

After a delay Crook moved again, toward a reported encampment of Sioux and Cheyennes across the Tongue River. For faster marching he left supply wagons behind.

By the afternoon of June 16, after the column had crossed the waist-high Tongue, muddy from spring rains, scouts began riding back from the advance with reports of finding the trail of "a very great village" ahead.

Troopers halted. Crows and Shoshones, able to reconnoiter without being seen and eager for vengeance, went forward to investigate.

After some time Bourke became aware of their return. "From the tops of the hills they yelled like wolves, [a] . . . signal among the Plains tribes that the enemy has been sighted."

Again the column moved—to the left, now, toward Rosebud headwaters and across high, gently rolling grassland. Approaching battle might have monopolized the thoughts of other men, but Bourke studied the landscape. Few trees added picturesqueness, but wild roses and blue phlox gave the greenery polka dots of various colors, and a variety of birds sang what seemed to Bourke to be a welcome—indicating that this lieutenant could admit to some chauvinism, after all. He reveled in the wild surroundings, then thought, without indication of sympathy he had shown for Apaches, "Yet this lovely country was abandoned to the domination of the thriftless savage, the buffalo, and the rattlesnake; we could see the last named winding along through the tall grass, rattling defiance as [it] sneaked away." Bourke might have added that Sioux reacted the same way.

No Indians appeared for a fight, but, like the rattlesnakes, they knew of the army's arrival, as was shown. That night the soldiers and their allies encamped in a little valley on the South Fork of the Rosebud, only a trickling stream at this location. They halted a short distance from where the river made an abrupt northward turn into a canyon. At daylight the next morning the column moved forward once more. As it neared the sharp curve the men were stopped for a brief rest. Bourke, who had been riding with the Crow scouts, was sitting with Crook near a spring when he heard a number of shots fired in hills off to his left—to northward—then more howls from hilltops nearby declaring that the enemy was in view—and in force, as Bourke soon realized.

Other shots fired on the army's left flank punctured the morning stillness. Soon two Crow Indians rode up to Bourke, who heard

211

them both yelling, "Sioux! Sioux!" He saw that one Crow had been badly wounded.

What happened after that has been debated even by eyewitnesses, but one action certainly followed: a mighty assault by angry Indians who had planned a trap. Shouted orders sent soldiers deploying for battle. Skirmishers took up positions to protect the herd of cavalry horses. On Crook's left, Crows and Shoshones, rallied by Lieutenant Bourke, met attackers in hand-to-hand fights, along with infantrymen and dismounted troopers. On the right, a battalion commander who led a counterattack described the scene.

> These Indians were most hideous, every one being painted in . . . colors and designs, stark naked, except [for] their moccasins, breechclouts and head gear . . . of feathers and horns; some of the horses being also painted, and the Indians proved then and there . . . the best cavalry soldiers on earth. In charging . . . towards us they exposed little of their person, hanging on with one arm around the neck and one leg over the horse, firing and lancing from underneath the horse's neck, so that there was no part of the Indian at which we could aim.
>
> Their shouting and . . . appearance . . . terrified the horses more than our men and rendered them almost uncontrollable before we dismounted and placed them behind . . . rocks.
>
> The Indians came not in a line but in . . . herds like the buffalo, and they piled in upon us until I think there must have been one thousand or fifteen hundred in our immediate front, but they refused to fight when they found us secured behind the rocks, and bore off to our left.

That was the direction toward Bourke and the Crows and Shoshones. There, too, infantrymen firing long rifles from behind a range of knolls were taking a mounting toll of attackers, but Bourke marveled at the boldness of the pressing Sioux and Cheyennes, who were led (as he learned later) by Crazy Horse, one of the greatest cavalry leaders in history.

After one charge the Shoshones counterattacked, urged on by one of their chiefs. Bourke went with them, fighting furiously, yet

212

still noticing how his Indian allies conducted themselves—so that he could write later:

> There was a headlong rush for about two hundred yards, which drove the enemy back in confusion; then was a sudden halt, and . . . many of the Shoshones jumped down from their ponies and began firing from the ground; the others who remained mounted threw themselves alongside of their horses' necks, so that there would be few good marks presented to the aim of the enemy. Then, in response to some signal or cry which . . . I did not understand, we were off again . . . right into the midst of the hostiles.

After that came more hand-to-hand fighting. From the distance, army sharpshooters held their fire. They were unable to distinguish between friendly and enemy Indians.

For hours dust and smoke swirled upward from the battlefield. Crazy Horse unleashed new attacks with fresh warriors, but Crook, who had one horse shot from beneath him, refused to retire. In midafternoon the attackers withdrew toward the reported location of their village. Crook, who might have ordered pursuit, instead recalled his men—possibly because of the casualty toll (as many as half a hundred dead or wounded) or because of dwindling rations and ammunition. After camping on the battlefield that night the General and his column departed southward the next morning, to find his wagons and to proceed to a base camp and there await resupply from Fort Fetterman.

Seventy or eighty northerly miles separated the site of the Battle of the Rosebud from the junction of the Yellowstone and Rosebud rivers, where—four days after Crook's fight—Gibbon's and Terry's columns united, on June 21. The distance might as well have been a thousand miles, as time proved. Crook, unaware of the exact location of the other columns, made no attempt to inform those commanders of his recent battle and of Crazy Horse's part in it. Had he done this, or had he been decisively successful against the Indians, fate might not have sneaked up on a previously favored son, as it would do soon.

Both Lieutenant Bourke and his general devoted part of Sunday, June 25, 1876, to hunting and fishing in the scenic Big Horn Mountains while waiting for supplies and reinforcements. Bourke, who usually reserved his notebook entries for grander subjects, kept records of fish caught by various officers, and "about this time [they seemed] to be almost the chronicle of a sporting club."

Three hundred miles northeast, in a general's quarters at inelegant Fort Lincoln, officers' wives pining for absent husbands sought some solace in an informal Sunday service held after the noon meal on the twenty-fifth. Libbie Custer, who could endure with silence almost any discomfort as long as she had her husband around, had given up to fresh weeping.

She was not alone. She had invited for company and maybe consolation other women then living in temporary widowhood because of those troublesome Sioux and Cheyennes flinging their challenges to westward. One young wife lay forlornly on a carpet, with her head cradled in the lap of another mourner. A woman sat at the piano.

They tried singing a few favorite hymns, but the sorrow only seemed to settle instead of lift—"some of [the songs] dated back to our childhood . . . when our mothers rocked us to sleep to their soothing strains."

With Custer present, Libbie had been inspired by these singing devotionals—the only religious services possible at Fort Lincoln. She and the General had rented a piano out of St. Paul and someone had contributed a Moody and Sankey songbook. The forty or so regulars in attendance always had joined in singing, with full voices. But that had been in less anxious moments, when inspiration and faith came easily.

Now the words brought only great depression.

> Tho' like a wanderer,
> The sun gone down,
> Darkness be over me,
> My rest a stone;
> Yet in my dreams I'd be
> Nearer, my God, to Thee,
> Nearer, my God, to Thee,
> Nearer to Thee!

General Terry's column had departed Fort Lincoln more than a month and a week earlier—on May 17. Custer, recently returned from the ignominy of that ineffectual testimony against Secretary of War Belknap, and later against President Grant, had ridden proudly at the head of his regiment while the band played "The Girl I Left Behind Me."

But Libbie would not be left behind until the following day. She had accompanied the General on the first march out, and her description of the long column as she saw it from the lead was remindful of Bourke's account of Crook's army leaving Fort Fetterman. "The cavalry and infantry . . . the scouts, pack mules, and artillery, and behind all the long line of white-covered wagons, made a column . . . some two miles in length. . . . The sun, mounting higher and higher as we advanced, took every little bit of burnished steel . . . and turned [it] into glittering flashes."

The first march ended at the bank of a small stream, where the men encamped. An army paymaster disbursed money due, so that each man could settle debts with the sutler and at this remote location not be enticed over to the various vices Bismarck offered for that hard-earned cash. The soldiers stuffed remaining money into pockets, and there most of it would be found, worthless, five weeks later.

On the following morning Libbie returned to Fort Lincoln with the paymaster and his escort. She could not shake off "a premonition of disaster."

In following days and weeks Indians knowledgeable about Terry's sortie frequently attacked outer pickets at Fort Lincoln, causing continual anxiety for the women occupants. Libbie's only cheer came from occasional letters sent back by the General.

> Forty-six Miles from Fort Lincoln,
> May 20th, 1876—9.15 P.M.

It is raining now, and has been since we started. The roads are fearfully bad. Here we are on the Little Muddy, after marching four days, and only forty-six miles from home. . . .

We have not seen any signs of Indians thus far, and hardly look for any for a few days yet. I have been extremely prudent

215

—sufficiently so to satisfy you. I go nowhere without taking an escort with me.

. . .

On Little Missouri, May 30th—10 P.M.

We had halted here for one day in order to determine the truth of the many rumors which you and all of us have heard so long and often, to the effect that the hostile Indians were gathered on the Little Missouri River, with the intention of fighting us here.

I suggested to General Terry to send out a strong scouting party up the river to find out all that could be ascertained. He left the matter to me, and [today] I took four companies of cavalry and a part of the scouts, and at five o'clock we were off. The valley of the river averages about one mile in width, hemmed in on both sides by impassable Bad Lands. The river is crooked beyond description.

To shorten the story, we marched the fifty miles and got back before dark, having settled the question beyond a doubt that all stories of Indians being here are the merest bosh. . . .

General Terry just left my tent a few moments since, and when I asked him not to be in a hurry he said, "Oh, I'll leave you, for you must be tired and want to go to bed." I did not tell him that I was going to write you before I slept.

. . .

Powder River, about Twenty Miles above its Mouth,
June 9, 1876.

Yesterday I finished a *Galaxy* article, which will go in the next mail; so, you see, I am not entirely idle. . . . It is now nearly midnight, and I must go to my bed, for *reveille* comes at three.

As a slight evidence that I am not very conceited regarding my personal appearance, I have not looked in a mirror or seen the reflection of my beautiful (?) countenance, including the fine growth of *auburn* whiskers, since I looked in the glass at Lincoln.

. . .

Mouth of Tongue River, June 17th.

On our march here we passed through some very extensive Indian villages—rather the remains of villages occupied by them last winter. I was at the head of the column as we rode through one, and suddenly came upon a human skull lying under the remains of an extinct fire. I halted to examine it, and lying nearby I found the [cavalry] uniform of a soldier. . . . The skull was weather-beaten, and had evidently been there several months. All the circumstances went to show that the skull was that of some poor mortal who had been a prisoner in the hands of the savages, and who doubtless had been tortured to death, probably burned.*

. . .

Mouth of Rosebud, June 21, 1876.

Look on my map and you will find our present location on the Yellowstone, about midway between Tongue River and the Big Horn.

The scouting party has returned. They saw the trail and deserted camp of a village of three hundred and eighty . . . lodges. The trail was about one week old. . . . I am now going to take up the trail where the scouting party turned back. . . . I feel hopeful of accomplishing great results. I will move directly up the valley of the Rosebud. General Gibbon's command and General Terry, with steamer, will proceed up the Big Horn as far as the boat can go.

June 22d–11 A.M.

. . . I have but a few moments to write, as we move at twelve, and I have my hands full of preparations for the scout. . . . Do not be anxious about me. . . . I hope to have a good report to send you by the next mail. . . . A success will start us all towards Lincoln. . . .

I send you an extract from General Terry's official order, knowing how keenly you appreciate words of commendation and confidence, such as the following: "It is of course impossible to give you any definite instructions in regard to this

* This information causes an observer to muse over the rumored abandonment of a wounded trooper in Crook's battle of March 17, 1876.

movement; and were it not impossible to do so, the Department Commander places too much confidence in your zeal, energy, and ability to wish to impose upon you precise orders, which might hamper your action when nearly in contact with the enemy."

That was the last letter Libbie received from her husband, and by the time she would read it he would have died with every member of five troops of the 7th Cavalry—231 men—whom he had led in an attack on a great Sioux village.

On that same Sunday, June 25, when she and other wives had sought consolation in hymn singing, and the same Sunday when Bourke and Crook had fished, the unpredictable Custer had attacked the village on his own, ignoring an order or at least a strong suggestion from Terry not to rush in, but to wait and to work in cooperation with the rest of the force under Terry and Gibbon that would be on the move nearby. Further, Custer had divided his own small force and had led those five troops of cavalry into a hillside fight against swarming, vengeful Sioux propelled by Crazy Horse's shout, "Today is a good day to die!" Custer and every officer and enlisted man with him were killed. The only army survivor was an officer's horse with a name that was ironically remindful of diehardism elsewhere—"Comanche."

Other units of the divided but furiously fighting 7th Regiment might have gone to Custer's aid—they were in the vicinity—but no one knew exactly where the General was, and, further, they were busy enough seeing after their own well-being, surrounded as they were. Some officers who could have led a rescue attempt were described later as wondering whether Custer might have withdrawn from the area. The ghost of Major Elliot and his detachment abandoned at the Battle of the Washita thus had returned, and it could have had more than a spectral role in Custer's own death.

On the morning of June 27 Gibbon and Terry and their men arrived, relieving still-besieged 7th Cavalry survivors, and Custer's earthly whereabouts finally became known.

In the Battle of the Little Big Horn the Sioux and Cheyennes won a great victory that lost them the war. Ironically, word of it reached the rest of the nation just as the citizenry had gone into serious celebration of the "Centennial"—one hundred years of independence from Great Britain.

The defeat shocked and enraged military men, including the former general who had been elected President (Grant blamed Custer for the tragedy), and it brought every available officer and man into a campaign that would climax with Crazy Horse's surrender (and, later, his controversial death while a prisoner) and with Sitting Bull's flight into Canada, where he would remain until surrendering several years later.

It also brought an unhappy army captain, William S. McCaskey, knocking at a door of the General's quarters at Fort Lincoln to bring word of Custer's death to Libbie.

On July 5, a sunny day, Libbie, who had slipped on a dressing gown when she heard the knock, ushered McCaskey into the parlor. Two other wives of regimental officers were there, in the same room where they had been singing and sorrowing on the afternoon of Sunday, June 25, while five entire cavalry companies and their commander were being annihilated.

The Captain read his words from a formal announcement. All three women seemed dazed. Libbie listened, then asked for a shawl, despite the day's heat. She felt that her own life might as well have been extinguished, too.

But at least her fear of spring had been overcome. She would live more than half a century longer, but the year's first growth of grass would lose the portentousness it once had possessed for her. On that July 5 when she heard of the General's death she was a young woman—thirty-four, slender, and pretty. She would never think of remarrying, but would instead live with "the echo of [his] voice" for inspiration, as she once wrote in a book dedication.

21

SUFFERING MUCH

Like the great Sioux Confederacy, the administration of U. S. Grant
had come and gone—its departure clouded by various scandals. Although most Americans regarded Grant himself as honest, he had
not been able to judge human character well, and many of his
friends and associates had taken advantage of their offices or of
their friendship with the President to reap personal reward. This
national calamity had combined with the Custer annihilation to
tarnish the brilliance of the 1876 centennial.

The United States was celebrating its first one hundred years of
growth—from a relatively narrow strip of land lying along the
Atlantic Coast to a broad belt extending across the continent to the
Pacific. A small meteor shower had burst upon the red, white, and
blue banner: thirteen stars had become thirty-eight. By 1876 the
United States had become the largest food-producing nation and
the world's leading industrial power.

But Americans were stung by world-wide taunts, partly inspired
by jealousy, that the United States surpassed other nations only in
corruption. By 1876 violence, war's aftermath, and unconstitu-
tional rule had left the nation rotten with fraud and graft. So many
officeholders were known to be dishonest that simply being active in
politics could stamp a man as a scoundrel.

Corruption ruled the Indian Bureau. An investigation soon to be
made would declare that Indian agencies existed simply as "a
license to cheat and swindle the Indians in the name of the United

States of America." President Grant had wanted to help Indians, but he had not devoted enough careful attention to the handling of this program—or any other, it seemed.

Nominated by Republicans in 1876 and elected after close and disputed voting was Ohioan Rutherford B. Hayes, a bearded, kindly-looking man and a wearer of ill-fitting clothes whose ordinary personality contrasted with the quirks of some predecessors: the emotionalism (especially in youth) of Lincoln and the alcoholic instability (particularly in antebellum days) of Grant.

Hayes withdrew the last federal troops from the South. He was a well-meaning man who considered his primary jobs as President to be those of reform, especially in regard to governmental employment, and "pacification," especially as it pertained to former rebels.

Hayes's reforms would help Indians only temporarily, and indirectly at that. His Secretary of the Interior, Carl Schurz, a native German of tactless honesty who peered at culprits from behind a pair of thick-paned spectacles, dismissed workers found guilty of pocketing money at Indian expense, but angry victims of Schurz's reform eventually brought about the man's political retirement.

Nor did Hayes's desires for peace help Indians much. His pacification was aimed southward, not westward. No administrative change ever seemed to be noticeable to Indians. One reason for this was that various political pressures precluded development of a consistent policy. Many Democrats observed without genuine sadness the mess made by Republicans of Indian programs. No one seemed sincerely willing to sacrifice for the welfare of native Americans—as two contemporary suggestions indicated. One, made by Comanche chief Ten Bears at an 1872 council, advised the Great White Father that since he had moved Indians so often with such unsatisfactory results he might try moving Texans, inasmuch as they were the main cause of most trouble anyway. Another ignored suggestion came in 1880 from a Wyoming resident who proposed transferring tribes to the Atlantic Seaboard, where Easterners whose hearts were saddened by the bad use of red people might better see after their welfare. This proposal met an especially silent reception on the East Coast.

All national benefits fell elsewhere than on Indians. They showered down upon favored whites. During Hayes's administration a depression that had come during the last years of Grant's second term would vanish. The nation would move further toward becoming an industrial society—a direction given impetus by the defeat of the agricultural South.

Railroad tracks already extended from coast to coast and were continuing to multiply, affording transportation of raw materials to manufacturing centers and distribution of finished products from there. This industrialization resulted in quick amassing of fortunes —and in some sharing (through philanthropies) that aided education and the arts.

Inventions improved the standard of living. Thomas Edison contributed a phonograph in 1877 and an incandescent light two years later. In 1879, also, a pioneer in mass merchandising, Frank W. Woolworth (while still in his twenties) opened his first five-cent store (in Utica, New York) and later added items costing a dime. Not only the economy boomed; so did population, increasing greatly through immigration.

Indians could contribute nothing to this progress, with the exception of getting out of its way. Squeezed further by the present and doomed by the future, several tribes felt forced to fight a number of futile "last stands" that characterized Indian relations during these years. Invariably the natives were further alienated by bureaucratic unconcern, mismanagement, or faithlessness—or all three.

One of the most needless small wars involved the Nez Percé Indians of the Far Northwest—red people who had extended friendship to pale-skinned strangers since the days of the Lewis and Clark Expedition and who boasted of never having killed a white man. But the passing years and flocking settlers brought mounting trouble to these long-time inhabitants of green Wallowa Valley (in present northeastern Oregon), and the United States Government sought to move the Nez Percés to a reservation in northwest Idaho, which would have opened their scenic valley of streams, grasslands, mountain forests, and a clear lake to white settlement. The Indians' chief, a peacefully inclined leader known in history as Old Joseph, protested the move, and he had persuaded Grant, while President, to issue an executive order declaring that the Wallowa Valley belonged to Old Joseph's people.

Two years later the order was revoked and the valley became public domain. Still the Nez Percés stayed, but they did not attack white newcomers until 1877, after two of their own tribesmen had been slain by settlers impatient because Indians still occupied the coveted land.

That same year, despite the disapproval of the new chief, Young Joseph (son of the old man, who had died in 1873), vengeful Nez Percé braves killed scores of settlers in reprisal. Their actions brought in a U. S. Army force led by General O. O. Howard (of Arizona Apache experience), who personally felt that the Nez Percés should have been left to their homeland, but who also obeyed military orders.

Joseph led his band in a fighting retreat, trying to reach Canada. With only three hundred warriors at most he often outfought and usually outwitted the Army, despite its possession of artillery and of telegraphic links that could be used for sending more troopers from various posts into the field to intercept the Nez Percés. Joseph took his people into the tangled mess of the Bitter Root Mountains, an area made almost impassable by deep ravines, huge boulders, and toppled trees, then out of those heights southward into Big Hole Basin, Montana, and eastward into Yellowstone Park, Wyoming— all the while fighting occasional battles with soldiers who had been summoned into position by telegraph, an occurrence of which Joseph was ignorant. After leaving Yellowstone he marched northward into the Bear Paw Mountains, near the Canadian border and presumed safety. But there, on October 5, 1877, he was forced to surrender. He and his people had traveled more than two thousand torturous miles while defeating or fending off the attacks of two thousand soldiers (more than three hundred of whom became casualties), with a loss to the Nez Percés themselves of more than two thirds of their battle force dead or wounded, and with that beloved valley home now gone forever. The government shipped Nez Percé survivors to the Indian Territory.

During the following summer a band of Bannock Indians, seeking to protect some southeastern Oregon land given them by treaty, attacked three white trespassers who were herding some two thousand head of cattle in the area. This precipitated another minor war that ended with the usual result.

The very next year, 1879, a motley group of Bannocks, Shoshones, and ragtag representatives of other tribes—all banded together in central Idaho under the designation "Sheepeaters"—made the mistake of leaving their craggy habitat and their usual austere diet of mountain sheep for some raiding into the more affluent, white-occupied valleys. The Army again ordered General Howard to punish the marauders, and they soon surrendered.

That same year also brought renewed conflict to Colorado, where Utes "revolted" after silver-seeking miners began flocking onto their land. Violence was brief but unusually brutal (including copious bloodshed, mutilations, and rapes of white women), but it all ended with the same inevitability.

The most poignant last stand, however, occurred in the Texas penitentiary at Huntsville, although Texans of that day did not appreciate the sadness of it.

After the Kiowa chief White Bear had been returned to prison he had hoped, as usual, for release, but only for a short time. The optimism of younger days had been eroded by time, disappointment, and the disappearance of the old way of life.

He had seen the end coming, finally, although it had been too late for him to guide his people into acceptance and survival—assuming he would have wanted to try. Shortly before his return to prison he had indicated this awareness to a group of Kiowa chiefs gathered at Fort Sill by picking up a handful of sand and as it sifted through his fingers saying, "The white men are as numerous as the sands in these hills. We may kill these [pointing to soldiers nearby], but others will come. The Indians' days are over."

Greater chiefs than White Bear would have managed to die in battle, but White Bear had seemed unwilling to make that sacrifice. Now, as an old man behind bars waiting out the turns of meaningless seasons, he probably wished he had gone out in glory.

Still, he had pride, or at least a broad stubborn streak. During his first imprisonment he and Big Tree had been assigned to chairmaking chores, but White Bear had refused to turn a hand, although Big Tree had complied. That was woman's work, convict

No. 2107 had scoffed, and the warden had refrained from insisting that he do it.

Now, back in prison, White Bear spent his early days looking down a long nose from the heights of Kiowa chieftainship at fellow convicts, and again no one knew exactly what to do about his snobbishness, since the situation was without precedent. He did eventually condescend to make small souvenirs like bows and arrows for sale to the public, but he probably did this out of sheer boredom.

White Bear heard about the Custer "massacre," as white men called it, and he learned further that a number of Kiowas had been shipped to a Florida prison as punishment for raiding. Those two bits of information would have dimmed in him any hope he might have had for his own parole.

When he realized fully the doom forced upon him he began to show age rapidly. Still, he never failed to impress visitors, including a feature writer from *Scribner's* magazine: "In the corridor of the penitentiary I saw a tall, finely formed man with bronzed complexion and long flowing hair, a man of princely carriage on whom even . . . prison garb seemed elegant. It was [White Bear], the great chief of the Kiowas. He [came] into the workroom where he was supposed to labor, but did no more than sprawl himself on a pile of oakum."

In autumn of 1878, the year after Chief Joseph had led his Nez Percés almost to safety in Canada and the same year that the Bannocks revolted futilely in Oregon, White Bear began showing great melancholy. Outside, beyond his reach, but not beyond his vision or his memory, he could see leaves on the many trees that shaded Huntsville taking on seasonal beauty, with yellows, fiery reds, browns. Some years ago at this time he would have been riding out with hundreds of warriors on buffalo hunts, gathering meat and clothing material for the coming winter.

People who observed White Bear that autumn of 1878 recalled later that he spent much time at the windows, peering northwestward, but they could not have envisioned the old life he was no doubt reliving. Nor would they have known the text of Ten Bears' speech at Medicine Lodge, which White Bear had heard and with which he certainly agreed whenever he chose to speak honestly to government men. "I was born upon the prairie where the wind blew free and there was nothing to break the light of the sun. I was born where there were no enclosures and where everything drew a free breath. I want to die there, and not within walls."

Two men said later that during an early-October talk with White Bear the Kiowan asked if they thought he would ever be released. The men, both white, knew he never could expect freedom again, and they told him so.

Not long after that a guard found White Bear near death from bleeding; he had cut into neck and leg arteries in an ultimate attempt to get out of the white world. The Chief was carried to the prison hospital, located on a second floor, was given emergency treatment to stop the blood flow, and was left lying on a cot near a window, alone. Sometime later he struggled to the window, plunged headfirst to the ground (on October 10, 1878), and died.

White Bear finally had won his freedom, and if Kiowan belief of that day proved true he had gone to an even better life than the old way that had been beyond his vision as he stared from those prison windows. Sometime after he had drawn his last earthly breath his spirit traveled westward, racing to overtake the sunset. It traversed a high mountain ridge, came upon a wide band of water, and crossed it.

On the opposite shore White Bear was met by relatives and friends who had preceded him. Some of these people had been watching from a height for the arrival of souls of persons they had known on earth. When they saw White Bear approaching they called eagerly to other friends of his, and they all joined in welcoming him to this land of joy and no parting or pain, where could be found plentiful game and green grass, and large, swift horses.

But whatever happened to White Bear's spirit, it did indeed leave this part of earth to men who had most recently won it.

Apaches made the most fanatical last stands. Their violence bloodied the southwestern United States and Sonora, Mexico.

Generals Howard, the erstwhile peacemaker, and Crook, the peace forcer, had transformed Arizona into a relatively tranquil place, but that pleasantness had not lasted long.

Not all Apaches had taken to the warpath, but even some cooperative bands had been antagonized into killing again by a variety of wrongs: inadequate rations; foolish attempts to place mutually hostile tribes on the same reservation; arbitrarily moving some bands from desirable locations to sterile, out-of-the-way wastelands; and troublemaking by an "Indian ring" (white men who benefited from army contracts and other government spending) designed to keep Arizona in turmoil. The names of Apaches who led these final outbreaks are well known today: Cochise, Mangas Coloradas and his son Mangas, Victorio, and Geronimo.

Geronimo has passed into history as the most notorious, but when Apaches embarked on their long-continuing series of last stands his name was not feared so much by settlers as were some others, because until late in his fighting career Geronimo had concentrated on raiding those despised people who had massacred his family: the Mexicans. But as the flow of settlers into Arizona increased and as the United States Government sought more and more to restrict roaming Apaches and to regulate their lives, Geronimo's hatred expanded to include white Americans along with Mexicans.

Years later, in his autobiography, he would state the primary reason for his emergence as a leader whose name came to mean desolation and death to enemies. "My people," he said, "were suffering much."

227

22

LONG BLACK HAIR

Quanah had foreseen the greater suffering his people certainly would have been forced to endure had they continued to defy inexorability, and he had led them to the reservation. A man determined to fight white encroachment might as well have held up his hand in a gesture implying "Halt!" and thus have sought to hold off winter snows and summer heat or to stop those timepieces of constant ticking that civilized people carried with them for purposes of getting somewhere on time, usually for the accumulation of wealth, real or imagined.

Pale-skinned authors writing during Quanah's time naturally credited the wisdom displayed by his surrender to the white blood that "enhanced" his veins' flow. Even his son, Baldwin Parker, was quoted in a 1930 document kept today in the University of Texas Archives as having said, "Quanah's white blood endowed him with superior intelligence and made him more resourceful." But Baldwin Parker was misquoted or was seeking to please white people—or he had been persuaded by earlier writings on racial superiorities. Close examination of his half-breed father showed that Quanah had remained largely Indian in attitude and intellect even while accepting the new existence. He simply had seen with his own Comanche eyes the accuracy of Billy Dixon's mile-long shot, and many other signs of what the future held, and he had compared with this Isatai's dismal protective prowess and other paucities. Half-red Quanah knew the way to survival, as did some other chiefs more

228

thoroughbred than he. But Quanah proved to be a rare type to whom loss of freedom meant no loss of character. He accepted the inevitable with dignity.

In a later sentence in that document Baldwin Parker attested to his father's purity of Indian thought: "Even after [surrender], Quanah was much opposed to the white man's ways and kept his tribe from adopting civilization and the Christian religion." Another man (this one white: O. W. Bronson, writing in *Outdoor Life*) visited Quanah during his years on the reservation and remarked on the physical Indian still obvious in him: "His movements are as lithe as a cat, and he walks with [seemingly] no exertion at all. His form is something wonderful to look upon, every muscle being developed to perfection. . . . He is straight as an arrow, taller than . . . average . . . and the color of his skin is very dark."

Quanah always spoke with pride about the way he had led his people off the warpath. He had brought them into Fort Sill without soldiers guarding them. The decision had been a voluntary one despite the pressures. In an interview Quanah later described the event and a final encounter with Colonel Mackenzie that had preceded (but had not forced) his surrender.

> I came into Fort Sill, no ride me in like horse or lead me by halter like cow. Me had big war; I fought . . . Mackenzie. He brave man, good soldier, but uses two thousand men; many wagons, horses, and mules. Me, I only had 450 braves, no supply train, ammunition and guns like him. I used this knife. Me see eight miles . . . lots of soldiers coming. I say, Hold on, no go over there. Maybe we go at night, maybe stampede troops' horses first. I stand my men around in circle. Me tell them to holler, shoot, and run. I gather 350 horses in one night. They find my trail next morning. I ready to fight, my men hide behind hill, shoot and run. Mackenzie no catch me.

The government assigned a part of the Fort Sill reservation to Quohadas, and, probably to encourage tranquillity, designated Quanah as chief of the Comanches—an act not really within governmental jurisdiction, but one that worked because Comanches already respected him and accepted his leadership. White men built him a two-story, thirty-two-room frame house—non-Indian shelter he nevertheless occupied with his several wives.

Quanah cooperated generally, but he avoided total acceptance of white civilization as urged upon him by government agents. Largely because of this the earliest attempts to "civilize" Comanches realized but scant success. During a visit to Washington, D.C., Quanah met one federal official who requested that he give up all but one wife and live like a white man. When the Chief failed to reply immediately the man repeated his suggestion, advising Quanah to go home, choose one wife, and order the others out.

Quanah finally answered. *"You* tell 'em which one I keep," he said, and he remained polygamous.

He also retained for his people as much independence as possible. When army recruiters sought to enlist Comanche braves for an all-Indian cavalry unit Quanah protested and kept his young men from joining, although other Indians enlisted. He argued that missionaries were constantly preaching to his people that war was wrong; therefore he saw no excuse for other white men to try to hire braves for fighting. He emphasized that the reason he had accepted reservation life was that he and his people were tired of war.

He did, however, approve of a Comanche police force to keep order on the reservation—after some initial hostility occasioned by his traditional view that a young man had no business telling an elder what or what not to do. In this instance he acted again to benefit his people: better that Comanches maintain themselves properly, he reasoned, than to have white men oversee all of this for them.

In time Quanah became a tribal judge—one of three natives appointed by the government (despite Quanah's multiple marriages) to hear cases involving Indians. In fulfilling his duties he showed close observation of, if not total affinity for, white colleagues. Quanah once gave this facetious description of his duties.

"You see," he said, illustrating with appropriate gestures as he went along, "me open desk and sit down in chair so—and lean back, and put feet up on desk and lighting seegar, and hold newspaper in front of me, all same white man. . . . Then by-m-by white man he come in and knock at door, and he say:

230

'Quanah, me want talk t'you a minute.' And me swing round in chair—so—and puff lots of smoke in his face and me say, 'What can I do for you today?'"

In the judicial job Quanah showed that his sense of humor was matched by intelligence and ability. He held the position for more than a decade after 1886 and won the esteem of both Indians and government officials—the only tribal judge to enjoy this success. Even when white-red relations became strained from time to time Quanah managed to retain the friendship of both factions.

But he did not dispense white justice. Along with the other two judges he looked at transgressions with an Indian's eye, viewing crimes as having been committed against individuals rather than against society. For that reason he concluded that the most appropriate punishment for an Indian man found guilty of the whites' crime of bigamy was payment of ten dollars and presentation of a pony to the first of the man's two wives. (Ironically, when Quanah was removed from the bench, it would result from his taking still another wife into his household, although this did not cause him loss of chieftainship or influence.)

The longer Quanah served as judge and as Comanche chief, the more "white" he seemed to become. His use of English improved somewhat, too, because the government had given him the services of a language tutor. His conversion to civilization seemed most pronounced after a trip to Texas to visit his mother's family (including Silas Parker, Cynthia Ann's brother who had escaped capture at Parker's Fort). Quanah returned to the reservation praising the white people he had met and painting a vivid word picture of their superior living standards.

His accounts only alienated fellow Comanches, who still considered Texans their eternal enemies. Some of the men suggested to Quanah that since he liked the land and its occupants so much he might remove himself from the reservation and make his permanent home in Texas. Quanah's reply reflected his usual honesty. "Down there," he said, "I just a plain Indian. Here I am great chief."

Nevertheless, impressions gathered during the trip stayed with him. He encouraged Indian youths to take advantage of educational opportunities, and he sought with renewed effort to smooth transitions to the new life. During this period he developed some friendships remarkable for an Indian with his rampaging background. Charles Goodnight and other cattlemen who had suffered a few losses to Quanah and his raiders during the earliest days of their ranching became close acquaintances, as did public officials ranging from small-town mayors to United States Presidents.

Through it all, Quanah remained Indian. He learned to wear a white man's suit, but he never looked Caucasian and obviously never wanted to. During an 1889 visit to San Antonio a reporter for the *Light* wrote (in the May 9 edition):

> The Chief wears a . . . suit of black broadcloth, neatly fitting his straight body. His shoes are the regular dude style, with toothpick toes. A gold watch, with chain and charm, dangles from his close-fitting vest. He wears a beautiful black beaver hat that is pulled down in front. The only peculiar item of his appearance is his long black hair, which he wears in two plaits down his back.

Nor did Quanah ever attune himself to some of civilization's refinements. He and a father-in-law named Yellow Bear visited Fort Worth in the 1880's, enjoyed saloon convivialities common to "that class of visitors" (a doctor wrote later), returned to the Pickwick Hotel in a state of utter drunkenness, and went to bed—Yellow Bear first. The older man extinguished the gaslight before retiring, but Quanah relit it to make his own preparations for sleeping. When he turned it out again he apparently left the stopcock open enough to allow some gas to leak out. Before dozing off, he said later, he detected an odd odor, but he pulled bedcovers over his head and shut out the smell.

Later he awoke—"aroused by a burning, parched sensation of the lips, mouth, and fauces [wrote the learned doctor who had twitted him about his drunkenness]; a horrible constriction throughout the air passages, pain in the chest, extending down the arms to the elbow; a feeling as if there were heavy weights bearing down upon the thorax; and all the frightful symptoms of a dangerous asphyxia. The venous system was already charged with it."

Altogether the discomfort was enough to persuade any Indian

never to drink a white man's whiskey again. Quanah sought to rouse Yellow Bear, but then he fainted. The next morning when a chambermaid entered the room Yellow Bear was dead and Quanah lay unconscious—and seriously ill. As soon as he had recovered enough to travel he hurried back to the reservation and home, despite doctor's advice to the contrary.

The Indian in Quanah also showed in his politics. In one speech he said:

> I [watch] both parties close, which is best? The Democratic Party is trying to work for good of all us. It looks at the rich man and poor man, the same. The Republican Party for rich man, but not the good poor man. The Republicans have all the offices—[hold] money tight. Democrats want them to turn loose.

To illustrate his remarks he held up two hands. His right hand, he said, stood for the Democratic way and for the Indian way.

As the reservation years came and went and Quanah acquired more white friends—and more prestige and power—his material holdings increased. He invested forty thousand dollars in a railroad with a name that honored him: the Quanah, Acme, and Pacific Railway. He enjoyed visiting the company's yards and mingling with the locomotives. He liked to caress and pat parts of engines and to boast, "My engine; my railroad."

He spoke with similar pride of a white community named for him: Quanah, Texas—begun with a town-lot sale in 1886. Soon after its establishment he responded to an invitation from its citizens and addressed them. "May the Great Spirit always smile on your new town," he said.

The community had been built near the southeastern end of the Texas Panhandle—just a few miles south of the Red River—in country that not many years earlier had belonged without dispute to Comanches and Kiowas and other peoples now dispossessed—the same as Comanches and Kiowas had, in fact, dispossessed earlier occupants. Changes now came with astonishing speed, as Quanah's friendly words to recent enemies showed.

Consider also Quanah himself. Born to a white woman who had been taken forcibly from the present to the past, he had advanced

233

in his own lifetime from Stone Age culture almost to a modernism that young Cynthia Ann Parker or her parents could not have envisioned when Parker's Fort was overrun in 1836.

Almost to modernism, but not quite. Once, after having been designated reservation chief of his tribe, Quanah decided to prepare a feast of cooked dog and to invite his many acquaintances to partake of the Comanche cuisine. When no one appeared at the banquet he lamented, "I thought I had more friends than this."

23

LIKE THE WIND

Those Indians never subdued by soldiers of the Spanish Empire and never exterminated by the Mexicans eventually stood longer than any others against the U. S. Army. Quanah's wild Comanches had been tamed and Crazy Horse's Sioux finally defeated, but some Arizona Apaches continued to fight—and not simply because of the violence inherent in their character.

Even their foe in battle, General Crook, sympathized with them. "During the twenty-seven years of my experience with the Indian question," he said once, "I have never known a band of Indians to make peace with our government and then break it, or leave their reservation, without some ground of complaint. . . . I have never yet seen one so demoralized that he was not an example in honor and nobility compared to the wretches who plunder him of the little our government appropriates for him."

Two notable injustices aroused the wrath of Apaches: the arbitrary removal of bands from homeland reservations to new and usually undesirable land elsewhere, and the existence of that ring of human parasites who turned governmental Indian appropriations to their own profit through various frauds and swindles—frequently accomplished with the connivance of lawfully appointed Indian agents.

The Apache called Geronimo, who had earlier concentrated his raiding in Mexico, was fully aware of all the injustices. Years before, he had heard about Mangas Coloradas' death after that chief had been taken prisoner while talking under a flag of truce, and Geronimo regarded this treachery as "the greatest wrong ever done to the Indians." Nothing he subsequently saw or heard really changed his mind.

Geronimo had no admiration for General Crook, a man some Apaches respected. Much later, when he heard that Crook had died, Geronimo would remark, "I think that General Crook's death was sent by the Almighty as a punishment for the many evil deeds he committed." Geronimo believed he knew Crook and all other white men thoroughly, and he distrusted them even more than had Mangas Coloradas or Cochise or any other Apache leader. Those chiefs had sometimes talked sincerely of peace with the "White-eyes," as Apaches called their newest enemy. Geronimo (a shaman, not a true chief) believed nothing worthwhile could come of it—only more Apache tragedy. But his name was slow to win renown among white Americans simply because he had devoted himself to making it known among Mexicans.

Another force besides wrath drove Geronimo into his fanaticism. As a Chiricahuan, he cherished his free-roaming life even more than did other Apaches, and he felt a stronger urge to fight against its loss. In some ways he resembled White Bear of the Kiowas: Geronimo despised compromise and seemed blind to its necessity in order for his people to survive. Like White Bear, he would lie and cheat to have his way, and his victims might be either white or red. But where White Bear weakened occasionally in moments of danger or in addressing stern-faced representatives of the faraway Great Father, Geronimo rarely showed any attitude other than a fighting one—as long as the odds gave him a reasonable chance for victory. Geronimo was a worthy representative of Chiricahuans, who were, in turn, appropriate occupants of the rough, arid desolation of southeastern Arizona and southwestern New Mexico—that brown wasteland they called home.

For a decade after Custer's defeat in the north these Apaches rampaged along the Mexican border. A few score of them demanded the attention of soldiers by the hundreds and even thousands. For a time after Victorio's death in Mexico a handful of Apaches displayed their desert superiority by creating border bedlam with a successful series of swift-striking raids carried out under the leadership of a rheumatic named Nana, who was about eighty years old.

Much of this latest trouble stemmed specifically from governmental selection (about 1876) of a reservation on which to concentrate large numbers of Apaches from many groups and bands. The chosen site—San Carlos, in southeastern Arizona (at the junction of the San Carlos and Gila rivers)—became known immediately for its hot, sickly climate, for its crowded conditions (by Indian standards, anyway), and for its inadequate ration issue. An army officer left this description of the place:

> A gravelly flat rose some thirty feet or so above the river bottoms and was dotted here and there by the drab adobe buildings of the agency. Scrawny, dejected lines of scattered cottonwoods, shrunken, almost leafless, marked the course of the streams. Rain was so infrequent that it took on the semblance of a phenomenon when it came at all. Almost continuously dry, hot, dust-and-gravel laden winds swept the plain, denuding it of every vestige of vegetation.

In addition to having been cursed by a dreadful climate the location was plagued by hordes of insects. Yet this was the place the government expected Apaches to inhabit in large numbers, and on which they were to learn farming. Worse (at least for governmental integrity) several bands had been promised reservations in other locations. Now they were collected and taken to San Carlos, invariably against their wishes. There some were forced to live near other bands with whom they had developed mutual animosities.

Before the days of San Carlos the reservation system had meant little to Geronimo and to a cohort (and cousin) named Juh, a Nedni Apache chief who accompanied him on many raids. They and their warriors would sneak off for raids into Mexico, remain away as long as they were successful, then return for brief periods— if only to escape the Mexicans. But when Geronimo learned he was to be moved to San Carlos he asked for a few days' delay (ostensibly to prepare kinfolk for the move), then he and Juh broke camp and took their people to Mexico and into the depths of the Sierra Madre. They divided into small groups under various leaders, as customary, and supported themselves by raiding—occasionally even into the United States. For months no one knew Geronimo's exact location until he struck, always unexpectedly.

Early in 1877, however, the Army learned he was hiding in New Mexico. San Carlos agent John Clum, a young Easterner whose religion had brought him to Arizona with an intention of making a contribution to peace, collected a strong force of Apache policemen, set out across the desert, found Geronimo, and forced his surrender. Clum brought his Apache in irons to San Carlos. The agent sympathized with many Indians, but he considered this one to be an incorrigible scoundrel, and he did not intend to let him escape.

That situation lasted only a short time. Soon afterward Clum resigned as the result of a political dispute, and Geronimo found himself irons-free again. He was released to join his family in what some naïve army officers thought would be for him a happy, agrarian retirement from the letting of blood here and there.

Clum's successor at San Carlos followed the bestowal of freedom with another presentation involving responsibility. Relying on a scheme that had worked with Quanah and the Comanches, he made Geronimo "captain" of the reservation Chiricahuas, hoping that the responsibility might bring character improvement, governmentally speaking.

But the new agent was dealing with Geronimo—one of the very last Indians in North America willing to accept white society's moral and geographical boundaries. After wallowing through a period of restlessness, Geronimo (accompanied again by Juh) led a group off the San Carlos reservation in 1878 toward those beloved south-of-the-border *sierras* and into the boundless life they offered. For more than a year they all raided, but not exactly in the carefree manner they had anticipated. They found that their food supply sometimes lacked the quantity even of the theft-riddled San Carlos rations; and their existence was becoming more precarious as more people, including other Apaches, proved willing to fight them with a hope of reward or with anticipation of establishing security and peace in a turbulent area.

In 1880 Geronimo and Juh came back across the border and agreed to go back to San Carlos, where meals came in handouts and nights passed without the interruption of sleep due to a variety of strange noises.

For a year or so the new tranquillity lasted—blissfully at first, then with less and less ecstasy. The usual complaints about skimpy rations began coming; the usual restlessness returned to old roamers. When soldiers shot a medicine man said to have been fomenting San Carlos Indians, Geronimo became jumpy as well as restless. When a strong cavalry force one day appeared in the vicinity he and Juh and other leaders collected their people and again raced for the Mexican border and the comparative safety of the Sierra Madre, using the darkness of a starlit night to get a head start on the troopers they knew would pursue them. "We thought it more manly to die on the warpath than to be killed in prison," Geronimo explained later.

The fleeing Apaches reached the Sierra Madre, then a few months afterward sneaked back across the border, returned to San Carlos, killed a white police chief and one of his Indian scouts, and "rescued" as many kin previously left behind as they could round up. They forced these people to go with them to Mexico, regardless of individual desires.

Most of the Indians thus redeemed would have preferred to remain in peace at San Carlos. They realized that their absences would in effect convict them as followers of Geronimo and of his uncompromising colleagues. Now they could not return to San Carlos without convincing authorities of their innocence in those two slayings—something they realized would be difficult, or impossible. They could only keep quiet and accompany their tribesmen into Mexico. One young Apache caught in this predicament wondered, "What had we done to be treated so cruelly by members of our own race?"

They all eluded Apache police and army troopers, captured several hundred sheep to roast and eat, stole horses for faster traveling, fought a hard skirmish with pursuing cavalrymen, then vanished into the Chiricahua Mountains—a desolate jumble of rocky heights and deep canyons, well known only to Apaches like themselves. From there they slipped into Mexico, as only they could have done. But once safe, as they supposed themselves to be, they relaxed too much. An American force that had followed them without stopping at the international border overtook them, and the Apaches were forced into a rear-guard fight (superbly directed by Geronimo) while those ahead fled—coincidentally, into ambush by Mexican soldiers acting on their own and not in unison with the Americans.

The Apaches' indiscretion cost them one hundred casualties (dead or captured), but most of these were women and children. Those who escaped the trap eventually reached the Sierra Madre and its plentiful grass, game, water, and canyons, into which few pursuers would venture for fear of being ambushed themselves.

After the Apaches had vanished from the scene of latest battle with their usual stealth their Mexican ambushers met their American pursuers; and Geronimo, watching from a distant height, hoped to see the two forces fight each other.

He was disappointed. The Mexican commander merely reported results of the battle, then protested the presence of United States troops on Mexican soil. The Americans withdrew northward.

Geronimo and his people crept into Sierra Madre depths again, split into those small groups so effective for raiding and fleeing (although they still maintained close communication with each other), and resumed the life they loved.

Then supplies became a problem again. Further (some Apaches said later), Geronimo missed the whiskey he had come to crave. He called a grand council of all Apaches in the mountains and proposed making a peace treaty with a town nearby—Casas Grandes, in Chihuahua. After that they could obtain supplies, including liquor. The Apaches agreed, some with great reluctance.

Geronimo the distrustful thus prepared to place his life in the hands of others—Mexicans at that: the same people who had initially summoned his yearning for vengeance by murdering his family years earlier. Either Geronimo placed surprising faith in human beings or he misunderstood the unity of Mexicans when it came to hating him and his people—or he did indeed thirst terribly for whiskey. He and Juh and a number of Apaches set out eastward toward Casas Grandes, descended from the mountain heights, established a camp several miles from town, and sent a woman as emissary to ask municipal officials to meet them for negotiations.

Such reasonableness brought success. The mayor of Casas Grandes approved a treaty, and his people welcomed the Indians

240

into town. For two days Apaches wandered about—tense at first, then, seeing the cordiality, completely relaxed. On the second night the Indian visitors drank themselves into a collective stupor and lay down along the banks of a river nearby rather than attempt to make the long journey back to camp.

Small-arms fire startled them. Mexicans had taken advantage of their helplessness to strike. The Apaches lost a dozen warriors (dead) and thirty women and children (captured—including a wife of Geronimo's). Survivors raced for the camp, found the people there already running for the mountains (having been alerted by the distant shots), caught up with them, and found collective security again only after they had returned to Sierra Madre recesses. In the future, Geronimo decided, his people would get their supplies by raiding.

Southwestern settlers remained in ignorance of Geronimo's plight. To them the Apache menace had worsened, and with this had come increased white nervousness. Now even friendly Apaches seemed likely to break out and join Geronimo's marauders, since the usual reservation injustices had continued. Further, the recent raid on San Carlos (when Geronimo and Juh returned to get their kin) had shown settlers the vulnerability of the entire border area.

Hoping to regain control, the Army reassigned the man who earlier had helped to establish comparative peace—George Crook. The General and his aide, Captain John Bourke (newly promoted), and other headquarters staff members returned to Arizona—to Prescott —in October 1882.

Bourke observed turmoil: "All the Apaches were again on the warpath or in such a sullen, distrustful state of mind that it would have been better in some sense had they all left the reservation and taken to the forests and mountains."

Bourke observed Crook begin working in his usual direction: seeking to talk a return to peace before embarking on military operations. Crook called a council, conferred with reservation chiefs, rectified as many grievances as he could (but, to their dismay, forbade the making of their intoxicant, *tiswin,* realizing what troubles could ensue from it), and brought some renewed stability to reservations. Then he turned his attention to Geronimo and the other fugitive Apaches in the Sierra Madre.

Crook and his staff recognized the hopelessness of border guarding with the scant numbers of soldiers available; so he—and they—began thinking of an alternative: going after the Indians in their own stronghold.

About this time (on March 21, 1883) a band of Sierra Madre Apaches led by a warrior named Chato ("Flat-nosed") killed three men near Tombstone while on a foray northward to capture fresh supplies of ammunition needed for their American-made weapons. Later they veered eastward, into New Mexico, killed a federal judge from Lordsburg and his wife, and took with them into Mexico the couple's six-year-old son.

During the raid, however, they lost a defector who was war-weary and angry at having been "rescued" from San Carlos against his will: a man named Tso-ay, later nicknamed "Peaches" by army personnel because of his surprisingly light complexion. This gave Crook an opportunity. He persuaded Peaches to agree to guide soldiers to those Sierra Madre hideouts. Next, Crook visited Mexican officials and received their approval for sending his troopers into the country to get Geronimo.

On May 1, 1883, Crook—and Bourke—crossed the border with fifty soldiers, two hundred Indian scouts, and Peaches, marching southward. For five days they traveled through a poor land where men labored hard to hack out a living. There they were greeted amicably by Mexican inhabitants weary of losing hard-earned necessities of life to raiding Apaches.

On May 7 they turned eastward, into the Sierra Madre and—as night fell on an awesome canyon they had entered—into near-darkness. One soldier caught an owl and leashed it to the pommel of his saddle, thus provoking a halt and ensuing complaints from Indian scouts who regarded the bird as a creature who would bring bad luck. The soldier released his owl; it fluttered off into the night. Placated scouts recommenced their march and continued until Crook stopped everyone at midnight for a rest.

The next day they went on up the canyon. Tracks of horses and cattle, increasing in numbers, attested to Peaches' reliability. The Apache obviously was taking them toward a major hideaway.

Description of terrain as provided by Bourke left small wonder that Geronimo had found refuge here. "The path wound up the face of the mountain and became so precipitous that were a horse to slip . . . he would roll and fall hundreds of feet to the bottom. At one of the abrupt turns could be seen, deep down in the canyon, the mangled remains of a steer which had fallen from the trail."

The path became even steeper. Six pack mules lost their usual sure footing and tumbled off the trail, but because of favorable terrain at the locations where they had happened to fall none was seriously injured. Later, more pack mules fell. Three suffered broken necks and died; two others were injured so seriously they had to be shot.

Some consolation came with the ruggedness: a plentiful water supply in the canyons, good grass, pine forests curtaining the sun that in lower regions had cooked men with flame-like rays. Nights became cold, however, and no fires were allowed.

In daylight marches Bourke could see trails angling off in every direction, all littered with cast-off material that once had belonged to Mexicans residing in the lands below: dresses, letters, saddles, bridles. Peaches stayed on one chosen trail, however, and seemed certain of his destination.

He led the expedition to a place deep in the mountains where a main camp had been located when he was with the Apaches. The site resembled a natural amphitheater. It was watered by a clear stream and shaded by pines, oaks, cedars. But now the occupants obviously had retreated farther into the rugged wilderness.

Crook's Apaches proposed (on May 10) going ahead alone. Mules and soldiers were proving to be a hindrance. Crook approved, first emphasizing to them that they should do everything possible to persuade their fellow tribesmen to surrender. The General wanted no fighting in this wild, unfamiliar region. But when the scouts (on May 15) encountered the first "hostiles"—two warriors and a woman—they fired immediately and missed. The three Indians fled, but the scouts surprised and attacked a main camp nearby. They killed nine occupants and captured five others.

Held captive in this camp was the six-year-old son of the slain Lordsburg couple, and some Indian frustrated and infuriated by the unexpected attack seized stones and beat the boy to death before fleeing with the others.

Crook's scouts burned the village and rounded up the livestock. A woman captured in the attack volunteered information that many of the holdouts wanted to return to reservation security, no matter how distasteful it had been once, and promised to solicit surrenders if her captors would release her.

The scouts let her go, then waited. In time the soldiers and pack animals came up and encamped with the scouts.

Just as the woman had foreseen, Apaches began coming in—a few at first, then more. Within a few days Crook could count 121 Indians who preferred reservation existence to the dangers of life in the Sierra Madre.

Geronimo was not among those who surrendered. At that time he was not even in the vicinity. He and a group of warriors had descended the eastern foothills again in the direction of Casas Grandes, seeking prisoners to exchange for Indian captives (including Geronimo's wife) held in that Chihuahuan town since the recent trickery.

This time they were being careful. When they crossed a frequently used road they walked on their heels for some distance to avoid leaving footprints.

Near Casas Grandes they captured six women—all wives of soldiers who manned the town garrison. Geronimo promised the women they would not be harmed, sent another woman into town with an offer to exchange prisoners, then, while he waited for an answer, began eating a meal of roasted meat.

Geronimo was sitting with a portion of beef in one hand and a knife in the other, an eyewitness recalled later, when he dropped the knife and announced to everyone as fact a vision that had just come to him. The U. S. Army, he said, had captured those kinfolk left behind at base camp, now 120 miles distant. The warriors attested to their faith in Geronimo by agreeing to return to the camp at once. They took the Mexican women with them.

While still a day away from base camp Geronimo voiced another prediction (according to the same eyewitness): tomorrow, he said, he and the warriors with him would encounter a man who would tell them that American soldiers were occupying the site. On the following day, in midafternoon, this happened as Geronimo was said to have prophesied.

The changed situation left Geronimo mostly helpless. After truce talks with General Crook and after several days of reflection and indecision Geronimo surrendered and promised to lead his people back to the reservation. Many months later they arrived there, but with 350 head of stolen cattle in tow. The stock had been taken in some Mexican raids of grand finality. Geronimo's colleague and cousin, Juh, was not among the returning Indians. He had been fatally injured earlier in a fall from his horse.

To Geronimo's surprise Crook collected all the stolen animals and sent them back to Mexico. His action angered the newly surrendered Indians and especially Geronimo, who argued that he had made peace with Crook, but not with any Mexicans.

At the same time, but without Geronimo's realization, Crook also antagonized Arizona settlers by bringing back these troublesome Apaches. The settlers would have preferred their extermination deep in the Sierra Madre.

Crook's theft (as Geronimo saw it) of the stolen cattle filled the doubtful Apache with renewed distrust. Further, the usual inadequacies of rations and other supplies developed. Some Indians forgot their troubles with *tiswin,* although liquor had been forbidden. Discontent spread and multiplied, even though many Apaches, Geronimo among them, had been moved from San Carlos eastward to a reservation with a better climate, at Fort Apache. Restlessness flooded the souls of an inherently restless people. The Army again appeared to be on the verge of moving in, for some unknown purpose that could only be harsh. Settlers spoke of their continued hate.

Geronimo began having still more visions, this time of imprisonment and eventual execution. He predicted dismal events ahead and urged other leaders to leave the reservation with him. Then he lied to them, saying that an army officer and an Indian scout had been killed (an event planned by Geronimo but not carried out) and that the Army intended to arrest them all for the crime.

That tilted the scales again in favor of flight (on May 17, 1885).

Geronimo and several other leaders took 150 men, women, and children off the reservation, toward Mexico. As they left they cut the telegraph wire. Later, when two duped chiefs learned of Geronimo's trickery they came close to executing him themselves, but they finally settled for departure from the main band.

Ironically, Apache scouts ordered out in pursuit of Geronimo came across the trail of one of these groups (led by a chief named Chihuahua), followed it, and attacked people who were mulling over a logical way to return to the reservation without being punished. This incident so infuriated Chihuahua that he commenced a series of bloody raids reminiscent of those led by Victorio, Nana, and others, and he left border inhabitants cringing in terror. Then Chihuahua, too, went into the Sierra Madre again with an intention of taking up the old life.

General Crook had hoped to make reservation existence more attractive for Indians, whether or not Geronimo and a few other leaders gave him credit for it. In working toward this goal he had inflamed much of white Arizona.

Extracts from two documents indicated his thinking. The first has been taken from a letter (dated January 5, 1885) Crook wrote to Herbert Welsh of Philadelphia, an official of the Indian Rights Association.

Our object should be to get as much voluntary labor from the Indian as possible. Every dollar honestly gained by hard work is so much subtracted from the hostile element and added to that which is laboring for peace and civilization. . . . I wish to say that the American Indian is the intellectual peer of most, if not all, the various nationalities we have assimilated to our laws, customs, and language. He is fully able to protect himself if the ballot be given, and the courts of law not closed against him. If our aim be to remove the aborigine from a state of servile dependence, we cannot begin in a better or more practical way than by making him think well of himself, to force upon him the knowledge that he is part and parcel of the nation, clothed with all its political privileges, entitled to share in all its benefits. Our present treatment degrades him in his own eyes, by making evident the difference between his own condition and that of those about him.

The second extract appeared in Crook's "Annual Report" for 1885.

It should not be expected that an Indian who has lived as a barbarian all his life will become an angel the moment he comes on a reservation and promises to behave himself. . . . I do not wish to be understood as in the least palliating their crimes, but I wish to say a word to stem the torrent of . . . abuse which has almost universally been indulged in against the whole Apache race. This is not strange on the frontier from a certain class of vampires who prey on the misfortunes of their fellowmen, and who live best and easiest in time of Indian troubles. With them peace kills the goose that lays the golden egg. Greed and avarice on the part of the whites . . . is at the bottom of nine-tenths of all our Indian trouble.

Now Crook had another military campaign to launch. Once more troopers guided by Apache scouts followed hostile Indians through ravines and canyons, over and around giant rocks, across mountain streams awash with runoff from heavy, late-spring rains (which also helped to hide trails). Ahead, the fleeing Chiricahuas left the usual mementos of their visits: murdered and sometimes mutilated settlers, stolen stock, goods seized to sustain Indian life. Further, the Apaches this time tried a new trick. Whenever pursuers came uncomfortably close they would throw them off by making "false camps"—starting small camp fires at some selected location, leaving one or two worn-out horses tethered in the vicinity, then dashing on while pursuers halted and prepared an ambush.

An army officer later described the difficulty of chasing Geronimo.

It is laid down in our army tactics . . . that twenty-five miles a day is the maximum that cavalry can stand. Bear this in mind, and also that here is an enemy with a thousand miles of hilly and sandy country to run over, and each brave provided with from three to five ponies trained like dogs. They carry almost nothing but arms and ammunition; they can live on the cactus; they can go more than forty-eight hours without water; they know every water hole and every foot of ground in this vast . . . country; they have incredible powers of endurance; they run in small bands scattering at the first indications of pursuit. What can the United States soldier, mounted on his heavy American horse, with the necessary forage, rations, and camp equipage, do . . . against this supple, untiring foe? Nothing, absolutely nothing. It is no exaggeration to say that these fiends can travel . . . at the rate of seventy miles a day . . . over the most barren and desolate country imaginable. One week of such work will kill the average soldier and his horse.

Crook's solution, as it had been earlier, was to rely on those Apache scouts. Now he sent two columns of them after Geronimo— one along the eastern slope of the Sierra Madre, the other along the western side. Whenever they found trails leading into the mountains they were to follow them.

One group located a camp and attacked (capturing fifteen women and children), but they did not find Geronimo. The hostile Apaches countered this, whether or not intentionally, by sending a small party of warriors northward past Crook's sentinels to the border country, where their raids terrorized settlers again and once more brought the collective wrath of Arizona settlers down on Crook. Meanwhile, the Apache scouts had found more camps and had attacked, taking prisoners, but Geronimo continued to elude them.

Then (in January 1886) the scouts came upon a main camp and after a surprise attack that caused few human casualties captured most of the Indians' horses and supplies. Such loss disheartened even Geronimo. After a chance battle between Mexican troops nearby and Crook's Apaches, commenced when identities were mistaken and ended when communication finally was established, the end began to grow near for the freewheeling Apache leader.

Geronimo's band had dwindled since coming into Mexico. Some of his people had been killed. Many had been captured (including

Geronimo's entire family, with the exception of an eldest son). Others had gone with the raiding party northward and had not returned. The only recognized leaders left were Geronimo, Naiche, and Chihuahua. Against their scant numbers was arrayed a large military force of Americans and Mexicans, and the Sierra Madre no longer terrified outsiders. "Our scouts had reported bands of United States and Mexican troops at many points in the mountains," Geronimo said later. "We estimated that about two thousand soldiers were ranging these mountains seeking to capture us." He also made an observation that typified his entire career: "It is senseless to fight when you cannot hope to win."

The time had come again, sadly, to talk about peace.

Captain Bourke, still with Crook, heard of Geronimo's desire to confer with the General. "Geronimo sent word that he would come in . . . at a spot he would designate. This was the Cañon de los Embudos, in the northeast corner of Sonora, on the Arizona line." Already encamped near that canyon was an American army detachment under the command of a Lieutenant Marion Maus, through whom Geronimo had sent his request to meet Crook.

Bourke accompanied Crook to the site, although the General wisely left most of his army behind. The sight of so many soldiers moving toward them would have sent the Apaches running again.

> The rancheria of the hostile Chiricahuas was in a lava bed [Bourke observed], on top of a small conical hill surrounded by steep ravines, not five hundred yards in direct line from [Lieutenant Maus's camp], but having between the two positions two or three steep and rugged gulches which served as scarps and counter-scarps. The whole ravine was . . . beautiful: shading the rippling water were smooth, white-trunked, long, and slender sycamores, dark gnarly ash, rough-barked cottonwoods, pliant willows, briery buckthorn, and much of the more tropical vegetation already enumerated.

Bourke saw Geronimo, Naiche, Chihuahua, and a number of their warriors approach Crook's camp, after some delay. Not all of them entered at once. They came in groups of four, five, or six—"all on the *qui vive,* apprehensive of treachery, and ready to meet it."

Crook's talk with Geronimo was held in a shady grove of cottonwoods and sycamores. Bourke and twenty or so others, including interpreters and a photographer, also attended. The Captain kept notes of what was said at the historic meeting, which ended (after some subsequent talks) with the surrender of Geronimo and all other hostile Apaches. Bourke heard with pleasure Geronimo's words, directed to Crook: "Once I moved about like the wind. Now I surrender to you and that is all."

But peace had not come, nor had Geronimo's surrender. That evening a Swiss-American adventurer named Bob Tribolet, acting as an agent of Arizona war contractors, came into the Apache camp selling mescal to the happily surprised Indians. Tribolet got them drunk and told them frightening stories of what the Army planned for them once they had been returned to the reservation.

Geronimo needed no other motivation. He and Naiche and a small number of Apaches fled again toward the mountains, although Chihuahua and the rest stayed with the soldiers.

"A beautiful commentary upon the civilization of the white man!" Bourke fumed.

Such treatment of Indians and an ensuing humiliation of Crook would leave the Captain smoldering for most of the rest of his life (which ended with his death June 9, 1896, while nearing the age of fifty). All War Department appreciation of Crook's earlier painstaking work with Geronimo vanished along with the skittish Apaches.

Chief of Staff Sheridan replaced Crook with an almost opposite in personality, General Nelson Miles, who launched an elaborate and costly campaign against thirty-three Apaches (including thirteen women) that eventually brought Geronimo's final surrender on September 4, 1886. As punishment Geronimo and many other Apaches, inexplicably including some warriors who had served as army scouts, spent time in a Florida prison before those who survived the dreadful, unaccustomed humidity there were returned to their families on the Chiricahua reservation—by that time established in present Oklahoma.

Bourke never mourned the treatment given Geronimo, but he did grieve for Crook's reputation and for the general treatment of Apaches. "There is no more disgraceful page in the history of our relations with the American Indians than that which conceals the treachery visited upon the Chiricahuas who remained faithful in their allegiance to our people," he said.

Years later Geronimo would add his own lament, tempered with a few well-greased words calculated to appeal to his white civilizers.

At least partly because of his previous failure to admit reality his Apaches had been moved far from home. This saddened him enormously.

> I know that if my people were placed in that mountainous region lying around the headwaters of the Gila River they would live in peace and act according to the will of the President [Geronimo would say near the end of his life]. They would be prosperous and happy in tilling the soil and learning the civilization of the white men, whom they now respect. Could I but see this accomplished, I think I could forget all the wrongs that I have ever received, and die a contented and happy old man. . . . If this cannot be done during my lifetime—if I must die in bondage—I hope that the remnant of the Apache tribe may, when I am gone, be granted the one privilege which they request—to return to Arizona.

24

TIME AT ITS WORK

Throughout the waning years of Indian resistance an interested observer from afar had been Lieutenant Robert Goldthwaite Carter, the dedicated young officer of earlier days who had sustained a painful leg injury during his mounted ascent of Blanco Canyon and who later had been released from the Army as "permanently disqualified." The leg had never ceased to cause him pain.

On the Wednesday, June 28, 1876, that Carter had been released—much against his will—Custer and those 7th Cavalry troopers the General had led into eternity had been dead for three days, although word of the tragedy had not yet reached Americans. Within a week of release Carter heard with what must have been shock and sadness of the Army's great defeat on the Little Big Horn.

Following that, news of happenings closer to home had come interspersed with other word from the frontier. About a month after the arrival of news of Custer's death Colorado was admitted as a state (on August 1, 1876), indicating again the inexorability of westward advancement despite the momentary setback inflicted by Crazy Horse, Sitting Bull, and the other Sioux.

Technical as well as geographical advancement continued. Americans welcomed a new god, machinery, and in their spirit of materialism began acquiring as many of his manufactures as they could. In 1876 appeared the first mimeograph (Thomas Edison's invention); in 1877 the first gasoline-driven horseless carriage

252

(George Selden's, but he later lost a patent war against Henry Ford); in 1878 a phonograph (Edison's); in 1879 a perfected electric light (Edison's); in 1880 the first successful roll film for cameras (George Eastman's); in 1882 the first electric fan (Schuyler Skaats Wheeler's); in 1884 the first fountain pen (Lewis Waterman's).

Educational facilities were multiplying, too. During the decade following 1880 these universities (among others) were established west of the Mississippi: University of Southern California, University of Dakota (now South Dakota), University of North Dakota, University of Texas, University of Arizona, Stanford University, University of Wyoming, University of New Mexico, and University of Idaho. None of them admitted illiterate Indians, although a scattering of reservation schools sought with great difficulty to give some native children a basic education, and an eastern institution of higher quality located at Carlisle, Pennsylvania, and opened November 1, 1879, strove to equip Indian youths for life in a white society.

Carter read, too, of Presidents who came and went—all without greatly influencing Indian relations out West, a fact that the various tribes would have corroborated, if asked. In 1880 Republican James A. Garfield, a vigorous, even-tempered man with a scholarly bent, was elected to succeed Rutherford Hayes, another Republican, but Garfield served little more than six months before he died (in 1881) of an assassin's bullet. Taking his place was fat, dapper, side-whiskered Chester A. Arthur, candidate for Vice-President on the successful 1880 Republican ticket and a lover of French cuisine who invariably rose late for a ten-o'clock continental breakfast.

Democrats finally broke the postbellum string of Republican presidential victories in 1884 with the election of Grover Cleveland, a man of notable obesity in a long line of fleshy Presidents. This was a triumph that must have pleased Democrat Quanah Parker of the reservation Comanches, even if few other Indians would have noticed the change.

Four years later Republican Benjamin Harrison—a reticent, hard-working noncharmer—defeated Cleveland, and Harrison saw to the admission of six states (more than any other President) that not so many years earlier had been populated almost entirely by Indians: North and South Dakota, Montana, Washington, Idaho, and Wyoming. In addition, his administration was responsible for opening large tracts of Indian land to white settlement.

In 1892 Democrats reversed their recent loss and returned Cleveland to the White House against the same Benjamin Harrison. But after that came more Republicans: self-contained William McKinley, assassinated during his second term, and ebullient Theodore Roosevelt, who (like Arthur) moved up from Vice-President.

Carter saw them all come and go, and he knew the intimacies of their administrations. He resided in Washington and kept himself informed of current happenings in the nation that he felt he had helped to build. Some events saddened him; others made him happy. Few left him unmoved; he usually had an opinion ready to express.

In 1884 came an event that saddened him. His old commander, Ranald Mackenzie, joined him in enforced retirement from military service, but for a different reason. Mackenzie's physical frailness, the rigors of Indian fighting, and the wearing demands of leadership —all combined with a high-strung temperament—seemed to have sapped his reason. When his irrationality became obvious friends sought to keep him from view until good sense returned—as they thought it would. Instead, his condition worsened, and he was committed to Bloomingdale Asylum, in New York. The following spring (of 1884) the Army retired him for disability contracted in line of duty. About five years later, while living with his sister on Staten Island, he committed suicide.

Carter had speculated that some mental lapse by Mackenzie had been responsible for the commander's failure to mention Carter's valor at Blanco Canyon in 1871—and responsible, too, for his negligence in failing to reprimand Captain Heyl, the officer who had taken his seven troopers out of the fight there. Mackenzie never did correct the error (as Carter considered it); so the now forgotten Lieutenant also devoted himself in his retirement years to gathering letters from surviving eyewitnesses in an effort to substantiate his claim to more consideration by the Army he had sought to serve well. He asked the War Department for proper recognition of his conduct at Blanco Canyon and for return to active duty—for anything that might get him and his stagnant personal affairs back into the mainstream of life—but his requests resulted only in continued silence by the War Department.

Once, in a mood of great depression, he wrote:

> It has been said by wise men, great writers, sages, and ancient philosophers that one should never . . . turn backward, but always live in the present, and look forward to one's future life, the past being forever dead and buried.
>
> That is excellent advice and philosophy for youth. Few young people do look backward, for their interest centers in their present work and ambitions, and their future lies before them full of gilded hopes and promises. But this chunk of wisdom does not always hold true with the aged, for while they are compelled to adjust themselves to the present, there are few, if any, rosy promises held out to them for a future— unless, with full faith, it is the one after life—especially if some event in that past life has been largely responsible for much of the sorrow, bitter disappointments, and blasted hopes in their selected career.

Carter's physical and mental condition precluded anticipation of any earthly life ahead of him. He could only look back and hope that he might persuade someone else in authority to look back, too, and reward him adequately for past service. But no one would join him.

The government actually devoted much more attention to the Indians it had paid Carter to kill, even if that attention continued to work against Indian welfare more often than not. No one seemed to have any effective ideas of how best to help people previously thought of as being blocks to progress that must be removed.

Generous distribution of rations and supplies made the recipients completely dependent on the government and, worse, caused them to assume that Washington realized it owed them a living and would follow through appropriately. Further, many of the goods received were not wanted or used by the recipients. Crude houses constructed for them remained empty while they slept in the tents to which they were accustomed. Men's trousers found no wearers until the new owner had first cut out the seat.

But moves to make Indians self-supporting through agriculture failed, too, because most reservations had been located in poor land not wanted by anyone else. Whenever drought or other natural disaster wiped out crops supplemental federal aid was slow to arrive—if it came at all.

Some Indians had a more effective solution to their problems, but unfortunately for them, this, too, failed to work. About three years after Geronimo's final surrender a solar eclipse (on January 1, 1889) excited still-superstitious Indians. A medicine man of the Nevada Piutes named Wavoka declared that the Great Spirit had used the eclipse as a sign that he, Wavoka, had been selected to lead all tribesmen back to their old existence. Indian dead would be returned to life, Wavoka said, and buffalo would again inhabit the Plains. This time, he added, white men's bullets would be ineffective, provided Indians had taken part in a ceremonial called the ghost dance.

Wavoka's pronouncements stimulated many Indians to dance—especially the Sioux. It also aroused renewed fear among whites who could recall recent uprisings and massacres with yesterday vividness. As a result, minor violence occurred. It ended with the shooting death of Sitting Bull (who had returned from Canada) by Indian police sent to arrest him in connection with all the ominous activity, and with an outbreak at Wounded Knee, South Dakota, that led to the killing or wounding of 176 Sioux (mostly women and children) by troopers of the 7th Cavalry, which happened to be Custer's old regiment.

Wavoka's solution to the "Indian problem" thus proved to have been of greatest harm to the Indians themselves. Nothing else worked, however, then or later; and today the resultant squalor associated with most reservations is well known—but scarcely nearer solution.

In 1901 officials became so concerned about tribal dependence on Washington for all necessities that the government ordered reservation superintendents to reduce food and clothing distribution, with the hope that the recipients might be encouraged to make up the difference by working.

The usual confusion resulted. Rations distributed to old and ill persons were shared with everyone, including the young and healthy. This was in accordance with Indian custom, which dictated that anyone who had food should pass it around to those who had none. Rations were consumed in a short time, requiring a period of near-starvation to be endured by everyone (including the old and ill) until arrival of the next distribution.

Government attempts to encourage Indians to help themselves within the structure of a new society thus proved largely futile, with some notable exceptions. Among them might have been included some activities of the old Apache leader Geronimo.

After he had been removed from Florida imprisonment to the new Chiricahua reservation in the Indian Territory and had accepted Christianity, his former enemies invited him to the 1904 St. Louis World's Fair—the "Louisiana Purchase Exposition," commemorating the hundredth anniversary of the event that eventually meant doom for thousands of Indians.

At first Geronimo refused to go, but promoters insisted. His presence would attract crowds and money. President Theodore Roosevelt intervened to promise Geronimo protection, and this won his consent. Geronimo went to St. Louis, remained six months, and showed an immediate grasp of moneymaking and what a bit of the white man's education could do to abet it.

> I sold my photographs for twenty-five cents [he said] and was allowed to keep ten cents of this for myself. I also wrote my name for ten, fifteen, or twenty-five cents, as the case might be, and kept all of that money. I often made as much as two dollars a day, and when I returned I had plenty of money— more than I had ever owned before.

At the same fair Geronimo also showed more tongue-in-cheek grasp of character than his hosts might have realized at the time. After visiting "The Pike" and its various amusements, including a Ferris wheel, he said:

> One time the guards took me into a little house that had four windows. When we were seated the little house started to move along the ground. Then the guards called my attention

to some curious things they had in their pockets. Finally they told me to look out, and when I did so I was scared, for our little house had gone high up in the air, and the people down in the Fair Grounds looked no larger than ants. The men laughed at me for being so scared. . . .

One day we went into another show, and as soon as we were in it, it changed into night. It was real night, for I could feel the damp air; soon it began to thunder, and the lightning flashed; it was real lightning, too, for it struck just above our heads. I dodged and wanted to run away, but I could not tell which way to go in order to get out. The guards motioned me to keep still, and so I stayed. In front of us were some strange little people who came out on the platform; then I looked up again and the clouds were all gone, and I could see stars shining. The little people on the platform did not seem in earnest about anything they did; so I only laughed at them. All the people around where we sat seemed to be laughing at me. . . .

. . .

I am glad I went to the Fair. I saw many interesting things and learned much of the white people. They are a very kind and peaceful people. During all the time I was at the Fair no one tried to harm me in any way.

After that Geronimo returned to the Indian Territory, still a prisoner of war and still wishing he and his people might be allowed to go back to Arizona.

Even had he been permitted this move, his way of life never could have been the same as it had been once. By this time Geronimo had become a farmer and an especially proud grower of fine watermelons, a member of the Dutch Reformed Church, and a teacher of Sunday school—all this and an ardent devotee of capitalism, too. In addition to the money he made selling autographs at the fair he accumulated piles of cash from the sale of bows and arrows and other articles hand-made by himself.

Geronimo became a great self-promoter. With the aid of S. M. Barrett, a school official of Lawton, Oklahoma, he produced his autobiography and dedicated it to his friend Theodore Roosevelt, then President. The book idea was largely Barrett's, however, and Geronimo cooperated only because Barrett agreed to pay him to tell his story—through a translator, Asa Daklugie, son of Juh.

During the storytelling sessions Geronimo showed Barrett something about Indian integrity.

> [Geronimo] soon became so tired of book making that he would have abandoned the task [Barrett said] but for the fact that he had agreed to tell the complete story. When he once gives his word, nothing will turn him from fulfilling his promise. A . . . striking illustration of this was furnished early in January, 1906. He had agreed to come to my study on a certain date, but at the appointed hour the interpreter came alone, and said that Geronimo was very sick with cold and fever. He had come to tell me that we must appoint another date, as he feared the old warrior had an attack of pneumonia. It was a cold day and the interpreter drew a chair up to the grate to warm himself after the exposure of the long ride. Just as he was seating himself he looked out of the window, then rose quickly, and without speaking pointed to a rapidly moving object coming our way. In a moment I recognized the old chief riding furiously (evidently trying to arrive as soon as the interpreter did), his horse flecked with foam and reeling from exhaustion. Dismounting, he came in and said in a hoarse whisper, "I promised to come. I am here."
>
> I explained to him that I had not expected him to come on such a stormy day, and that in his physical condition he must not try to work. He stood for some time, and then without speaking left the room, remounted his tired pony, and with bowed head faced ten long miles of cold north wind—he had kept his promise.

Geronimo survived that ordeal, and for three more years he sought permission to return to Arizona. In a story printed in the Tucson *Daily Star* (December 6, 1908) he was quoted as saying, "I want to go back to my old home before I die. Tired of fight and want to rest. Want to go back to the mountains again."

Little more than a year later (on February 17, 1909, when about eighty) he died in the post hospital at Fort Sill from the effects of

259

exposure. He had traveled in a buggy to Lawton to sell a bow, had spent the money on whiskey, and during a return journey undertaken in freezing rain had fallen, drunk, out of the buggy. He had lain in the road all night before being discovered still alive. Not even an Apache could survive such an ordeal as that.

Like Geronimo, Quanah the Comanche numbered among his friends President Theodore Roosevelt, whom he entertained once with a five-day wolf hunt. Quanah visited the White House during Roosevelt's tenure and found one Republican administration, at least, to his liking.

But Quanah continued to refuse to become totally white, and during all of his reservation life he remained more Indian in many ways than had Geronimo. Meanwhile, and not far away, former Kiowa Chief Big Tree—the onetime fellow inmate of White Bear's in the Texas penitentiary—had commenced a life of Christianity that would lead to his teaching Sunday school and serving as deacon in the Rainy Mountain Baptist Church (near Mountain View, Oklahoma) until his death in 1929.

Quanah never accepted Christianity, although he numbered Christian missionaries among his many friends, and his son, White Parker, became a Methodist minister. On one occasion the wife of a Fort Sill Indian agent described for him the religion of his mother's parents and aroused enough interest in Quanah so that he asked how he might take the same religion.

A beginning, she answered, would be to give up all but one of his several wives.

"In that case," he answered, "I keep my religion."

His religion eventually went into establishment of the Native American Church, which utilized narcotic peyote buttons in worship.* Quanah had learned somewhere, perhaps during a trip to Mexico, that the bitter-tasting buttons produced color visions and dreams, and he claimed that these fantasies gave him and his people inspiration from God. That belief became popular among Quanah's people, but most religious Comanches today are said to claim a Protestant faith.

* The 200,000 members of this church are still (in 1975) allowed under law to chew peyote during tribal ceremonies.

Quanah himself called on a Baptist and a Mennonite to officiate at a 1910 reburial service near Cache, Oklahoma, for his mother, whose remains had been disinterred at his request (but only after local opposition had been overcome) from Old Fosterville Cemetery in Anderson County, Texas, for removal to a new grave site near Quanah's home. The United States Government allocated one thousand dollars for the work, including money for a new monument. Speakers at the Oklahoma service included Quanah himself, whose words were quoted in *Chronicles of Oklahoma:*

> Forty years ago my mother died. She captured by Comanche nine years old. Love Indian and wild life so well no want to go back to white folks. All same people anyway, God say. I love my mother. I like white people. . . . I want my people follow after white way, get educated, know work, make living when payments stop. I tell um know white man's God. Comanche may die tomorrow or ten years. When end come then they all be together again. I want to see my mother again, that's why when Government U. S. gave money for new grave, I have this funeral and ask white folks to help bury. Glad to see so many my people here at funeral. That's all.

Quanah said he wanted to be buried next to his mother someday, and within months his wish was granted. In February 1911 he became ill during a visit and returned home near death—hopelessly so, in everyone's apparent opinion.

Quanah died an Indian. A quickly summoned medicine man—not Isatai—prayed, "Father in heaven, this, our brother, is coming." With his arms he embraced Quanah, flapped his hands, and imitated an eagle's call.

Within minutes Quanah died. Women wailed their lament—three surviving wives among them. His people dressed him the way he had looked years earlier when a warrior chief roaming the Staked Plain, and they buried him. The United States Government paid for a red-granite monument that declared Quanah Parker was "Resting here until day breaks and shadows fall and darkness disappears."

In Washington, the forgotten lieutenant who had identified Quanah as the chief he once fought felt no sadness, no nostalgia

261

when he read of Quanah's death and the government's solicitude in regard to the marker. Robert Goldthwaite Carter's emotion was instead one of frustration and anger, tinged with self-pity—a usual social repellent, but in Carter's case at least understandable.

Carter felt that way even though his letter writing and evidence gathering had persuaded the War Department to acknowledge the value of his services. Mackenzie, for whatever reason, had ignored him, but Carter had collected sufficient evidence from fellow officers to persuade War Department officials to brevet him captain (on February 27, 1890) for gallantry in an 1873 action during Mackenzie's expedition into Mexico and to award him the Congressional Medal of Honor (on January 23, 1900) for his fight at Blanco Canyon against the chief Carter identified as Quanah.

But Carter wanted more. The years of his life that should have been the most productive had been full of agony for him. His injured leg had not only pained him; it required frequent medical attention, for which he was forced to spend some of his poor pay as a retired first lieutenant while at the same time striving to support a family.

Finally surgery progressed to a point where an army doctor believed he could relieve the pain and the disability by an operation. The doctor succeeded (in 1901), and Carter requested a return to active duty, together with past promotions he would have received and the ensuing higher pay. He volunteered for service in the Philippines, then a theater of United States military operations (against native guerrillas, following American take-over of the Islands after the 1898 war with Spain).

Bureaucracy stymied him. Government officials all the way to the President ignored his request or contended they lacked authority to approve it. At the top, Theodore Roosevelt suggested trying an enabling act of Congress, but War Department people frowned. This would establish an unfortunate precedent, they said. Carter continued on the retired list as a brevetted captain and fumed about how the Republic treated those who had served it to the best of their ability.

Theodore Roosevelt's March 4, 1905, inaugural parade exasperated him further. Carter joined a multitude of Washingtonians who watched it.

A total of 35,000 Americans representing virtually every vocation paraded down Pennsylvania Avenue in a chilly wind for more than three hours. Roosevelt reviewed them from a stand near the White House.

Carter also watched them come: bands and other marching units, Rough Riders, mounted cowboys, governors given more sedate transportation, United States Military Academy cadets.

Midway in the parade Carter was amazed and angered to see the fellow citizens packed around him paying utmost attention and tribute to a group of mounted Indians seemingly dressed for another war on the Great White Father, who was applauding them as energetically as any other spectator. The Indians rode their richly adorned horses directly in front of Carter, and he saw (six years before that chief's death) Quanah, the Comanche who had helped to give him his cursed disability; Geronimo (four years before his death), slayer of many army men and white citizens; and others.

Carter might have read later the Washington *Post* description of those Indian chiefs that day as a real-life "Remington's picture"; but Carter, following orders that had originated in this same city of Washington, had seen reality—and something of it was lacking here. He could only reflect that most of the "good Indians" he saw in the parade "had dipped their hands in many a white settler's blood on the once far off borderland of the West."

The Indians passed on along Pennsylvania Avenue—out of Carter's vision, but still not out of his life. After Quanah had brought his mother to Oklahoma for reburial Carter read about some federal government generosity: allocating money for a tombstone. Once more he lost his restraint and whatever selflessness remained to him, and he wrote:

> Generous government, indeed! Could a generous government afford to do less for a "gallant officer" of the Army who had almost sacrificed his life in an effort to promote the settlement of that wild, uninhabited, savage-infested territory. . . . If Congress . . . could bestow a $1,000 monument to honor the white mother who bore this implacable half-breed Comanche . . . it could certainly have done a simple justice to . . . one officer who was . . . ready, for the sake of peace and civili-

zation in that far-off Texas Panhandle, to risk his life in what
has . ... . proved to be something more than a mere story.

But Congress did not hear Carter. Instead, after Quanah's own
death (within a matter of months) it appropriated another fifteen
hundred dollars for a memorial to that Comanche chief.

Another white survivor of the Indian wars had been having
financial troubles. After General Custer was reported killed his
widow Libbie had begun receiving a pension amounting to thirty
dollars a month. This pittance certainly afforded scant consolation,
but no amount of money probably could have consoled her immediately following that summer of 1876.

She moved to New York and sought to lose herself in the masses
of humanity there, but unpleasantness always seemed to seek her
out. She read or heard many critical remarks aimed at Custer's
alleged indiscretion at the Little Big Horn, and each of them
overwhelmed her. Her own considerable ability to gossip and to ac-
cuse had until now been checked by the General for reasons of
diplomacy, but with Custer gone she began to indulge herself in
spiteful remarks aimed at her late husband's critics.

About a year after Custer's death his body was taken from its
battlefield grave and reburied at West Point. Libbie steeled herself—
something not at all easy for her to do now—and attended the ceremony.

Most of her physical discomfort, however, was caused by the
small pension, which became lost quickly in New York living—and
much sooner than she was able to lose herself in the masses there.
Eventually she wrote her old friend General Sherman, asked for an
increase to fifty dollars, signed her letter "Desolate me," and
received the additional allowance.

Later her economic situation began to brighten. Her stepmother
died and left her some money. Then Libbie began writing, and the
royalties helped pay for a cottage at Onteora, in the Catskill Mountains. The hero in her books always was the same man: General
George Armstrong Custer. Libbie's productions were nonfiction,
but her depiction of Custer usually was subject to dispute by his
critics.

Her hero worship became even more pronounced with the passage of time. One book (*Tenting on the Plains*, 1895) she dedicated

TO HIM

WHOSE BRAVE AND BLITHE ENDURANCE

MADE THOSE WHO FOLLOWED

HIM FORGET,

IN HIS SUNSHINY PRESENCE,

HALF THE HARDSHIP AND THE DANGER

—thus ignoring the time when many enlisted men from Custer's command deserted because of his unreasonable marches.

Libbie contributed much to Custer's enduring fame by keeping his name before the public at a time when it might otherwise have vanished from American lips and by washing the memory of him clean of some dubiousness—feats well within reach of a seemingly helpless woman writing for emotional nineteenth-century readers. Except for Libbie's efforts the name Custer might be but little better known to today's readers than the name George Fetterman, an officer who led a force against Sioux, Northern Cheyennes, and some Arapahos in an 1866 battle that (as in Custer's fight) ended with no white survivors.

As the years passed Libbie's financial situation continued to improve. She traveled continually, but she always returned to Onteora for summers; and wherever she was, she always glorified the General. Fifty-five years to the day after Custer died on the Little Big Horn—and the anniversary of that day she and other officers' wives had been trying to assuage their anxiety at Fort Lincoln with hymns like "Nearer, my God, to Thee"—she acceded to a request by journalists for an interview. The New York *Times* carried a story in its edition of June 26, 1931.

Less than three years after that Libbie Custer joined her long-absent husband. She died April 6, 1933, within two days of her ninety-second birthday, and was buried beside the General at West Point.

Robert Goldthwaite Carter outlived her. The Army never had returned him to duty, but a son, Robert D. Carter, had served in the

Philippines, on the Mexican border, and in France during the First World War—before retiring as a lieutenant colonel in 1918.

Brevet Captain Carter lived on and on, beyond the death of his wife, Mary, in November 1923. After that he moved into the Army and Navy Club—in 1924, the same year, incidentally, that Congress finally declared that every last native Indian be counted as a citizen of the United States. But Carter never forgot the "injustice" done to him, especially after he had observed several administrations striving to right prior wrongs done to the same Indians he had been ordered to fight.

The Franklin Roosevelt administration did the best single job of improving the Indians' situation—in 1934, with the passage of an Indian Reorganization Act. This rectified what proved to have been a mistake foisted upon the tribes half a century earlier (in 1887) by a well-meaning Massachusetts sympathizer, Senator Henry Dawes, who concluded that Indians would be best served and their parcels of earth kept in utmost safety by a "Severalty Act" dissolving tribes as legal units, distributing tribal lands among individual members (160 acres to families, 80 acres to unmarried persons—none of the land to be sold for twenty-five years), and returning to the government left-over acreage that would then become open to white settlement. But this left tribesmen lost, generally, with no familiar organization supporting them and with no economic base. Franklin Roosevelt's advisers recognized the misfortune, and their Indian Reorganization Act reinstated old authority by returning to tribal ownership lands open to sale and by allowing reservation inhabitants to organize for self-government.

More than a year after Indian reorganization Carter, aged ninety, was still living.

That Civil War veteran survived to see the advent of air warfare, the emergence of armored divisions from his own beloved cavalry, and the coming of Adolf Hitler. In 1935 Hitler rejected the Versailles Treaty of World War I and ordered conscription in Germany. That same year Italy invaded Ethiopia; meanwhile, Japanese troops were three years into their take-over of the Chinese mainland. The military monster Germans called *Führer* would give countless young lieutenants an opportunity to fight, and many of them would suffer personal damage much greater than Carter's disabling wound.

Carter died January 4, 1936, and was buried in Arlington National Cemetery. Fortunately for whatever earthly peace of mind had remained to him to the last, he did not live to read about two ensuing events.

In 1957 Lieutenant Carter's old adversary, Quanah, was reburied (along with his mother) in the post cemetery at Fort Sill, and the Comanche chief received full military honors—all at government expense, of course. White men had taken his land once again—this time the old Post Oak Mission Cemetery, where he had lain for nearly half a century, but needed now for guided-missile expansion. Six of Quanah's seven surviving children attended the rites,* as did many senior army officers. One of the speakers at the funeral was the Fort Sill commanding officer, a major general.

Six years later the pitifully few remains of the Kiowa chief Carter had escorted to Atoka, Oklahoma—White Bear—were exhumed from "Felon's Field" outside the walls of the Texas penitentiary at Huntsville and were taken, too, to the post cemetery at Fort Sill. There, near the Kiowa reservation, they were reburied at the request of White Bear's grandson, James Auchiah (of Carnegie, Oklahoma), with full military honors—again, at considerable expense to the late Bob Carter's government.

White Bear's removal had required an act by the Texas Legislature. In debate the bill had been vigorously opposed by a representative from once-victimized Parker County; he called White Bear "murderous." But the bill, after approval had been voted, was signed by Governor John Connally.

Except for the Parker County legislator few persons harbored any grudges against White Bear. Most Texans, in fact, never had heard of him—an example of time at its work.

At Fort Sill soldiers not unlike the ones who once had aimed taunts and rifle fire at old White Bear stood at attention, while other soldiers saluted the once great "orator of the Plains" with ceremonial volleys.

Even the Parkers, red and white, seem to have forgotten old

---

* Quanah's last surviving son, Thomas Titah Parker, died July 1975.

animosities. Members of the family meet at yearly reunions now—usually in odd years at the site of Parker's Fort in Texas and in even years in Oklahoma, somewhere near the grave of the half-breed Comanche chief whose birth came as a result of one solution to social problems more impressive than anything any number of bureaucrats are likely to devise.

EPILOGUE

RED ANTS, COYOTES, AND
CATTLEMEN

The Medicine Lodge and Laramie treaties failed in their immediate purpose of bringing peace to the Plains, but both contributed to accomplishment of the long-range objective: to stop Indian interference with white expansion throughout desirable areas of the United States.

In its treatment of native inhabitants the United States eventually put itself on an approximate level with Australia, where the original population of 300,000 aborigines (estimated) decreased rapidly after 1788 because of ruthless treatment and exploitation. About 1880, in response to growing humanitarian pressures, the various Australian states began to make provisions for protection. Now the numbers of half-blooded (or greater) aborigines (79,620 in 1966) are increasing.

Canada offered a more humane example. The government there promised Indians less than did the United States, but it delivered what had been promised with greater integrity. Canada carefully kept liquor from Indians, refrained from annexing their lands without genuine consent, meted out equal punishment to lawbreakers both red and white, named Indian administrators to lengthy tenures and ably administered Indian funds, bestowed citizenship earlier on more advanced tribesmen, and generally displayed consistency and honesty in dealings—especially when compared to United States Government conduct after the Medicine Lodge and Laramie treaties.

269

Failure of those treaties to bring peace was not, however, a one-sided responsibility.

Ranking army officers like Custer sometimes ignored treaty terms (as Custer did in his attack at the Battle of Washita), and junior officers could only follow orders. Carter and others like him fought because of belief in the righteousness of their cause; Bourke and other reluctant officers because of duty; women like Libbie Custer followed their men blindly because of devotion.

But the other side had several devious leaders, too—like White Bear, who promised peace but almost immediately continued his raiding. Of greater integrity were Quanah, who scoffed at the treaty signing because he suspected the terms would mean nothing at all, and even Geronimo, who was not included (then) on invitation lists.

The Medicine Lodge and Laramie treaties indeed proved to be harbingers of bad days for North American Indians: first a series of Plains fights (and no peace at all) that spelled their doom as warriors; then an extended period of bungling by bureaucrats who put into practice a variety of theories about how best to care for a once proud people.

Since history has a way of putting events in proper perspective, most Americans commiserate today with the poor Indians, now that the old death songs have been sung and scalps rest in general safety, but had some people possessed more humility and perception in the past they might have learned something from the once despised savages that could have served society well today: a universal tendency among tribesmen to share and to make life for everyone as comfortable as possible, an ensuing avoidance of hard competition for essentials, a concern for the very young and affection and respect for the very old, an ability to live with nature and not despite it, and an abhorrence of waste—following the Indian tradition of taking nothing more from the earth than was essential to sustain life.

In the 1930's, with both buffalo and grass gone from the Plains and the soil there torn by men thinking little farther ahead than the next crop, drought and high wind inevitably created a dust bowl still remembered by many onetime farmers who fled to city jobs during those years.

Quanah appeared to have foreseen some of this decades earlier, during a July 4, 1898, speech at Hobart, Oklahoma. He said, "We love the white man, but we fear your success. This pretty country you took away from us, but you see how dry it is now. It is only good for red ants, coyotes, and cattlemen."

Three quarters of a century later the English historian Arnold Toynbee added an ominous postscript.

> Man's plundering of nature now threatens him with pollution and depletion. In so-called developed countries like those of Western Europe, the United States, and the Soviet Union and Japan, growth is going to cease.
>
> They are going to find themselves in a permanent state of siege in which the material conditions of life will be at least as austere as they were during the two world wars. The wartime austerity was temporary: the future austerity will be perennial and it will become progressively more severe.

NOTES ON THE CHAPTERS
AND BIBLIOGRAPHY OF SOURCES

If the source of a quotation is identified in the text no further reference to it appears in these notes.

Complete bibliographic information appears here with the first reference to a source. Thereafter a word or a number enclosed in parentheses and placed following a short reference to any source refers to the section or to the chapter where first mention occurs.

A PERSONAL PREFACE

A few paragraphs in this section appeared in the author's contribution (among twelve others) to *Growing Up in Texas* (Austin: Encino Press, 1972).

Sky Walker's role in the raid near Jacksboro was not known outside Kiowa circles until years after that event.

The versions of Geronimo's Apache name were found in the following places: "Goyathlay," *Webster's Guide to American History* (Springfield, Mass.: G. & C. Merriam Co., 1971); "Go khlä yeh," *Geronimo's Story of His Life,* edited by S. M. Barrett (New York: Duffield, 1907); both "Goyakla" and "Goyahkla," *I Fought with Geronimo,* by Jason Betzinez with W. S. Nye (New York: Bonanza Books, 1959).

Most other Indian names can be found spelled in various ways. There are, for instance, still other spellings for Indian names of White Bear, Sitting Bear, and Big Tree not given in this preface. In every case, whichever spelling was chosen has been used consistently.

Description and Sitting Bear's quotations are based on several eyewitness accounts: a statement dated January 12, 1921, by John B. Charlton (who was corporal of the guard that day) given to Captain Robert G. Carter, by then a retired officer of the 4th Cavalry, for use in Carter's book, *On the Border with Mackenzie* (Washington: Eynon Printing Co., 1935); an account by Lieutenant R. H. Pratt (who was Fort Sill officer of the day when Sitting Bear began his trip from that post to Texas) in "Some Indian Reminiscences," *Journal of the U. S. Cavalry Association,* October 1905, and another account by Lieutenant George Thurston (who was officer of the day for the escorting 4th Cavalry) in an official report kept in Department of the Army archives, both quoted in *Carbine & Lance: The Story of Old Fort Sill,* by W. S. Nye (Norman: University of Oklahoma Press, 1937); and an authoritative intermediate study by James Mooney in "Calendar History of the Kiowa Indians," *Annual Report,* Vol. 17, Part I (Washington: Bureau of American Ethnology, 1898).

The Kiowa society of bravest warriors has been given different spellings: Ko-eet-senko, Koisenko, and still other variations besides Kaitsenko (as used here, without hyphens following the "a" and the "t"), which comes from Mooney's history, where also may be found the Kiowa version of Sitting Bear's death song and its English translation.

That song, too, has appeared in different versions. See (among other publications on Kiowas) *The Ten Grandmothers,* by Alice L. Marriott (Norman: University of Oklahoma Press, 1945).

1 THE GREAT WESTERN PIONEER

Thoreau's quotation is from *The Works of Thoreau,* selected and edited by Henry Seidel Canby (Boston: Houghton Mifflin, 1946).

A panorama of United States history (with many illustrations), including a description of this period, appears in the first volume of *Life in America,* by Marshall B. Davidson, Vols. 1–2 (Boston: Houghton Mifflin, 1951). Some specific dates and facts in this chapter are given as they appear in *Encyclopedia of American Facts and Dates,* edited by Gorton Carruth and associates (New York: Crowell, 1962), and in *Webster's Guide to American History* (Preface). Estimates for Civil War casualties and costs are from *Webster's Guide.*

For detailed descriptions of Washington during this time see (among other publications) *Washington Cavalcade,* by Charles Hurd (New York: Dutton, 1948), and *Your Washington and Mine,* by Louise Payson Latimer (New York: Scribner's, 1924).

A number of biographies of Andrew Johnson have been written, including *Andrew Johnson, Plebeian and Patriot,* by Robert W. Winston (New York: Holt, 1928), and (more recently) *The First President Johnson,* by Lately Thomas (New York: Morrow, 1968), in which appeared Johnson's statement about peace. Condensed biographies of Johnson and other Presidents may be found in *Facts about the Presidents,* by Joseph Nathan Kane (New York: H. W. Wilson, 1968), and *The Presidents of the United States,* by Maxim Ethan Armbruster (New York: Horizon, 1969).

About the middle of the twentieth century (or soon thereafter) some historians began a revision of Reconstruction interpretation. They labeled Andrew Johnson a villain and Radical Republicans heroes, contending that if Radical Republicans had been successful in imposing harsher Reconstruction terms on the South, national progress, especially in civil rights, would have been swifter. For a recent presentation of this view see *A Compromise of Principle: Congressional Republicans and Reconstruction, 1863–1869,* by Michael Les Benedict (New York: Norton, 1974).

2 LET US HAVE PEACE

The Medicine Lodge Peace Council has been the subject of many books and articles. Included among them are the following references:

Bury My Heart at Wounded Knee, by Dee Brown (New York: Holt, Rinehart and Winston, 1971); *The Comanche Barrier to South Plains Settlement,* by Rupert N. Richardson (Glendale, Calif.: Arthur H. Clark, 1933); *Fighting Indians of the West,* by Martin F. Schmitt and Dee Brown (New York: Scribner's, 1948);

Life of "Billy" Dixon: Plainsman, Scout and Pioneer, by Olive K. Dixon (Dallas: P. L. Turner, 1927); *Medicine Lodge,* by Nellie Snyder Yost (Chicago: Swallow Press, 1970); "Medicine Lodge Peace Council," by Alfred A. Taylor, in *Chronicles of Oklahoma* (published by the Oklahoma Historical Society), Vol. 2, 1924; *My Early Travels and Adventures,* by Henry M. Stanley, Vol. 1 (New York: Scribner's, 1895); *Satanta and the Kiowas,* by F. Stanley (Borger, Texas: Jim Hess Printers, 1968); "Satanta," by Carl Coke Rister, in *Southwest Review,* Autumn 1931; "The Significance of the Jacksboro Indian Affair of 1871," also by C. C. Rister, in *Southwestern Historical Quarterly* (published by the Texas State Historical Association), January 1926; and *The Treaty of Medicine Lodge,* by Douglas C. Jones (Norman: University of Oklahoma Press, 1966).

Nellie Yost gives a history and a description of the present town of Medicine Lodge and of the surrounding area in her book. Brown (in *Bury My Heart at Wounded Knee*) writes from the Indian viewpoint about the Medicine Lodge Peace Council and the Sand Creek massacre, and he quotes the words of White Antelope's death song. Dixon (who was the "teen-age U. S. Army employee from West Virginia") is the source of some personal observations—used with care. His account, prepared many years later, contains some obvious errors. For example, he called Satanta (White Bear) "Satank" ("Sitting Bear"), and he described the arrival of Cheyennes at the council site as the arrival of all tribes represented, giving the date as October 28, 1867. But he was obviously referring to the arrival of Cheyennes on October 27.

In the first volume of Henry M. Stanley's book may be found his personal observations of Medicine Lodge and the transcripts of many speeches there, including lengthy talks by White Bear. F. Stanley (no relation) also quotes White Bear's orations. Jones's book is a narrative based on the accounts of Henry M. Stanley and other journalists present.

The U. S. Army officer who commanded a force that once camped near the medicine lodge "in the absence of its owners" was General George Armstrong Custer, who wrote about it in *My Life on the Plains* (New York: Sheldon, 1874), a book later republished, edited and with an introduction provided by Milo Milton Quaife (Lincoln: University of Nebraska Press, 1952)—"by arrangement with The Lakeside Press, R. R. Donnelly & Sons Co., Chicago, who are the sole proprietors of its special contents."

Combined with the description of White Bear as left by West Virginian Dixon is some other personal information regarding that chief found in James Mooney's "Calendar History of the Kiowa Indians" (see Prologue notes) and in Rister's "Satanta," which also contains White Bear's quoted complaint about the buffalo killers. Mooney mentions the raid by White Bear (who was wearing his army officer's uniform) on General Hancock's post—Fort Larned.

Exaggerated accounts of the peace commissioners' arrival at Medicine Lodge have appeared. Some authors have written of an attempt to impress the natives with military might (not entirely logical considering the small numbers) and an ensuing reaction by thousands of mounted Indians who went through intricate cavalry maneuvers without audible commands, to show off their own ability and power. (Obviously, however, the Indians could and did operate effectively as a unit—and in large numbers—on horseback.) The arrival scene actually was less awesome than all that.

The long oration by White Bear ("remember [White Bear], the white man's friend") appeared in the *Tri-Weekly Austin Republican,* December 17, 1867. (A transcript is kept in the University of Texas Archives.) Henry M. Stanley quoted the speech, too, but erroneously attributed it to "Satank"—not Satanta—and his mistake has been duplicated by other authors.

3 RED RAIDERS

Sources of general information on Quanah referred to in this section (in addition to Medicine Lodge Peace Council sources listed for Chapter 2) are these:

"Parker, Quanah" entry in *The Handbook of Texas,* Vol. 2, edited by Walter Prescott Webb and others (Austin: Texas State Historical Association, 1952); *Quanah Parker: Last Chief of the Comanches,* by Clyde L. Jackson and Grace Jackson (New York: Exposition Press, 1963); "Quanah Parker: The Last Great Chief," by J. Evetts Haley, in *Men of Fiber* (El Paso: Carl Hertzog, 1963); and "Typescript Life of Quanah Parker, Comanche Chief, by His

Son Chief Baldwin Parker . . . Through J. Evetts Haley, August 29, 1930"—document in the University of Texas Archives.

Other notes on Quanah and his tribesmen:

Quanah Parker's year of birth has been given as anywhere from 1845 to 1852. The latter date appeared on his grave marker, but it probably would have made him too young to have been a Comanche subchief at the Medicine Lodge Peace Council. A date in the 1840's is likelier. His mother (captured in 1836 at the age of nine) would have been twenty-five in 1852—rather old to bear a first child. Further, most accounts agree that Quanah's mother became the wife of Peta Nocona when she was eighteen—which would have been about 1845.

"Quohada" has been spelled differently by other writers (typical, of course, of most Indian names): Kwahadi, Quahadi, Cohoite, and so on. Peta Nocona can be spelled in other ways, too.

The frowning Indian known to us today through old photographs and sketches (like Quanah's and White Bear's, referred to in this section) often had a reason for his scowl. Few Indians wanted to be photographed (some absolutely refused), and they showed their reluctance by their looks.

Quanah himself later gave white authors the estimate of "seven hundred" Indians as having taken part in the attack on Parker's Fort, apparently having heard the figure from his father or from other Indians present.

Sources of general information on the Parker's Fort attack and the ensuing captivity and recapture of Cynthia Ann Parker referred to in this chapter are these:

"The Capture of Cynthia Ann Parker," by J. Marvin Hunter, in *Frontier Times*, May 1939;

The Comanche Trail of Thunder, by Gene Fallwell (Dallas: Highlands Historical Press, 1965), with commentary and corrections appended by Eugene G. O'Quinn, great-grandnephew of Cynthia Ann Parker—copy in the Eugene C. Barker Texas History Center of the University of Texas;

Cynthia Ann Parker: The Story of Her Capture, by James T. DeShields (San Antonio: Naylor, 1934)—first published in 1886, with some obvious errors that still remain in this and other reprintings, but still considered an important book on the subject, written while many participants were still living;

Dream of Empire: A Human History of the Republic of Texas, 1836–1846, by John Edward and Jane Weems (New York: Simon and Schuster, 1971), in which appeared part of the account of the Parker's Fort raid also used by the same author in this book;

"Early Times in Texas and History of the Parker Family, As Told By Ben J. Parker of Elkhart, Texas"—typescript copy in Parker Family Papers in the Eugene C. Barker Texas History Center at the University of Texas;

The Fall of Parker's Fort, by James T. DeShields, edited by Matt Bradley (Waco, Texas: E. L. Connally, 1972)—an extract from DeShields' *Border Wars of Texas,* published in 1912;

"Frank Gholson's [Eyewitness] Account of the Death of Nacona [*sic*] and Rescue of Cynthia Ann Parker—original [manuscript] in hands of Mrs. Cade Williams, Hamilton, Texas. Dictated by Frank Gholson to Felix Williams about 1931 . . . contributed by James D. Carter"—copy in the University of Texas Archives;

History of Texas from 1685 to 1892, Vol. 2, by John Henry Brown (St. Louis: L. E. Daniell, 1893);

James H. Baker's description of the recaptured Cynthia Ann Parker and the moccasin story—from his diary, excerpted in the Dallas *Morning News,* November 28, 1937.

L. S. Ross's account of the recapture of Cynthia Ann Parker—original given by Ross to the Texas Collection of Baylor University, copy in the University of Texas Archives;

Narrative of the Capture and Subsequent Sufferings of Mrs. Rachel Plummer . . . Written by Herself (Houston [n. p.], 1844), an account republished by James W. Parker in 1926 (Palestine, Texas) and reprinted several times since then in pamphlet form, most recently by E. L. Connally (Waco, Texas: Texian Press, 1968).

"Parker, Cynthia Ann" entry in *The Handbook of Texas,* Vol. 2 (for complete bibliography see *Handbook* reference earlier in these Chapter 3 notes);

"Parker History," documents in the J. E. Taulman Papers in the University of Texas Archives; and

"Parker's Fort," another document in the Taulman Papers.

Information on the other white captives whose experiences might be compared with those of Cynthia Ann and John Parker came from the following sources. The fourteen-year-old boy captured by Comanches: *Lost and Found; or Three Months with the Wild Indians,* by Ole T. Nystel (Dallas: Wilmans Brothers, 1888)—reprinted most recently with introduction and notes by Derwood Johnson (Clifton, Texas: Bosque Memorial Museum, 1967). The ten-year-old boy (Herman Lehmann) captured by Apaches: *Indianology,* by J. H. Jones (San Antonio: Johnson Brothers, 1899), and in a second version entitled *Nine Years among the Indians,* by J. Marvin Hunter (Austin: Von Boeckmann-Jones, 1927). The most recent version is in *The Last Captive,* by A. C. Greene (Austin: Encino Press, 1972). Incidentally, after Lehmann fled from the Apaches and joined the Comanches, Quanah adopted him—and later persuaded him to return home to his white family.

Other notes on the Parker's Fort attack and the ensuing captivity and recapture of Cynthia Ann Parker:

The story of the warning given Parker's Fort by the friendly Indian was told by Dan Parker, Sr., of Elkhart, Texas, and can be found in the "Parker History" documents in the Taulman Papers (see reference above). Dan Parker, Sr., did not mention the possible dishonest dealing, but other documents suggest it—and W. W. Newcomb, Jr., referred to the possibility in *The Indians of Texas* (Austin: University of Texas Press, 1961).

Mrs. Rachel Plummer said that before the attack two Indians left the waiting group and walked toward the fort, pretending to seek a treaty. Benjamin Parker then strode out to meet them, she added. Other accounts have differed. Used here are what seemed to this author to be the most logical details.

The baby thrown into "a cluster of cactus" belonged to Mrs. Plummer, who was pregnant when captured. This horror happened six months later (and after the birth of the baby), but is included here as an example of the brutalities Comanches could inflict on their enemies—especially Texans, who (the Indians claimed) had stolen their best lands. The captivity ruined Mrs. Plummer's health, and she died soon after her release, without knowing what had become of her son, James Pratt Plummer, who would be ransomed and freed late in 1842. (Incidentally, Mrs. Plummer's aunt, Elizabeth Kellogg, was ransomed by Sam Houston for $150 six months after capture.) For a grim reference to Indian rape that women endured see "The Battle of Wood Lake," by Noel M. Loomis, in *Great Western Indian Fights* (Lincoln: University of Nebraska Press, 1966).

DeShields (in *Cynthia Ann Parker*) quoted Len Williams about talking with the captive girl in 1840, and he quoted Victor M. Rose. Newcomb, in *The Indians of Texas*, described a Comanche birth. L. S. (Sul) Ross described the recapture of Cynthia Ann Parker in his journal, later given to Baylor University. The long quotation is his own, except that he wrote, "Indians do not have blue eyes," but surely would have said, ". . . don't have."

Ross presumed he had killed Peta Nocona, but history proved him wrong. Most authorities today accept evidence that Nocona was not present and that he died later, as Quanah himself would assert in time.

Quanah's daughter, Mrs. Neda Parker Birdsong, explained to Paul Wellman how Ross probably had made his mistake. (The explanation appeared in *Chronicles of Oklahoma*, June 1934; Wellman spelled the name Nokoni, as have other authors.)

> Peta [Nocona] and the warriors were not within miles of this place when Ross and his Rangers won their "victory" over this band of women with babies in their arms, and a few Mexican servants.
>
> One of the Mexican servants who was helping the Comanche women was owned by Peta [Nocona] and was Cynthia Ann's personal servant. . . . This man was known as Joe (or Jose) [Nocona], much as we would say "[Nocona's] Joe."

Ross saw the Mexican, who was dressed like a Comanche, prepare to fight despite the odds against him, and he heard the man begin singing a death song. Ross shot him, then inquired of women prisoners the man's name. "Joe [Nocona]," they told him, and Ross presumed that he had killed the chief named Nocona.

To complete the Chapter 3 notes, which are lengthy here because details regarding the capture and recapture of Cynthia Ann Parker have started many an argument among individuals who know the story, are these two further observations:

The "early Texas historian" to whom Isaac Parker told the story of his identification of Cynthia Ann (by pronouncing her name) was Homer S. Thrall. A copy of Thrall's account can be found in the University of Texas Archives.

For the naming of Parker County after Cynthia Ann's Uncle Isaac (in 1855, five years before her recapture) see *Texas Almanac and State Industrial Guide, 1974–1975* (Dallas: A. H. Belo Corporation, 1971).

4 DISHONEST WORDS AND BROKEN PROMISES

Many books have been written about Custer and especially about his Little Big Horn fight (which is not retold again in detail in this narrative). For two biographies of the man—the first more favorable than the second—see: *Custer,* by Jay Monaghan (Boston: Little, Brown, 1959), and *Glory-Hunter: A Life of General Custer,* by Frederic F. Van de Water (Indianapolis: Bobbs-Merrill, 1934). See also Custer's own book, *My Life on the Plains* (2). In it, however, Custer refrained from discussing his court-martial and other unpleasant subjects. The 1952 University of Nebraska Press reprint of *My Life on the Plains* (also 2) included a brief biography of the General by Milo Milton Quaife and the quoted admission by Custer of his error as officer of the guard at West Point.

Books by Elizabeth Custer that discuss Custer and his campaigns (always glowingly) include these two: *Boots and Saddles: or Life in Dakota with General Custer* (New York: Harper, 1885) and *Tenting on the Plains, or, General Custer in Kansas and Texas* (New York: Harper, 1895).

Elizabeth Custer's nickname, "Libbie," has been spelled "Libby" by some authors. She spelled it "Libbie" in her two books listed above.

Regarding the "wholesale overnight desertion," Custer (in his own book) said forty soldiers deserted, but official records do not indicate so many men fled on that one occasion.

Van de Water quoted Sheridan's note to Elizabeth Custer (about Lee's surrender table) from a 1929 biography, *The Life of General*

Custer, by Milton Ronsheim. The note has been quoted also in earlier writings.

The telegram from Sheridan requesting Custer's return to command was quoted by Custer himself in *My Life on the Plains.*

5 RED MOON

The first two thirds of this chapter is based largely on Custer's own account of battle preliminaries in *My Life on the Plains* (2). That particular material rings true, mostly, and shows no obvious self-serving purpose. But when Custer recounted the Battle of the Washita itself he was obviously thinking of his reputation. For that reason some other narratives have been relied on, too: *Sheridan's Troopers on the Borders,* by DeB. Randolph Keim (Philadelphia: David McKay, 1885), in which appeared Sheridan's order to Custer quoted herein; "Some Reminiscences of the Battle of the Washita," by E. S. Godfrey, in *Cavalry Journal,* October 1928, which contained the "incriminating" quotation regarding Custer's lack of concern for Major Elliot and the details of withdrawal to the music of "Ain't I Glad to Get Out of the Wilderness," and other information; *Indian Fights and Fighters,* by Cyrus Townsend Brady (New York: McClure, Philips, 1904)—a book later reprinted with an introduction by James T. King (Lincoln: University of Nebraska Press, 1971); Van de Water's *Glory-Hunter* (4); Monaghan's *Custer* (4); and two comparatively recent descriptions of the Battle of the Washita, in Nye's *Carbine & Lance* (Prologue) and Brown's *Bury My Heart at Wounded Knee* (2).

Other notes on this chapter:

The Kansas statistics for Indian depredations appeared in Brady's *Indian Fights and Fighters.*

Custer's spelling for Major Joel Elliot (consistently with one "t") has been used, although the last name has often appeared as "Elliott."

Some authors have asserted that the Cheyenne war party trail was made instead by latecomers straggling into Black Kettle's village for the winter. But even Cheyenne survivors told of the war party's return and of the ensuing celebration.

Most secondary accounts until recently have accepted Custer's statement that his 7th Regiment killed "103 warriors." Evidence is clear, however, that many of those "103 warriors" were women and children. Black Kettle's wife, for example, certainly was a victim, but her death is not accounted for in Custer's statistics. Brown, in *Bury My Heart at Wounded Knee,* accepts figures showing that only eleven of the 103 slain Indians were warriors.

Two comparatively recent accounts of the battle from the Indian viewpoint have appeared, in Nye's *Carbine & Lance* and in Brown's book. Nye interviewed one or two Indian survivors years later and wrote that the scalp dance with those throbbing drums had lasted until the midnight immediately preceding Custer's attack on the village. But Custer, who had reached the vicinity at midnight, did not report hearing any drums, although in *My Life on the Plains* he did quote a prisoner as saying that the night before the attack the villagers had been celebrating the war party's return "until a late hour." Brown does not mention the night's scalp dance, but he does tell about Black Kettle's visit with Hazen and his return to the village on November 26, the day before the attack—the same day (Nye said) the war party returned.

Nye and Brown differ on who fired the single shot in the village. Nye said it came from a sleepy Indian sentinel who had dozed off after the night's dancing and had been alerted first by a dog's bark, then by a woman's shout of "Soldiers!" Brown said that Black Kettle fired it (after hearing a woman call out, "Soldiers! Soldiers!") to awaken the village, but that Black Kettle hoped to confer with the attackers and assure them of his peaceful intent.

Custer (in *My Life on the Plains*) quoted Black Kettle's captured sister as having said that Black Kettle fired the shot to rally warriors. Research into primary-source material can turn up information to support any of these statements (and others, too), but the account as written in this chapter has been based on the most logical assumptions. Black Kettle probably fired the shot to awaken his people with the hope that they might escape. His background of working for peace, surviving Sand Creek, censuring those war parties (and so on) precluded any attempt by him to rally his warriors to fight furiously.

Some probing into Indian accounts by Nye, who was assigned in the early 1930's to write an official history of Fort Sill, described the last hours of Major Elliot and his men. The story appears in detail in *Carbine & Lance*. Other accounts also exist.

6 RED SUN

Walter Prescott Webb's observation quoted here appeared in his book *The Great Plains* (New York: Ginn, 1931). He discussed at some length Spanish attempts to exterminate hostile enemy tribes like the Apaches. For another, more detailed account of this period and a history of Apacheria, see *The Last Americans,* by William Brandon (New York: McGraw-Hill, 1974), where appeared the quoted description of torture inflicted on Apache prisoners.

The Spanish name for the chief known as "Red Sleeves" has often appeared as Mangus-Colorado and Mangas Colorado. Mangas Coloradas would be the correct Spanish spelling.

The name of the Confederate governor of Arizona who ordered extermination was John R. Baylor. Frederick W. Turner III, in an introduction to *Geronimo: His Own Story* (New York: Dutton, 1970), quoted Baylor's order. In the first volume of *The Handbook of Texas* (3)—in the entry for "Baylor, John Robert"—appears information regarding his recall because of his harsh Indian policies.

James Carleton commanded the "California Column." His order was included in the first series, fifteenth volume of *The War of the Rebellion: A Compilation of the Official Records of the Union and Confederate Armies,* Series I–IV, Vols. 1–70 (Washington, D.C.: Government Printing Office, 1880–1901), and was quoted (in greater detail than here) by Brown in *Bury My Heart at Wounded Knee* (2).

Geronimo's quotations are from his own book, first published in 1907 (Preface). Authors have differed on his age, but Geronimo himself gave his year of birth: 1829 (in June, in "No-doyohn Canyon, Arizona," near the headwaters of the Gila River).

Some other books on the colorful Apache chief, his people, and his land—in addition to Betzinez' *I Fought with Geronimo* (Preface)—are these: *The Apache Indians,* by Frank C. Lockwood (New York: Macmillan, 1938); *An Apache Life-Way,* by Morris E. Opler (Chicago: University of Chicago Press, 1941); *Chasing Geronimo: The Journal of Leonard Wood, May–September, 1886* (Albuquerque: University of New Mexico Press, 1970); *The*

Conquest of Apacheria, by Dan L. Thrapp (Norman: University of Oklahoma Press, 1967); *The Truth about Geronimo,* by Britton Davis (New Haven: Yale University Press, 1929); and *The Geronimo Campaign,* by Odie B. Faulk (New York: Oxford University Press, 1969).

7 A BREEZE THAT WHISPERED

Virtually all of this chapter as it concerns Custer (including his quotations and the note from Hazen) has been based on information contained in his own book, *My Life on the Plains* (2). Facts supporting Hazen's argument about White Bear's (and the Kiowas') innocence, however, appeared in Hazen's pamphlet, *Some Corrections to My Life on the Plains* (St. Paul, Minn.: privately published, 1875). Custer and Hazen had not been on friendly terms for years, and when Custer's book appeared criticizing Hazen for softheartedness toward Indians, Hazen published his "proof" (and it seemed to be that) showing himself to be right and Custer wrong.

See Stanley's biography of White Bear (2) for details regarding the chase, arrest, and release. See also *Satanta,* by Clarence Wharton (Dallas: Banks Upshaw, 1935), although Wharton's book must be read with particular care because overcompression has resulted in some misleading statements.

In Sheridan's announcement of the Washita victory the General spelled it "Arapahoes," as did Hazen and Custer in every plural reference to that tribe. For style consistency this has been changed to "Arapahos." (Other similar, minor style corrections have been made throughout the text, but words have not been otherwise altered.)

The quotation from Grant's inaugural address appeared in *Ulysses S. Grant,* by John A. Carpenter (New York: Twayne, 1970), where also is discussed in some detail Grant's Indian policies.

8 BEWILDERING KALEIDOSCOPE

Some specific personal information on Lieutenant John Bourke appears in *American Authors, 1600–1900,* edited by Stanley J.

Kunitz and Howard Haycroft (New York: H. W. Wilson Co., 1938), and in the first volume of *Dictionary of American Biography,* edited by Allen Johnson (New York: Scribner's, 1936). Some characteristics (such as his curiosity, devotion to study, and so on) have been deduced after reading his writing.

Virtually all of the rest of the chapter has been based on information contained in Bourke's *On the Border with Crook* (New York: Scribner's, 1891)—a book quoted often and recently reprinted (Lincoln: University of Nebraska Press, 1971).

9 HAPPINESS AND HARSHNESS

Personal information on Carter came from three main sources: the entry for "Carter, Robert Goldthwaite," in the first volume of *The Handbook of Texas* (3); from Carter's own book (which he published himself), *On the Border with Mackenzie* (Prologue); and from J. C. Dykes's foreword to a reprint of that same book (New York: Antiquarian Press, 1961).

Personal information on Mackenzie came from the entry for "Mackenzie, Ranald Slidell" in the second volume of *The Handbook of Texas* (3), and from Carter's book, which also yielded most of the rest of the information (including quotations) used in writing this chapter.

10 ABILITY TO PROJECT

Except for the quotations of Lieutenant Whitman and his surgeon (the source of which has been given in the text) most of this chapter is based on John Bourke's *On the Border with Crook* (8).

11 INSPECTION ALONG THE BUTTERFIELD TRAIL

The story by the newspaper correspondent who reported from Jacksboro, Texas, appeared in the Austin (Texas) *Daily Journal,* July 11, 1871. His story was dated June 30. A copy of this clipping has been kept in the University of Texas Archives, along with other newspaper accounts.

Information that appeared in Carter's *On the Border with Mackenzie* (Prologue) provided the foundation for most of this chapter, and his conversation with General Sherman has been quoted as Carter remembered and recorded it.

Occasionally, however, Carter erred in minor details. In his book, written much later, Carter said that Fort Belknap was deserted when he passed through it. General Sherman, writing immediately after his own visit, said that a small detachment of soldiers remained there, and Sherman recommended to Washington that this small garrison and certain others along his inspection route be made more comfortable and confident.

Carter was also mistaken in saying (in his book) that he left Fort Richardson "May 17" to meet Sherman. He left on May 18—the same day Sherman later arrived at the fort and the same day the wagon train was attacked on Salt Creek Prairie.

W. S. Nye, in *Carbine & Lance* (Prologue), has told the most complete story from the Indian view of the raid inspired by Sky Walker. Nye based his account on interviews with a participant still living in the 1930's and with other Indians who had some tribal knowledge of the event.

12 PRIDE BEFORE DESTRUCTION

The newspaper account from Jacksboro appeared in the Austin *Daily Journal* May 17, 1871. Lieutenant Carter's quotation about acting as General Sherman's secretary (with punctuation and capitalization changed slightly for easier reading) appeared in his book *On the Border with Mackenzie* (Prologue), which also provided the foundation for narrating his other experiences in this chapter.

Lawrie Tatum, in *Our Red Brothers* (Philadelphia: Winston, 1899), quoted White Bear's admission of leading the attack on the wagon train and recounted other details of that notable interview. The Chief's oration has been quoted many times, usually with slight variations but with substance remaining the same. Nye, in *Carbine & Lance* (Prologue), quoted Tatum's rough notes of White Bear's talk, as kept by the Oklahoma Historical Society.

13 SENTENCE OF DEATH

The description of Fort Sill as Carter saw it is based on two sources: information he provided himself in his book *On the*

Border with Mackenzie (Prologue), which was the basis also for other narration in this chapter concerning the Lieutenant; and on period information contained in Nye's history of the fort, *Carbine & Lance* (Prologue).

For two detailed histories of Kiowa Indians see *The Ten Grandmothers* (Prologue) and *The Kiowas,* by Mildred P. Mayhall (Norman: University of Oklahoma Press, 1962).

Refer to Prologue notes for information about the sources of the story of Sitting Bear's death. (Lieutenant Carter did not see the shooting of that Indian chief, but he did question witnesses immediately after the event, and he gathered material on the incident for half a century afterward. Nye also questioned eyewitnesses.)

The quoted description of the courtroom where White Bear and Big Tree were tried is from Carter's observation of it. Proceedings were recorded in Volume A of *Minutes of the 43rd Judicial District of Texas,* Jacksboro. J. W. Wilbarger, in *Indian Depredations in Texas* (Austin: Hutchings Printing House, 1889), also described the trial and quoted proceedings at some length—as many other authors have done: C. C. Rister (2), F. Stanley (2), and others, most of them with minor variances in quotations. Mid-July 1871 editions of the Austin *Daily Journal* (among other newspapers) carried reports of the trial, sent by correspondent E. F. Gilbert. The defense statement by Thomas Ball quoted here was as recorded by Lieutenant Carter, who also quoted the jury foreman in rendering the verdict. (Carter wrote his account of the trial years later, but he used diaries and notes kept at the time it transpired to refresh his memory. In some instances when he was not an actual eyewitness he relied on information compiled by questioning others and by reading related material, but he had a commendable record of striving for accuracy.)

Other notes:

District Attorney S. W. T. Lanham's son, Fritz, later served in the U. S. House of Representatives.

The name of the Jack County sheriff at that time was Michael McMillan.

White Bear and Big Tree had two attorneys for their highly unpopular defense. One was Thomas Ball (mentioned in the text); the other was J. A. Woolfork.

14 TRIUMPH AND SUFFERING

With one exception all direct quotations in this chapter are given as Carter recorded them in either of two books he wrote: *On the Border with Mackenzie* (Prologue) or *Tragedies of Cañon Blanco: A Story of the Texas Panhandle* (Washington: Gibson Brothers Printers, 1919). The first book, incidentally, included all of the material contained in *Tragedies of Cañon Blanco,* with some slight differences in wording.

An exception to the above paragraph: A Comanche participant named Cohaya described Carter's defense at the ravine to W. S. Nye more than half a century later, when Nye was researching for *Carbine & Lance* (Prologue). The quotation about bullets sounding like "the roar of a sling" is his.

Generally, this account of the fight at Blanco Canyon is as Carter said he saw it.

Other notes on this chapter:

The story of Captain Heyl's flight is as Carter told it. Not surprisingly, Carter never forgave Heyl for his action, and the Lieutenant had nothing good to say about him afterward. Heyl himself might have given a somewhat different account. Certainly the fact that Heyl spurred his horse across the ravine when others halted argued against total cowardice.

Carter said that during the fight at the ravine he presumed the "large and powerfully built" Comanche chief to have been either Shaking Hand (Mow-way) or Big Bear (Parra-o-coom). Cohaya, talking to Nye, recalled that Big Bear was there and led the Indians. Years after the fight an army officer who talked with Quanah said that Quanah admitted to him he had led the attack himself, and this information was passed on to Carter.

At another time, during conversation with another army officer, Quanah said he still had Mackenzie's gray pacer stolen that night at Blanco Canyon, and he offered to return the animal. (See *Tragedies of Cañon Blanco,* page 23, footnote.)

Carter's fight at the ravine was recorded in a bit of Comanche history. The Lieutenant himself told of it in *Tragedies of Cañon Blanco:*

Lieutenant John A. McKinney, of the 4th Cavalry (killed in

the fight with Dull Knife's band of Northern Cheyennes in a [canyon] of the Big Horn Mountains, November 25, 1876), told [me] that when he was at Fort Sill in 1872 the Comanches brought in a buffalo robe with a pictograph on it representing [the] scene. It was at the moment of [Private] Gregg's fall from his horse, and the [horse's] running into . . . Indian lines. [I] was shown firing at Quanah. Five Indians were shown dead on the ground, just the number they admitted they lost. [I] endeavored later to secure this robe, but could get no trace of it either through the two interpreters or the Indian agent.

15   LIKE FIGHTING WILD ANIMALS IN A TRAP

This chapter has been based entirely on material in Bourke's *On the Border with Crook* (8).

16   OLD ENEMIES

The first part of this chapter (pertaining to Apaches) is based on Bourke's *On the Border with Crook* (8).

The Modoc war has been the subject of several books, including these: *Wigwam and War-path,* by Alfred B. Meacham (Boston: Dale, 1875); *The Modocs and Their War,* by Keith A. Murray (Norman: University of Oklahoma Press, 1959); *The Indian History of the Modoc War and the Causes That Led to It,* by Jeff C. Riddle (San Francisco: Marnell, 1914); and a recent one, *Burnt-Out Fires: California's Modoc Indian War,* by Richard Dillon (Englewood Cliffs, N.J.: Prentice-Hall, 1973).

Brief discussion of Colonel Mackenzie's career on the frontier in 1871–76 may be found in "General Ranald Slidell Mackenzie: Indian Fighting Cavalryman," by Edward S. Wallace, in *Southwestern Historical Quarterly,* January 1953.

Carter's experiences have been based on information contained in *On the Border with Mackenzie* (Prologue).

Two sources for the fight at Beecher Island (and Jack Stillwell's long journey to solicit help) include these: *Thrilling Days of Army Life,* by George A. Forsyth (New York: Harper, 1900), and Cyrus Townsend Brady's 1904 book, *Indian Fights and Fighters* (5), in which he devoted several chapters to Forsyth's fight. It was an event of great renown, however, and has been recounted in many other publications.

17 A DAKOTA BLIZZARD

Elizabeth Custer's own account of the Dakota blizzard appeared in the second chapter of her 1885 book, *Boots and Saddles* (4).

In it she described the faint illumination of a light placed in the window of her cabin (the light that attracted the lost and freezing soldiers), but she did not specifically identify it as a candle (as in this chapter)—which it no doubt was. The light could have come from a "spirit lamp" filled with alcohol. That commodity was, however, so scarce (as has been shown later in the chapter) that she probably would not have used it.

Some of the direct quotations that appeared in her book have been paragraphed and punctuated differently here, for easier reading, but have not been revised otherwise.

18 STRONGER MEDICINE

Sources of information about Indian resentment against buffalo hunters and about their other complaints are these:

The American Bison, by Martin S. Garretson (New York: Zoological Society, 1938); *The Extermination of the American Bison,* by W. T. Hornaday (Washington, D.C.: Smithsonian Institution, 1889); *The Southwestern Frontier,* by Carl C. Rister (Cleveland: Arthur H. Clark, 1928); and these books referred to earlier: *Bury My Heart at Wounded Knee* (2) and *Satanta* (7), by Wharton.

Sources of information about the Adobe Walls fight: *Bad Medicine and Good,* by W. S. Nye (Norman: University of Oklahoma Press, 1962); *The Buffalo Hunters,* by Mari Sandoz (New York: Hastings House, 1954); "The Comanche Indians and the Fight at Adobe Walls," by Rupert N. Richardson, in the fourth volume of *Panhandle-Plains Historical Review,* 1931; and these books referred to earlier: *The Handbook of Texas* (3), entries for "Adobe Walls," "Adobe Walls, First Battle of," and "Adobe Walls, Second Battle of"; *Bury My Heart at Wounded Knee* (2); *Carbine & Lance* (Prologue); *Fighting Indians of the West* (2);

Life of "Billy" Dixon (2); *Quanah Parker* (3), by Jackson and Jackson; and *Satanta and the Kiowas* (2), by Stanley.

Random notes:

The story of Isatai's role in Adobe Walls appeared in detail in *Carbine & Lance*. Nye interviewed some survivors who had known Isatai.

The story of the buffalo hunters' defense at Adobe Walls has been recounted by Bat Masterson and other participants. They differ in some details, as do secondary accounts. The version that appears here is based largely on Dixon's account, in *Life of "Billy" Dixon*. Some authors have said that Dixon's 1,538-yard shot came on the second day of siege, and others said on the first, but Dixon (who certainly should have known) declared that he made it on the third day. Dixon also said that the bugler serving the Indians was a Mexican, not a Negro deserter from the 10th Cavalry (as others claimed).

Details of the reaction to Quanah's attack at Adobe Walls and the subsequent military subjugation it soon brought may be found in the *Annual Report* of the Commissioner of Indian Affairs for 1874.

19 INEXORABILITY

For a detailed examination of Custer's involvement in feuds with Belknap, Grant, and others, see *Glory-Hunter* (4).

Narration of the wintry train trip from St. Paul into Dakota has been based largely on information contained in *Boots and Saddles* (4).

20 A GOOD DAY TO DIE

The parts of this chapter in which Bourke figures have been based on his book, *On the Border with Crook* (8), with an exception. He wrote largely of what he saw in the Battle of the Rosebud, but some of his secondhand material contained obvious inaccuracies that have been corrected after referring to the following accounts, which also served to provide other supplementary information:

"The Battle of the Rosebud," by J. A. Leermakers, in *Great Western Indian Fights* (3); *Crazy Horse,* by Mari Sandoz (New

York: Knopf, 1945); *General Crook: His Autobiography,* edited by Martin F. Schmitt (Norman: University of Oklahoma Press, 1960); *My Story,* by Anson Mills (Washington: privately printed, 1918); and *With Crook at the Rosebud,* by J. W. Vaughn (Harrisburg, Pa.: Stackpole, 1956).

(Incidentally, no two accounts of the Rosebud battle seem to agree. Selection and—it is hoped—logic went into the brief story presented here.)

The parts of this chapter in which Elizabeth Custer figures have been based on her book *Boots and Saddles* (4), with an exception. The account of her receiving news of her husband's death is based on information contained in *Custer* (4).

Random notes:

Bourke spelled the scout's name Gruard, instead of Grouard.

The battalion commander who led a Rosebud counterattack "on the right" was Anson Mills. The quoted description appeared in his book, mentioned above.

Elizabeth Custer did not quote the words (of the second verse) of "Nearer, My God, to Thee," but she specifically mentioned it as one of the hymns sung.

Custer's letters appeared as an appendix to *Boots and Saddles.*

21 SUFFERING MUCH

Favorable description of the 1876 centennial is based on information contained in *Pictorial History of American Presidents,* by John and Alice Durant (New York: A. S. Barnes, 1969). Unfavorable description immediately following is based on material found in *Rutherford B. Hayes: Statesman of Reunion,* by H. J. Eckinrode, assisted by Pocahontas Wilson Wight (New York: Dodd, Mead, 1930), which also offers a detailed biography of Hayes. Several books cover the Nez Percé history and uprising in detail. Two are *"I Will Fight No More Forever": Chief Joseph and the Nez Percé War,* by Merrill D. Beal (Seattle: University of Washington Press, 1963), and *The Nez Percé Indians and the Opening of the Northwest,* by Alvin M. Josephy, Jr. (New Haven: Yale University Press, 1965). Other titles recounting last stands and events that preceded them are *The Bannock Indian War of 1878,* by George Francis Brimlow (Caldwell, Idaho: Caxton

Printers, 1938); *The Last War Trail: The Utes and the Settlement of Colorado,* by Robert Emmitt (Norman: University of Oklahoma Press, 1954); and a chapter entitled "Last Stands" in *The Compact History of the Indian Wars,* by John Tebbel (New York: Hawthorn, 1966).

Stanley (2) and Wharton (7) wrote in detail of White Bear's penitentiary experience. The quotation from the *Scribner's* writer was reproduced first by Wharton (who erred, incidentally, in giving the year of White Bear's death as 1876; it was 1878). Thomas C. Battey, in *The Life and Adventures of a Quaker among the Indians* (Boston: Lee and Shepard, 1875), described Kiowa belief in life after death.

For a recent biography of Geronimo—one inevitably based on Geronimo's own autobiography—see *Geronimo,* by Alexander B. Adams (New York: Putnam's, 1971). The quotation about Geronimo's people "suffering much" appeared in the autobiography edited by S. M. Barrett (Preface).

22 LONG BLACK HAIR

Baldwin Parker's statements are from "Typescript Life of Quanah Parker" (3). The document does not offer so much fresh information on Quanah as one might expect.

Plentiful quotations from Quanah may be found in journals and newspapers published around Fort Sill during his reservation chieftainship—for instance, in *Sturms Oklahoma Magazine* (May 1911—his description of judicial duties), in the *Daily Oklahoman,* and in smaller papers like the Woodward, Oklahoma, *News* (December 14, 1894—"Here I am great chief").

Editors of that time seemed to have been intrigued with Quanah.

More quotations and interviews have appeared in *Indian Pioneer History* (Vol. 71—cooked dog; Vol. 89—Quanah's surrender and Quanah on Democrats and Republicans), published by the Oklahoma Historical Museum. Jackson and Jackson, in their book *Quanah Parker* (3), reproduced much of this material, including many of the quotations used here. Another source of direct quotations: *Quanah Parker: Last Chief of the Comanches,* by Charles H. Sommer (privately printed, 1945). Sommer was president of the Quanah, Acme, and Pacific Railway.

For still more information on Quanah see *Quanah: The Eagle of the Comanches,* by Zoe A. Tilghman (Oklahoma City: Harlow, 1938), although as a nonfiction account that book should be examined carefully; much of it has been fictionalized.

For details of Quanah's justice rendering see "Quanah Parker, Indian Judge," by William T. Hagan, in *Probing the American West* (Santa Fe: Museum of New Mexico Press, 1962); for details of Quanah's gaslight trouble see "Poisoning by Coal-Gas, of Two Comanche Chiefs," by Dr. H. W. Moore, in *Daniel's Medical Journal* (February 1886).

The date of Quanah's visit to Fort Worth, incidentally, was December 21, 1885. The account of his near-death at that time as given here has been based on Dr. Moore's report. There are other versions that differ in minor details.

People (including personal friends of Quanah) have not agreed on the number of wives he had at any given time. Charles Goodnight said a total of six. William T. Hagan, author of the article listed above, said his marriage to a seventh wife resulted in his dismissal as judge. A newspaper correspondent writing from Cache, Oklahoma (in the Wichita Falls, Texas, *Times* of March 1, 1951), said To-pay (then surviving) was one of seven wives officially listed by the Indian agency. Others (as the correspondent spelled them) were Tonarcy, Weckeah, Chony, Mah-cheet-to-wooky, A-er-wuth-tak-um, and Coby. The writer added that some historians also record an earlier marriage (that soon ended in separation) to To-ha-ye, a Mescalero Apache. Still others say Quanah had a total of five wives. But there is no doubt about the accuracy of Quanah's demanding that the admonishing government official tell his wives "which one I keep." That story has been repeated many times—most recently in first person by Quanah's widow To-pay, then his last-surviving spouse, quoted in the Wichita Falls *Times* of May 28, 1956.

23 LIKE THE WIND

General Crook's statement about comparative "honor and nobility" of Indians appeared in *Massacres of the Mountains: A History of the Indian Wars of the Far West,* by J. P. Dunn (New York: Harper, 1886).

All quotations attributed to Geronimo are from his autobiography, edited by S. M. Barrett (Preface).

A standard study of Apaches is *An Apache Life-Way* (6), by Morris E. Opler, who also wrote other significant books on Apaches. Another well-known title on this subject is *The Conquest of Apacheria* (6). A more recent examination, one accompanied by many illustrations by the author, is *The People Called Apaches,* by Thomas E. Mails (Englewood Cliffs, N.J.: Prentice-Hall, 1974).

The officer's description of San Carlos is from *The Truth about Geronimo* (6).

The quotation concerning cruelty "by members of our own race" is from Betzinez' (and Nye's) *I Fought with Geronimo* (Preface).

For another (short) history of the Geronimo period see *Crimson Desert: Indian Wars of the American Southwest,* by Odie B. Faulk (New York: Oxford, 1974).

Tso-ay ("Peaches") has been spelled many different ways: Tzoe, by Betzinez, for example. (Bourke called him Pahayotishn.)

Crook's campaign as given here has been based largely on Bourke's *On the Border with Crook* (8) and his *An Apache Campaign in the Sierra Madre* (New York: Scribner's, 1886). (All quotations attributed to Bourke appeared in either of those two books.)

Betzinez told of Geronimo's return to Casas Grandes and of his "visions" during the journey.

For more details of Bob Tribolet's interference with Geronimo's surrender see Adams' *Geronimo* (21) and Bourke's books (among others).

Crook's 1885 writings in defense of Indians have been quoted as reproduced in *On the Border with Crook,* where also appeared the officer's description of the difficulty of chasing Geronimo.

24 TIME AT ITS WORK

Dates and events that Carter would have been aware of (given toward the first of this chapter) are based on statistics in *Encyclopedia of American Facts and Dates* (1). Detailed discussion of Presidents referred to during that same time may be found in *From Hayes to McKinley: National Party Politics, 1877–1896,* by H. Wayne Morgan (Syracuse, N.Y.: Syracuse University Press, 1969). The rest of the chapter pertaining directly to Carter (including direct quotations attributed to him) came from material in his *On the Border with Mackenzie* (Prologue) or his *Tragedies of Cañon Blanco* (14), with one exception stated below.

Edward S. Wallace's "General Ranald Slidell Mackenzie" in *Southwestern Historical Quarterly* (January 1953) detailed the last years of Mackenzie's life, although the author did not specify suicide as the reason (now acknowledged) for death.

For one discussion of the "Indian problem," then and now, see *The Indians of the Southwest: A Century of Development under the United States,* by Edward Everett Dale (published in cooperation with the Huntington Library, San Marino, Calif.; Norman: University of Oklahoma Press, 1949). A description of the difficulties encountered in bringing a white education to Indian children may be found in Battey's *The Life and Adventures of a Quaker among the Indians* (21). A recent discussion of the "Indian problem" from an Indian viewpoint (including comments on the Dawes Severalty Act and the 1934 Indian Reorganization Act) may be found in *Custer Died for Your Sins,* by Vine Deloria, Jr. (New York: Macmillan, 1969).

Adams, in his *Geronimo* (21), quoted the December 6, 1908, Tucson *Daily Star.*

Quanah's quotation about keeping his wives and his religion appeared in *Captain Lee Hall of Texas,* by Dora Neill Raymond (Norman: University of Oklahoma Press, 1940). Information regarding Quanah's taste for peyote has appeared in many publications, including an edition of the Wichita Falls *Times* of November 5, 1961, reporting the gift (from a local citizen) to the Fort Sill Museum of Quanah's gilded jewel case in which he carried peyote buttons.

Jackson and Jackson, in *Quanah Parker* (3), found that most Comanches today claim to be Protestants.

In the first volume of *Chronicles of Oklahoma* (2) appeared details of Quanah's death. Baldwin Parker, in his typescript (3), also presented much the same material.

Information about Carter's awards was included in the entry under his name in the first volume of *The Handbook of Texas* (3).

NOTES

(Incidentally, Carter's son, Robert D. Carter, died in the early 1930's.)

In his biography of Custer, Monaghan (4) also recounted briefly Elizabeth Custer's life as a widow, including her request (and the quoted "Desolate me") sent to General Sherman.

Quanah's reburial received widespread mention in the press, including a story in the *Daily Oklahoman* of August 10, 1957.

White Bear's reburial was the subject of numerous stories in Texas newspapers, including (among others) the Houston *Post* of April 30 and June 5, 1963; the Houston *Chronicle* of June 28, 1963; the Dallas *Morning News* of June 29, 1963; and the Dallas *Times Herald* of June 30, 1963. The representative who opposed White Bear's removal to Oklahoma was James Cotten of Weatherford.

EPILOGUE: RED ANTS, COYOTES, AND CATTLEMEN

Australian statistics are from *Encyclopedia of Australia,* compiled by A. T. A. and A. M. Learmonth (London: Frederick Warne, 1968). Canadian description is based on *Uncle Sam's Stepchildren,* by Loring Benson Priest (New Brunswick, N.J.: Rutgers University Press, 1942).

Quanah's statement appeared in Vol. 87 of *Indian Pioneer History.* Jackson and Jackson, in *Quanah Parker* (3), quoted it. Toynbee's prediction was contained in an Associated Press story datelined London; it appeared in many North American newspapers published April 15, 1974.

ACKNOWLEDGMENTS
AND PICTURE CREDITS

My appreciation to these individuals in the following cities for assistance in various areas during the preparation of this book:

Austin, Texas: Joe Frantz, Chester Kielman, Jones Ramsey, Donald Weems, Dorman Winfrey.

Chicago, Ill.: D. L. McGuire.

Fort Worth, Texas: Curtis Nunn.

Houston, Texas: Ann Waldron.

Lincoln, Neb.: Virginia Faulkner.

New York, N.Y.: Lauretta Bonnell, Walter Bradbury, Carl Brandt, Rachel Cochran, Jack Lynch, Lawrence Reed, Granville Walker, Edith M. Wells.

Norman, Okla.: Mavis Yoachum.

Phoenix, Ariz.: Ramona Weeks.

Temple, Texas: Mr. and Mrs. J. E. Weems, Sr. (my parents).

Texas City, Texas: Ron Tester.

Waco, Texas: John Banta, Victor Jeffress, Bon-Jean White.

Washington, D.C.: A. A. Hoehling, Elizabeth Layton, Andrew Oerke, Barbara Ringer.

Sources of pictures are as follows:

White Bear—section of a larger photograph in National Anthropological Archives, Smithsonian Institution.

Sitting Bear—section of a larger photograph (by William S. Soule in 1870) that appeared in *Texas under the Carpetbaggers,* by

ACKNOWLEDGMENTS AND PICTURE CREDITS

W. C. Nunn (Austin: University of Texas Press, 1962), from files of the Texas Collection, Fort Worth *Star-Telegram.*

Quanah—section of a larger photograph in National Anthropological Archives, Smithsonian Institution.

Cynthia Ann Parker—section of a larger photograph, original of which is in the Texas Collection of Baylor University.

Old Camp Grant—section of a larger photograph in the National Archives.

Hostile Sioux—photograph by J. C. H. Grabill, 1891, near Deadwood, South Dakota. Library of Congress.

Pack Train—section of a larger photograph in the Arizona Historical Society, Tucson, used by special permission.

Emigrant Train Attacked—wood engraving by Nichols (after Champney) in *Ballou's,* August 15, 1857. Library of Congress.

Buffalo Herd—lithograph by Endicott & Co., 1862, after W. J. Hays. Library of Congress.

Plains Railroad Depot—wood engraving in *Leslie's,* December 11, 1869. Library of Congress.

Major General Custer and Libbie—section of a larger photograph in the National Archives.

Custer's Black Hills Expedition—section of a larger photograph in the National Archives.

Sod House—photograph by S. D. Butcher, 1887. Library of Congress.

Black Hawk City, Colorado—photograph by George D. Wakely. Library of Congress.

Winter Camp—photograph by E. S. Curtis. Library of Congress.

United States Cavalryman—section of a larger painting by Frederic Remington. Library of Congress.

Geronimo, Naiche—section of a larger photograph by C. S. Fly in the National Archives.

Geronimo at Surrender—section of a larger photograph by C. S. Fly (made March 25, 1886) in the National Archives.

Bourke, Clark—section of the same photograph from which "Geronimo at Surrender" (above) was taken. Geronimo sat off to the left of the camera, as photographer Fly faced them all.

Robert G. Carter—photograph in his later years, from his 1935 book, *On the Border with Mackenzie.*

INDEX

301

311

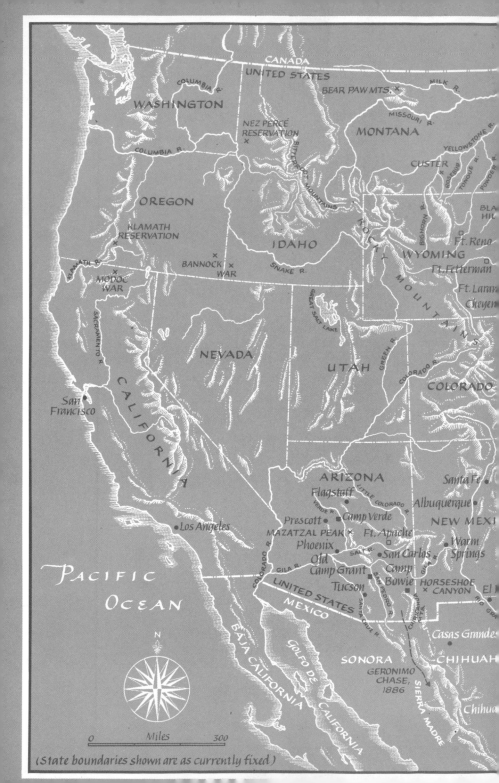